"This book is for every person who is appalled by evil but conflicted in how to respond to it in a way that honors Jesus, the Prince of Peace. It is not just for pacifists. It is for skeptics, war hawks, liberals, and conservatives—but is not for the faint of heart, for in the end it is a clarion call to take the cross as seriously as we have taken the sword."

—**Shane Claiborne**, author, activist, and founding partner
of The Simple Way

"In recent years I've traveled often to the Holy Land, where unholy violence continues to beget more violence. This book affirms the wisdom of the peacemakers I've met—both Israelis and Palestinians—who refuse the path of violence. With their active witness in mind, I fully endorse Ron's call to an organized, active campaign of nonviolence."

—**Lynne Hybels**, advocate for global engagement,
Willow Creek Community Church

"Whether or not one is a pacifist—I am not—one has something to learn about the power of nonviolent protest and resistance from Dr. Sider's careful and thoughtful study of successful nonviolent movements against tyranny and oppression. He shows that sometimes nonviolence is the most effective way—and therefore the right way—to overcome injustice and protect its victims. In my view, that isn't always the case, but Dr. Sider does the Christian community and everyone a great service in reminding us that sometimes nonviolence is the best option."

—**Robert P. George**, Princeton University

"Nonviolence has not been given the large scale study and trial it deserves. I hope this book of case studies inspires more people to seek the knowledge and training that Christian action for justice requires."

—**David Neff**, speaker, writer, and former editor-in-chief
of *Christianity Today*

"Ron Sider provides a profound and illuminating account of the effectiveness of nonviolent, grassroots movements that challenge unjust and discriminatory social practices. He concludes with a summons to faith communities to equip themselves for generating and sustaining such movements in their own responses to oppressive social systems that abuse vulnerable human beings in the contemporary world."

—**Thomas W. Ogletree**, Yale Divinity School

"Sider presents a compelling case for vastly increased investment by Christian churches and other faith traditions in the development of effective nonviolent strategies for resisting violent oppression and accomplishing social change. This convincing book makes an important contribution to a critical debate."

—**Marie Dennis**, co-president, Pax Christi International

"There are few people better qualified to write a book on this topic than Ron Sider, whose steadfast work for peace and justice for more than forty years never ceases to inspire me. I encourage anyone who cares about the future of humankind and wants to live out Jesus's call to be a peacemaker to read this book."

—**Jim Wallis**, author of *The (Un)Common Good*, president of Sojourners, and editor-in-chief of *Sojourners* magazine

"Thoroughly documented and clearly written. It explains how all persons can discern nonviolence to be both strategically and morally preferable to violence. A valuable resource for understanding peacemaking as a needed skill."

—**Edward LeRoy Long Jr.**, Drew University

"This book is an inspiring addition to Ron Sider's magisterial collection of writings, and in many ways a capstone to his consistent witness for peace. I strongly recommend this important contribution to the literature of Christian peacemaking—that is, Christian discipleship."

—**David P. Gushee**, Center for Theology and Public Life, Mercer University

"The facts are in: nonviolent action is often more effective than the use of force in the quest for justice. Sider argues powerfully that both pacifist and just war Christians should join together in struggles for such nonviolent change."

—**David Hollenbach, SJ**, Boston College

"Ron Sider is a vigorous and well-informed advocate for nonviolent action as the best way forward as we confront the deep problems of the twenty-first century. I am happy to recommend this book very strongly both to peace activists who are looking to deepen their historical and theological knowledge of the basic issues and to theologians who are searching for a more experiential and pragmatic approach than what a simple reiteration of pacifist convictions offers."

—**John Langan, SJ**, Kennedy Institute of Ethics, Georgetown University

nonviolent action

WHAT CHRISTIAN ETHICS DEMANDS
BUT MOST CHRISTIANS
HAVE NEVER REALLY TRIED

RONALD J. SIDER

Foreword by Richard J. Mouw

BrazosPress

a division of Baker Publishing Group
Grand Rapids, Michigan

Published by Brazos Press
a division of Baker Publishing Group
P.O. Box 6287, Grand Rapids, MI 49516-6287
www.brazospress.com

Printed in the United States of America

Library of Congress Cataloging-in-Publication Data
Sider, Ronald J.
    Nonviolent action : what Christian ethics demands but most Christians have never really tried / Ronald J. Sider.
        pages cm
    Includes bibliographical references and index.
    ISBN 978-1-58743-366-5 (pbk. : alk. paper)
    1. Nonviolence—Religious aspects—Christianity—History. I. Title.
BT736.6.S53 2015
241'.697—dc23   2014040103

15 16 17 18 19 20 21   7 6 5 4 3 2 1

To all the courageous pioneers who have demonstrated
that nonviolent action works

contents

foreword

There was a time when, as a defender of Just War theory, I got into heated arguments with pacifists. I still argue about the differences between us, but not with the same degree of passion as in the past. I owe the decreased intensity in my feelings on the subject to what I learned from the late Mennonite ethicist John Howard Yoder, who convinced me that the real divide concerning the use of violence was not between pacifists and Just War defenders. Both of those viewpoints, Yoder pointed out, insist that it is extremely important to subject questions about the legitimacy of violence to strict moral examination. Their disagreement is about whether that kind of examination ever permits the use of military violence. Together, though, these two perspectives stand in radical opposition to those for whom "winning at any cost" is the supreme concern, as well as to the views of the defenders of a pragmatic "national interest" approach.

Yoder obviously would have been pleased if those of us in the Just War camp were to convert to pacifism. But short of achieving that goal, he pushed us to be very strict and consistent in how we employed the criteria for giving moral approval to specific military ventures. In response to those urgings, I came to see that if we are genuinely rigorous in our adherence to Just War doctrine, we would approve of far fewer military campaigns than our past record has shown.

Take Just War teaching's "proportionality" criterion: the military means that we employ should be proportionate to the overall goals we are attempting to achieve. If your teenager locks himself in his bedroom, one way to get him to open the door is to set the house on fire. But that would obviously be a case where the proposed means are disproportionate to the intended result.

What should be clear to all of us these days is that participating in warfare causes serious psychic damage to those who engage in combat. Broken marriages, post-traumatic stress, nightmares, guilt and shame, suicides—this has become the stuff of daily news reports about the experiences of American veterans returning from combat duty. Military campaigns cause much devastation to large populations around the world. But they also have a serious impact on the soul of a nation that sponsors those campaigns—often, if not always, significantly out of "proportion" to intended goals.

In any event, pacifists and Just War defenders have a lot of work to do together. We need to find sensible and feasible alternatives to the use of military violence. We need to cultivate together what the Greeks called *phronesis*, practical wisdom. Or, to put it in New Testament terms, we need to seek together the gift of *discernment*.

Ron Sider has always been a gifted Christian discerner. While he has never been reluctant to argue for his basic pacifist perspective, that has never kept him from working hard to bring us together for common action on the convictions that we share as persons who profess a deep desire to be faithful followers of Jesus Christ.

This marvelous book is an excellent exercise in Christian *phronesis*. It provides us with many exemplary stories of moral courage. And when those accounts are about Ron's own participation, he offers candid testimonies about the hopes and fears that have accompanied his activism. But there are some highly instructive historical examples as well, with some clear evidence that nonviolent strategies have had surprisingly positive results in difficult situations.

Ron Sider has much to teach us about moral courage. But he also makes it clear that sometimes we need to wed our moral sensitivities to political and economic savvy. This wise, balanced, and inspiring book is a richly instructive guide for all who have pledged their allegiance to the Savior who is also the Prince of Peace.

Richard J. Mouw,
professor of Faith and Public Life and former
president of Fuller Theological Seminary

July 2014

acknowledgments

I could not have completed this book—at least not in any reasonable amount of time—without the help of a number of gifted graduate students at Palmer Seminary at Eastern University, where I teach. Lori Baynard, Heather Biscoe, David Fuller, Rebecca Hall, Stefanie Israel, Rachel Lesher, and Howard Pinder served (in their capacity as Sider Scholars) as helpful assistants, doing research on different chapters. In addition, David Fuller typed and retyped successive versions, becoming expert at deciphering my handwriting. To each of them I offer my special thanks.

I also want to thank Bob Hosack, my editor and friend at Baker, for his help and wisdom over many years. He has been an important part of making my long partnership with Baker Publishing Group a very satisfying experience.

introduction

There are only two invincible forces in the twentieth century—the atom bomb and nonviolence.

Bishop Leonidas Pranao[1]

What good would it do for three kayaks, three canoes, and a rubber dinghy to paddle into the path of a Pakistani steamship? For a tiny fishing boat with unarmed, praying Americans aboard to sail toward an American battleship threatening Nicaragua? For an eighty-year-old woman in a wheelchair to stop in front of advancing Filipino tanks? Or for nonviolent protesters to defy the Communist rulers of the Soviet Empire?

Soviet Communism collapsed. The tanks stopped, and a nonviolent revolution succeeded. The American battleship left, and the threat of invasion faded. And the US shipment of arms to Pakistan stopped.

Those are just a few of the many dramatic successes of nonviolent confrontation in the last several decades. Everyone, of course, knows how Mahatma Gandhi's nonviolent revolution defeated the British Empire and how Martin Luther King Jr.'s peaceful civil rights crusade changed American history. There have been scores upon scores of instances of nonviolent victories over dictatorship and oppression in the past one hundred years. In fact, Dr. Gene Sharp, the foremost scholar of nonviolence today, has said that the twentieth century saw a remarkable expansion of the substitution of nonviolent struggle for

1. Quoted in Adolfo Pérez Esquivel, *Christ in a Poncho: Testimonials of the Nonviolent Struggles in Latin America*, ed. Charles Antoine, trans. Robert R. Barr (Maryknoll, NY: Orbis Books, 1983), 87.

violence.[1] More recent scholarship has not only confirmed Sharp's comment[2] but also shown that nonviolent revolutions against injustice and dictatorship are actually more successful than violent campaigns.[3]

Surely these facts suggest a crucial area of urgent exploration in the twenty-first century. The twentieth century was the bloodiest in human history. No one who lived through or studies that vicious century needs to be reminded of the horror of war and violence. A violent sword killed more than two hundred million people in the twentieth century alone. One scholar estimates that eighty-six million people died in wars fought between 1900 and 1989. That means two thousand five hundred people every day, one hundred people every hour, for ninety years.[4] Genocide and mass murder by governments killed approximately one hundred twenty million more.[5] The mushroom cloud reminds us of greater agony yet to come unless we find alternative ways to resolve international conflict. A method that destroys more than two hundred million people in one century and threatens to wipe out far more is hardly a model of success. For all of us, from the ordinary layperson to the most highly placed military general, it is obvious that the search for peaceful alternatives is a practical necessity.

It is also a moral demand. Christians in the Just War tradition (a majority since the fourth century) have always argued that killing must be a last resort. All realistic alternatives must be tried before one resorts to war. After a century in which Gandhi, King, and a host of others demonstrated that nonviolent action works, how can Christians in the Just War tradition claim that the violence they justify is truly a last resort until they have invested billions and trained tens of thousands of people in a powerful, sustained testing of the possibilities of nonviolent alternatives?

Pacifists have long claimed that there is an alternative to violence. How can their words have integrity unless they are ready to risk death in a massive nonviolent confrontation with the bullies and tyrants who swagger through human history?

1. Gene Sharp, *The Politics of Nonviolent Action*, 3 vols. (Boston: Porter Sargent, 1973), 1:98.

2. Stephen Zunes, Lester R. Kurtz, and Sarah Beth Asher, eds., *Nonviolent Social Movements: A Geographical Perspective* (Oxford: Blackwell, 1999), 1–3.

3. See chapter 11, "Truly Testing the Possibilities of Nonviolent Action—for the First Time in Christian History."

4. Jonathan Glover, *Humanity: A Moral History of the Twentieth Century* (New Haven: Yale University Press, 2000), 47.

5. R. J. Rummel, "War Isn't This Century's Biggest Killer," *Wall Street Journal*, July 7, 1986; Rummel, *Statistics of Democide: Genocide and Mass Murder Since 1900* (Piscataway, NJ: Transaction Publishers, 1997).

In short, the concrete victories of modern nonviolent campaigns, the spiraling dangers of lethal weapons, and the moral demands of Christian faith bring into focus a clear imperative. It is time for the Christian church—indeed, all people of faith—to explore, in a more sustained and sophisticated way than ever before in human history, what can be done nonviolently.

This does not mean that one must be a pacifist to engage in serious exploration of the possibilities of nonviolence. One can conclude reluctantly that we still must possess nuclear weapons and at the same time fervently desire to substitute nonviolent strategies for violent ones wherever possible. This book does not deal with the old debate between pacifists and Just War theorists— precisely because that debate need not be settled for both to join together in a new, sustained testing of the possibilities of nonviolence.

More and more top Christian leaders, denominations, and councils are calling for a vast new exploration of what can be accomplished through nonviolent action. The National Association of Evangelicals in the USA, Pope John Paul II, the General Assembly of the Presbyterian Church (USA), the World Council of Churches, and the Vatican's Pontifical Council for the Promotion of Christian Unity have urged this expanded investigation.[6]

The purpose of this book is to promote that exploration. Parts I–III tell some of the most dramatic stories of successful nonviolent resistance to injustice, oppression, and dictatorship. Part IV pleads for action—now.

But first, a brief word on terminology. Nonviolence is not passive nonresistance; nor is coercion always violent. Nonlethal coercion (as in a boycott or peaceful march) that respects the integrity and personhood of the "opponent" is not immoral or violent.[7] By "nonviolent action," I mean an activist confrontation with evil that respects the personhood even of the "enemy" and therefore seeks both to end the oppression and to reconcile the oppressor through nonviolent methods.

"Nonviolent action" refers to a vast variety of methods or strategies. It includes things from verbal and symbolic persuasion through social, economic,

---

6. See chapter 11, "Truly Testing the Possibilities of Nonviolent Action—for the First Time in Christian History."

7. See the helpful discussion and literature cited in Duane K. Friesen, *Christian Peacemaking and International Conflict: A Realist Pacifist Perspective* (Scottdale, PA: Herald Press, 1986), 143–57. See also Ronald J. Sider, *Christ and Violence* (Scottdale, PA: Herald Press, 1979), chap. 2, esp. 44–49; David Cortright, *Gandhi and Beyond: Nonviolence for a New Political Age*, 2nd ed. (Boulder, CO: Paradigm, 2010), 26–27, 121–23.

and political noncooperation (including boycotts and strikes) to even more confrontational intervention. Gene Sharp describes 198 different tactics in his classic analysis of nonviolent action.[8] This book does not focus exclusively on any one strategy. Concrete situations demand a unique mix of tactics.

We turn now to stories of heroic struggle and astounding success.

8. Sharp, *Politics of Nonviolent Action*, 2:117–435.

proving it works

From Early Beginnings to Stunning Success

Kenneth Boulding's "first law" is simple: "What exists is possible."[1] From before the time of Christ to the present, hundreds of successful instances of nonviolent action have occurred. Recounting these stories demonstrates that nonviolent action works.

In Part I, I briefly review a few of the earlier nonviolent campaigns; next I explore more carefully how Mahatma Gandhi and Dr. Martin Luther King Jr. drew global attention to the power of nonviolent action; then I show how daring people applied the developing tactics of nonviolent action in Nicaragua and the Philippines.

1. Kenneth Boulding, quoted in Jerome D. Frank, *Sanity and Survival: Psychological Aspects of War and Peace* (New York: Vintage Books, 1968), 270.

1

early developments

Passive resistance can be so organized as to become more troublesome than armed rebellion.

The Times of London, 1861

The full story of unarmed daring has yet to be written.[1] Here I do not try to fill that gap, for that would require a vast library rather than a short chapter. Instead, I briefly sketch some of the early, and largely unknown, instances of successful nonviolent action.

Perhaps the earliest recorded example of nonviolent resistance occurred in Egypt about three thousand five hundred years ago. The Pharaoh ordered the execution of all Hebrew baby boys. In response, the Hebrew midwives chose civil disobedience, refusing to obey the ruler's command.[2]

1. Among the best are Gene Sharp, *The Politics of Nonviolent Action*, 3 vols. (Boston: Porter Sargent, 1973); Sharp, *Waging Nonviolent Struggle: 20th Century Practice and 21st Century Potential* (Boston: Porter Sargent, 2005); Peter Ackerman and Jack DuVall, *A Force More Powerful: A Century of Nonviolent Conflict* (New York: Palgrave, 2000); Stephen Zunes, Lester R. Kurtz, and Sarah Beth Asher, eds., *Nonviolent Social Movements: A Geographical Perspective* (Oxford: Blackwell, 1999); Kurt Schock, *Unarmed Insurrections: People Power Movements in Nondemocracies* (Minneapolis: University of Minnesota Press, 2005); David Cortright, *Gandhi and Beyond: Nonviolence for a New Political Age*, 2nd ed. (Boulder, CO: Paradigm, 2010); James C. Juhnke and Carol M. Hunter, *The Missing Peace: The Search for Nonviolent Alternatives in United States History* (Kitchener, ON: Pandora Press, 2001).

2. Exodus 1:15–2:10. Zunes, Kurtz, and Asher suggest that this incident may be the earliest recorded instance of nonviolent action (*Nonviolent Social Movements*, 3).

▪ Two Examples from the First Century

In AD 26, Pontius Pilate, the new Roman governor of Judea, outraged the Jews by bringing into Jerusalem military standards emblazoned with the emperor's image. Since the military standards with Caesar's image violated Jewish teaching, the religious leaders begged Pilate to remove the ensigns from the holy city. What happened is best told by the first-century Jewish historian Josephus:

> Hastening after Pilate to Caesarea, the Jews implored him to remove the standards from Jerusalem and to uphold the laws of their ancestors. When Pilate refused, they fell prostrate around his house and for five whole days and nights remained motionless in that position. On the ensuing day Pilate took his tribunal in the great stadium, and summoning the multitude, with apparent intention of answering them, gave the arranged signal to his armed soldiers to surround the Jews. Finding themselves in a ring of troops, three deep, the Jews were struck dumb at this unexpected sight. Pilate, after threatening to cut them down, if they refused to admit Caesar's images, signaled to the soldiers to draw their swords. Thereupon the Jews, as by concerted action, flung themselves in a body on the ground, extended their necks, and exclaimed that they were ready rather to die than to transgress the law. Overcome with astonishment at such intense religious zeal, Pilate gave orders for the immediate removal of the standards from Jerusalem.[3]

Nonviolent intervention worked.

A few years later, the Jews won an even more striking nonviolent victory. Caligula was the first Roman emperor to require that his subjects worship him as a god during his lifetime. In AD 39, Caligula sent Petronius to Jerusalem with three legions of soldiers to install his statue in the temple in Jerusalem. Outraged, the Jews organized a primitive version of a nationwide strike. Refusing to plant crops, tens of thousands of Jews took part in a "sit-in" in front of the residence of Petronius, the Roman legate. For forty days they protested nonviolently. Jewish leaders summoned for private persuasion remained firmly united with their people. They would all rather die, they insisted, than permit such a desecration of their temple.

This courage and commitment so impressed Petronius that he decided to risk his life and ask the emperor to change his mind. Caligula was furious. He

3. Josephus, *Jewish War* 2.171–74 (*Josephus: The Jewish War and Other Selections*, ed. Moses I. Finley, trans. H. St. J. Thackeray and Ralph Marcus [Union Square, NY: Twayne, 1965], 201–2).

sent a messenger commanding Petronius to commit suicide. Very soon after dispatching this messenger, however, Caligula himself was murdered. Fortunately, strong winds delayed the emperor's messenger, who arrived with the fatal letter twenty-seven days after Petronius had learned that Caligula was dead.[4]

Nonviolent direct action had succeeded again.

Attila and the Pope

In the middle of the fifth century, the conquering Attila marched to the very gates of the Eternal City. Having swept through central and eastern Europe in a bloody campaign, Attila hungered for the ultimate prize, Rome. His reputation preceded him. Terrified Romans believed that "the grass never grew on the spot where his horse had trod."[5] Facing this powerful warrior stood a demoralized Roman army and a daring Roman bishop.

Some stories portray Pope Leo I riding a mule, leading a small group toward Attila's advancing army. Armed only with a crucifix and a papal crown, the brave Leo directs his men in song as they advance. Finally, they face the enemy— their backs to the Roman wall, their exposed fronts to the "barbarians." Now the incredible happens. Attila, alarmed and confused, turns tail and runs— never to be seen again![6] Nonviolent peacekeeping at its pristine best? Perhaps, although many of the details likely are legendary.

But modern historians do believe that Leo the Great, accompanied by a Roman senator and other official ambassadors, did confront the invading Hun. Whether the negotiators were unarmed, singing, and riding mules is open to doubt. What *is* certain is the success of the mission. According to Edward Gibbon, in his classic work on the Roman Empire, "The pressing eloquence of Leo, his majestic aspect and sacerdotal robes, excited the veneration of Attila for the Spiritual father of the Christians."[7] The two parties managed to hammer out an acceptable treaty. The invading army withdrew.[8] Leo the Great's

---

4. This story is told in Josephus, *Jewish Antiquities* 18.257–309; *Jewish War* 2.184–203.

5. Edward Gibbon, *The Decline and Fall of the Roman Empire*, 3 vols. (New York: Random House, 1954), 2:289.

6. Lanza del Vasto, *Warriors of Peace: Writings on the Technique of Nonviolence*, ed. Michel Random, trans. Jean Sidgwick (New York: Knopf, 1974), 197.

7. Gibbon, *Decline and Fall*, 2:293. See also T. Walter Wallbank and Alastair Taylor, *Civilization Past and Present*, 7th ed., 3 vols. (Glenview, IL: Scott, Foresman, 1976), 1:215.

8. Attila was discovered dead in his bed soon after this incident. He had expired during one of his many honeymoon celebrations.

willingness to intervene directly and face a brutal warrior with overwhelming military might probably saved Rome from destruction.

■ Neglected History

Over the intervening centuries, there were undoubtedly examples of nonviolent action. Unfortunately, that history has attracted fewer historians than have the bloody battles of the Charlemagnes and Napoleons. But one should not assume from the relative silence of the history books that these centuries were free from any form of nonviolent resistance.

The American Revolution offers a striking illustration of this historical oversight. Almost every American knows about General George Washington and his military victories in the War of Independence. Only a very few realize how successful nonviolent resistance to British tyranny had been even before a shot had been fired. But scholarly study has demonstrated that by 1775 nine of the American colonies had already won de facto independence by nonviolent means.[9]

The nonviolent struggle in Hungary in the latter part of the nineteenth century is another exciting, yet relatively unknown, chapter in the emerging history of nonviolent action. Between 1850 and 1867, Hungarians resisted Austrian imperialism nonviolently and eventually succeeded without violence after armed revolt had failed miserably. In 1849, Austria crushed a popular, violent Hungarian rebellion against Austrian domination. The next year, however, a prominent lawyer, Ferenc Deàk, led the whole country into nonviolent resistance. Church leaders disobeyed Austrian orders. People refused to pay Austrian taxes, boycotted Austrian goods, and ostracized Austrian troops. So successful was the nonviolent resistance that *The Times* of London declared in an editorial on August 24, 1861, "Passive resistance can be so organized as to become more troublesome than armed rebellion."[10] In 1866 and 1867, Austria agreed to reopen the Hungarian parliament and restore the constitution.[11]

9. Walter H. Conser Jr. et al., eds., *Resistance, Politics, and the American Struggle for Independence, 1765–1775* (Boulder, CO: Lynne Rienner, 1986). See also Juhnke and Hunter, *Missing Peace*, 35–52.

10. Quoted in William Robert Miller, *Nonviolence: A Christian Interpretation* (New York: Association Press, 1964), 239.

11. For the story, see Miller, *Nonviolence*, 230–43, and the short summary in Ronald J. Sider and Richard K. Taylor, *Nuclear Holocaust and Christian Hope: A Book for Christian Peacemakers* (Downers Grove, IL: InterVarsity; New York: Paulist Press, 1982), 235.

Far away in the Andes Mountains, another nonviolent victory occurred in the nineteenth century. In his book *Warriors of Peace*, Lanza del Vasto describes the incident in this way:

> When relations between Argentina and Chile deteriorated, the two armies marched toward each other through the high passes in the Andes. But on each side, a bishop went ahead of the troops. The bishops met and exchanged the kiss of peace in the sight of the soldiers. And instead of fighting, they sealed a pact of alliance and perpetual friendship between the two nations. A statue of Christ, His hand raised in blessing, stands on the mountain to commemorate this victimless victory.[12]

By courageously placing themselves between two opposing armies, these peacekeeping bishops doubtless averted bloodshed.

■ A Growing Vision

Dr. Gene Sharp, longtime researcher at Harvard University's Center for International Affairs and founder of the Albert Einstein Institute, has pointed out that the twentieth century witnessed an astonishing increase in the use of nonviolence.[13] Some of the key figures are household names around the world: America's Martin Luther King Jr., India's Mahatma Gandhi, Poland's Lech Walesa, the Philippines' Cory Aquino. Many more are less familiar. But all have contributed significantly to a growing awareness of nonviolent alternatives.

A Brazilian soldier, Colonel Rondon, is one of the less well-known heroes. By the early 1900s, the Chavante tribe was violently resisting its Brazilian oppressors. The hatred and brutality were mutual. But Colonel (later General) Cândido Rondon, an officer in Brazil's army, determined to deal with the Chavante people in a radically new, nonviolent way. Rejecting the "Shoot the Indians on sight!" policy of the past, Rondon instructed his men, "Die if you must, but never kill an Indian."[14]

Success did not come overnight. Members of Rondon's peacekeeping force were wounded, some of them severely. Yet the "Indian Protective Service"

12. Del Vasto, *Warriors of Peace*, 202.
13. Sharp, *Politics of Nonviolent Action*, 1:98.
14. See Charles C. Walker, *A World Peace Guard: An Unarmed Agency for Peacekeeping* (New Delhi: Academy of Gandhian Studies Hyderabad, 1981), 65; Allan A. Hunter, *Courage in Both Hands* (New York: Ballantine Books, 1962), 90.

organized by Rondon lived up to its name. Finally, in 1946, the Brazilian government signed a treaty with the Chavante people. Rondon's protective service had taken no Chavante lives since its founding some forty years earlier.[15] The treaty permitted the construction of a communication system through the Chavantes' jungle home, over which Rondon telegraphed a friend, "This is a victory of patience, suffering and love."[16]

While Rondon experimented with peacekeeping in the field, philosophers expounded it in the public forum. In 1910, the renowned philosopher William James published "The Moral Equivalent of War." In this article he proposed the conscription of young people for a war against "nature" and for social welfare.[17] James had little time for idealistic visions; he suggested,

> Pacifists ought to enter more deeply into the aesthetical and ethical point of view of their opponents. So long as antimilitarists propose no substitute for war's disciplinary function, no *moral equivalent* of war . . . so long they fail to realize the full inwardness of the situation. And as a rule they do fail. The duties, penalties, and sanctions pictured in the utopias they paint are all too weak and tame to touch the military-minded.[18]

To be sure, James was not advocating a new "peace army." He simply saw his plan as having tremendous social value. Yet many today view James's essay as the antecedent of the idea of the modern peacekeeping force.[19]

Developments between the Two Great Wars

Not only in India (see chap. 2) but in other parts of the world as well, nonviolence was discussed and tested in the 1920s and 1930s.

In 1920, the Germans used nonviolence successfully to defeat a coup d'état. On March 13, 1920, right-wing troops seized Berlin, the capital of Germany, and declared a new government. Spontaneously, tens of thousands of Berliners began a strike. The next day, a ringing call for a general strike echoed throughout Germany:

15. Walker, *World Peace Guard*, 65.
16. Quoted in Hunter, *Courage*, 92.
17. See the analysis in Arthur Weinberg, ed., *Instead of Violence: Writings by the Great Advocates of Peace and Nonviolence throughout History* (New York: Beacon, 1963), 303.
18. William James, "The Moral Equivalent of War," in William James, *The Moral Equivalent of War, and Other Essays*, ed. John K. Roth (New York: Harper & Row, 1971), 10.
19. Walker, *World Peace Guard*, 65–66.

The strongest resistance is required. No enterprise must work as long as the military dictatorship reigns. Therefore, stop working! Strike! Strangle the reactionary clique! Fight by all means to uphold the Republic. Put all mutual discords aside. There is only one way to prevent Wilhelm II from returning: The whole economy must be paralyzed! No hand must move! No proletarian must help the military dictatorship. The total general strike must be carried through![20]

Even though some workers were shot, almost everyone went on strike. The bureaucracy refused to run the government. Within four days, the leader (Wolfgang Kapp) fled to Sweden, and the rebellion collapsed. Even though the police and army had failed to resist the coup, even though the coup succeeded and the rebels seized the machinery of government, they were unable to govern. Why? Because the people would not obey. Massive nonviolent resistance had defeated armed soldiers.[21]

In the 1930s, James's idea of action that would be the moral equivalent of war took one small step toward reality. When Japan invaded Manchuria in 1931, the League of Nations demonstrated its weakness by doing almost nothing. Even when the Chinese launched a total boycott of Japanese goods and Japan responded with brutal repression, the League of Nations failed to respond. At this juncture an amazing letter appeared in the London *Daily Express*. Signed by three well-known church people, the letter urged, "Men and women who believe it to be their duty should volunteer to place themselves unarmed between the combatants [in China]. . . . We have written the League of Nations offering ourselves for service in such a Peace Army."[22] The League of Nations secretary, General Eric Drummond, responded quickly, noting that the organization's constitution prohibited consideration of "private" proposals. At the same time, however, he promised to circulate the idea among the press in Geneva.[23] Editorials mushroomed worldwide. "The suggestion that such an army might suitably interpose itself between the forces of two peoples at war is both intelligent and apt," remarked the British newspaper *The Guardian*.[24] Across the ocean, *Time* magazine scoffed at foolish "Occi-

20. Quoted in Anders Boserup and Andrew Mack, *War without Weapons: Non-Violence in National Defence* (New York: Schocken Books, 1975), 123–24.

21. Sharp, *Politics of Nonviolent Action*, 1:79–81.

22. Quoted in Gene Keyes, "Peacekeeping by Unarmed Buffer Forces: Precedents and Proposals," in *Peace & Change* 5, nos. 2–3 (1978): 3–4.

23. Walker, *World Peace Guard*, 67.

24. Quoted in Keyes, "Peacekeeping," 4.

dentals willing to go to Shanghai and heroically interpose themselves between the fighting Orientals."[25]

Back in Britain, however, the proposal gained support. General Frank Percy Crozier, a decorated veteran of the Western Front, volunteered almost immediately.[26] Approximately eight hundred others followed, forming an organization called the Peace Army.[27] This army, unfortunately, existed mostly on paper and never actually served in Shanghai. Still, a precedent had been set. The proposal for a peace army had drawn marked attention, and fire, from around the world.

▪ Battling Hitler Nonviolently

Brave appeals for a nonviolent peace army did not, however, prevent the planet from slipping into the deadliest world war in human history. But even in those years, indeed precisely in many of the countries under the brutal thumb of Adolf Hitler, nonviolent resistance took place, and often it succeeded.[28]

Hitler easily conquered Norway and established Vidkun Quisling as his puppet in 1940.[29] But when Quisling tried to establish fascist institutions, massive nonviolent civil disobedience erupted. Teachers risked their lives, refusing to teach fascist propaganda. Labor unions struck and sabotaged machinery, even though their leaders were imprisoned and killed. Almost all the Lutheran clergy resigned from the state church, which Quisling tried to control. When the Gestapo demanded that the Catholic archbishop withdraw his signature from a letter supporting the defiant Lutheran clergy, he replied, "You can take my head, but not my signature."[30] Quisling failed in his attempt to impose fascism through the schools and church. Norwegians succeeded in saving more than half of the country's Jews.

25. Quoted in ibid.

26. A general turned pacifist, Crozier greatly admired Gandhi and saw the Peace Army as an outgrowth of Gandhian principles.

27. Keyes, "Peacekeeping," 4.

28. See Ackerman and DuVall, *Force More Powerful*, chap. 5; Sharp, *Waging Nonviolent Struggle*, chaps. 9–10.

29. For a summary and the bibliographical sources, see Sider and Taylor, *Nuclear Holocaust*, 238–41. See also Paul Wehr, "Nonviolent Resistance to Nazism: Norway, 1940–45," *Peace & Change* 10, nos. 3–4 (1984): 77–95; Wehr, *Conflict Regulation* (Boulder, CO: Westview Press, 1979), 69–100, which has a good study of the Norwegian communications network.

30. Quoted in Eivine Berggrar, "Experiences of the Norwegian Church in the War," *The Lutheran World Review* 1, no. 1 (1948): 51.

Resistance was even more successful in this regard in Denmark, Finland, and Bulgaria.[31] A secret tip-off concerning the impending arrest of Danish Jews enabled the Danes to hide and then smuggle 93 percent of the Danish Jews to neutral Sweden. Although allied with Germany, Finland refused to deport its Jews, even when Hitler's chief of security police threatened to cut off Finland's food supply. "We would rather perish together with the Jews," Finland's foreign minister told the astonished Heinrich Himmler.[32]

Also a German ally, Bulgaria initially passed anti-Jewish legislation. But massive resistance to anti-Jewish measures emerged at every level of society, from peasant to priest. The metropolitan of the Bulgarian Orthodox Church hid the chief rabbi in his home. Another Orthodox bishop told the Bulgarian king that he would lead a massive campaign of civil disobedience against deportation, "including personally lying down on the railroad tracks before the deportation trains."[33] Not one of the fifty thousand Bulgarian Jews fell into Hitler's hands.

▍Overthrowing Dictators

Nonviolence toppled two dictators in Central America in 1944.

General Maximiliano Martínez seized power in El Salvador in 1931.[34] The next year, he savagely crushed a peasant revolt, killing thousands. For thirteen years, the tyrannical autocrat ruled. In early 1944, he put down a revolt, torturing some and killing others. In response, university students spread the idea of a nonviolent general strike. Within two weeks, doctors, lawyers, engineers, teachers, shopkeepers, and railway workers left their posts. The economy ground to a halt. After a short period, Martínez resigned and fled to Guatemala, where he explained his resignation:

> In the first few days of April, I defeated the seditionaries with arms, but recently they provoked a strike. Then I no longer wanted to fight. Against whom was I

31. For the sources, see Sider and Taylor, *Nuclear Holocaust*, 242–46.

32. Quoted in Nora Levin, *The Holocaust: The Destruction of European Jewry, 1933–1945* (New York: Schocken Books, 1973), 401.

33. Quoted in Frederick B. Charry, *The Bulgarian Jews and the Final Solution, 1940–1944* (Pittsburgh: University of Pittsburgh Press, 1972), 90.

34. For the story, see Patricia Parkman, "Insurrection without Arms: The General Strike in El Salvador, 1944" (PhD diss., Temple University, 1980); Ackerman and DuVall, *Force More Powerful*, chap. 6.

going to fire? Against children and against youths . . . ? Women also were enlisted in the movement and in this way I no longer had an objective at which to fire.[35]

General Jorge Ubico had ruled Guatemala with an iron fist since 1931. Unfortunately for him, when El Salvador's dictator fled to Guatemala in May 1944, he brought along a contagious example of nonviolent resistance. The widespread opposition to Ubico's tyranny took heart. First students, then schoolteachers went on strike. When cavalry charged a silent procession of women and killed a schoolteacher, a total strike occurred in the capital, Guatemala City. Workers stopped. Businesses and offices closed. The streets were deserted. On July 1, 1944, Ubico gave up.[36]

Nor are the victories in El Salvador and Guatemala isolated examples. Nonviolent general strikes have overthrown at least seven Latin American dictators in the twentieth century.[37] When ruthless military dictators "disappeared" as many as thirty thousand people in Argentina in the 1970s, a movement of mothers (*Las Madres de la Plaza de Mayo*) dared to protest and march in peaceful demonstrations that eventually contributed to the collapse of the dictatorship.[38]

■ A Canoe Blockade of American Ports

On July 14, 1971, three kayaks, three canoes, and a rubber raft blocked the path of a huge Pakistani freighter steaming in to load arms at the port of Baltimore.[39] The next day, the Foreign Affairs Committee of the US House of Representatives voted to withhold all military and economic aid from Pakistan. A dramatic form of nonviolent intervention had played its part.

The Bengalis of East Pakistan (now Bangladesh) had chafed under the domination of West Pakistan. In December 1970, the Awami League, which championed greater autonomy for East Pakistan, won a clear electoral victory. In response, the

35. Parkman, "Insurrection," 169.

36. See Sharp, *Politics of Nonviolent Action*, 1:90–93; Sharp, *Waging Nonviolent Struggle*, chap. 11.

37. See Elizabeth Campuzano et al., *Resistance in Latin America: The Pentagon, the Oligarchy and Nonviolent Action* (Philadelphia: American Friends Service Committee, 1970).

38. Ackerman and DuVall, *Force More Powerful*, 267–78; Pam McAllister, "You Can't Kill the Spirit: Women and Nonviolent Action," in Zunes, Kurtz, and Asher, *Nonviolent Social Movements*, 26–29.

39. For this story, see Richard K. Taylor, *Blockade: A Guide to Non-Violent Intervention* (Maryknoll, NY: Orbis Books, 1977).

Pakistani dictator unleashed his army on East Pakistan on March 25, 1971. By the time the war ended, a million Bengalis had been killed, twenty-five thousand women had been raped, and nine million refugees had fled to India.[40]

As the Pakistani army continued to rampage through Bengal, the US government denied that it was aiding Pakistan. But it was. The United States was shipping large amounts of war material to Pakistan from American ports on the East Coast.

In *Blockade*, an exciting book that reads like a first-rate novel, Richard Taylor describes the daring adventure of the "nonviolent fleet" that helped stop this flow of arms. Taylor and other Philadelphia Quakers decided to dramatize the US shipment of arms by paddling their canoes in front of the steamship *Padma* as it came into the Baltimore harbor to load arms for Pakistan. Obviously, their lives were at risk. As it turned out, they were plucked out of the water by the US Coast Guard, which then escorted the *Padma* to dock. But the news coverage of their action contributed to the vote by the House Foreign Affairs Committee the next day. And the next week, the blockaders flew to Miami and persuaded the longshoremen there not to load any more arms destined for Pakistan.

The action then moved to Philadelphia. More canoes blockaded another Pakistani ship, the *Al Ahmadi*, as the longshoremen watched. The blockaders' daring persuaded the dockworkers to refuse to load the ship, thus shutting the port of Philadelphia to all Pakistani ships, regardless of their cargo.

Finally, in early November, the Nixon administration ended all shipment of arms to Pakistan. Obviously, many factors led to that decision. But the activity of the "nonviolent fleet" clearly played a part.

This chapter has skipped quickly over a long history of daring experimentation with alternatives to war. We explored only a few of the stories of nonviolent resistance.

We could have looked at John Adams's insistence, after his extremely dangerous nonviolent struggle to contain the fighting at Wounded Knee (1973), that "at times a person has to fight for nonviolence."[41] We could have examined the Alagamar Land Struggle in Brazil (late 1970s) and Archbishop Dom Helder Camara's chasing of the landlord's cattle off the peasants' fields.[42] We

---

40. Ibid., xiii.
41. John P. Adams, *At the Heart of the Whirlwind* (New York: Harper & Row, 1976), 119.
42. See Hildegard Goss-Mayr, "Alagamar: Nonviolent Land Struggle," *IFOR Report*, July 1980, 15–16.

might have noted the massacre that never occurred in Rio de Janeiro in 1968 because "a dozen priests offered themselves as the first victims."[43] We could have explored the Philadelphia Quakers' nonviolent police force at the Black Panthers Convention in 1970.[44] And we could have reviewed the overthrow of the Shah of Iran in 1978–79 by overwhelmingly nonviolent methods after violent revolution had failed earlier in the decade.[45]

Even this brief historical sketch demonstrates beyond dispute not only that nonviolent direct action exists but also that it often succeeds. That is an irrefutable part of the historical record. The many stories in subsequent chapters will underline that fact in powerful ways.

43. Penny Lernoux, *Cry of the People: The Struggle for Human Rights in Latin America— The Catholic Church in Conflict with U.S. Policy* (New York: Penguin Books, 1982), 313–14.

44. See Lyle Tatum, "Friendly Presence," in *Liberation without Violence: A Third-Party Approach*, ed. A. Paul Hare and Herbert H. Blumberg (Totowa, NJ: Rowman & Littlefield, 1977), 92–101.

45. See Erica Chenoweth and Maria J. Stephan, *Why Civil Resistance Works: The Strategic Logic of Nonviolent Conflict* (New York: Columbia University Press, 2011), chap. 4, esp. 110–18.

2

gandhi

Defeating the British Empire

My non-violence does not admit of running away from danger and
leaving dear ones unprotected.

Gandhi

The modern story of successful nonviolent action begins with Mahatma Gandhi (1869–1948).[1] He persuaded vast numbers of Indians
to embrace his vision of nonviolent protest. The result was victory
over the most powerful empire of that time and independence for India.

Beginning in the early seventeenth century, Britain increasingly dominated
more and more of the Indian subcontinent. By the latter half of the nineteenth century, Britain effectively controlled, through either direct rule or client
princelings, the entire area from present-day Pakistan to Burma. The British
considered India the crown jewel of their vast, far-flung empire.

---

1. Among the vast number of books on Gandhi, see Stanley Wolpert, *Gandhi's Passion: The
Life and Legacy of Mahatma Gandhi* (New York: Oxford University Press, 2001); Mohandas K.
Gandhi, *Gandhi's Autobiography: The Story of My Experiments with Truth by M. K. Gandhi*,
trans. Mahadev Desai (Washington, DC: Public Affairs Press, 1948); Dennis Dalton, *Mahatma
Gandhi: Nonviolent Power in Action* (New York: Columbia University Press, 2000); and the
other books cited below. I thank Heather Biscoe for her helpful research for this chapter.

15

The Indians were less enthusiastic. Many British policies harmed Indians economically as they benefited Britain. As nationalist sentiment swept the globe, more and more Indians dreamed of independence. With some frequency in the previous centuries, violent rebellions had protested British rule. By the early twentieth century, radicals within the Indian National Congress (the primary organization for nationalist politics) were urging violent revolution against the British. Instead, persuaded by Gandhi, they adopted nonviolent action.

Gandhi's use of nonviolent protest began in South Africa, where he lived for two decades. Born in India and trained as a lawyer in London, Gandhi moved to South Africa in 1893 to practice law in its minority Asian community. The writings on nonviolence by the great Russian author Leo Tolstoy had already deeply impressed Gandhi. So when the South African government adopted racist legislation against the Indian community, Gandhi organized a nonviolent campaign. Thousands went to jail—Gandhi himself, three times. In 1914, the government gave in and withdrew the offensive laws. The South African experience transformed Gandhi into a confident political leader with a strong vision of the theory and effectiveness of nonviolent action.

Gandhi called his method *satyagraha*—a conscious rejection of the then widely used phrase "passive resistance." Combining the Hindu terms for truth (*satya*) and forcefulness (*agraha*), Gandhi coined the term in 1906 during his vigorous but nonviolent resistance to South Africa's racist laws against Indians. "Truth-force" might be a good short translation of *satyagraha*. "It means forceful but nonviolent social action to realize and uphold truth."[2]

Satyagraha operates under the principle of *ahimsa*, which is the absence of hatred. *Ahimsa* is all-encompassing; it is not just the absence of violence, but the absence of hatred in any sense, including resentment and retaliation. This kind of "nonviolence" does not just avoid harming others; it also has no desire for harm to come to any living thing.[3] It is as much a state of the heart as it is a state of outward activity. *Ahimsa* respects the life even of one's opponent.

Courage and self-sacrifice were central parts of Gandhi's understanding of *satyagraha*. Gandhi despised cowardice. He famously said that if the only choices are cowardice or violence, then certainly one should choose violence.[4]

2. David Cortright, *Gandhi and Beyond: Nonviolence for a New Political Age*, 2nd ed. (Boulder, CO: Paradigm, 2010), 19.

3. Joan V. Bondurant, *Conquest of Violence: The Gandhian Philosophy of Conflict* (Princeton, NJ: Princeton University Press, 1988), 112–13.

4. Cortright, *Gandhi*, 31.

But Gandhi insisted that there was always a third option: courageous, non-violent resistance to evil.

> My non-violence does not admit of running away from danger and leaving dear ones unprotected. Between violence and cowardly flight, I can only prefer violence to cowardice. I can no more preach non-violence to a coward than I can tempt a blind man to enjoy healthy scenes. Non-violence is the summit of bravery. And in my own experience, I have had no difficulty in demonstrating to men trained in the school of violence the superiority of non-violence.[5]

That path, of course, frequently involves great self-sacrifice. Oppressors often respond to nonviolent protest, no matter how wrapped in love, with violence. But Gandhi realized that the resulting suffering of the nonviolent protestors is often precisely what makes nonviolent action so powerful. Sometimes willingness to suffer at the hand of violent oppressors begins to soften their hearts. More often, the self-sacrifice wins the hearts and minds of bystanders near and far. "The purer the suffering," Gandhi said, "the greater the progress."[6] Drawing on Hindu philosophy, Gandhi also believed that self-sacrifice led to purification that "promotes non-attachment to physical, bodily wants."[7] Hence came Gandhi's extreme assertions, including sexual abstinence, after 1906.

By the time Gandhi returned to India in 1914, he had also embraced a vision of *swaraj* (self-rule) for India. Rejecting the claim of Indian nationalists that independence could come only through violence, Gandhi insisted that nonviolent action was the path to *swaraj*. But *swaraj* meant so much more than national independence. It meant not only abandoning misguided Western ways (clothes, technology, even medicine) but also transforming what was wrong in Indian life: widespread poverty, child marriage, mistreatment of women, caste and religious prejudice, and contempt for physical labor. Manual labor, a simple lifestyle, purification through fasting, a "love for all things Indian," and improvements in education and public health were all part of the path to self-rule.

5. Quoted in George F. Estey and Doris A. Hunter, *Nonviolence: A Reader in the Ethics of Action* (Waltham, MA: Xerox College Publishing, 1971), 92.

6. Quoted in Cortright, *Gandhi*, 28.

7. Ibid., 30. That view finally is grounded in the Hindu monist belittling of the natural world, which is very different from the Judeo-Christian understanding of the goodness of creation. Contrary to what Cortright (ibid., 60) says, it is certainly not the case that the Christian understanding of *agape*, selfless love, "is similar to the Hindu concept of non-attachment." Rather, *agape* affirms the goodness and value of the material world, whereas monist nonattachment does not.

When Gandhi returned to India in 1914, he spent a year traveling around the country (by third-class train) to see how poor Indians lived.[8] He also established communities (ashrams) where people began to live his vision of *swaraj*: living simply, making their own Indian handspun clothes, doing manual labor, and embracing "untouchables" (the dreadfully oppressed persons at the bottom of Indian society).

Gandhi soon started launching nonviolent campaigns (*satyagrahas*) to protest injustice against peasants and workers. In 1918, a strike and fast that he organized on behalf of poorly paid textile workers won better wages. Unlike most of the leaders of the Indian National Congress, who were well-educated, upper-class persons, Gandhi worked with the poor, leading campaigns against injustice, building schools, improving hygiene, and promoting native crafts. Gandhi slowly became famous throughout India.

Gandhi's first nationwide nonviolent campaign came in 1920–22. The elite leaders of the Indian National Congress realized that they needed Gandhi's popularity and skills in organizing and strategizing. They planned a day of fasting and prayer for April 6, 1920. All across the country people stopped work. Tragically, some protests turned violent, and the police responded with force, killing hundreds in the city of Amritsar. Shocked, Gandhi fasted for three days in penitence.

But Gandhi also developed a more vigorous rejection of any ongoing British rule of India. He plunged into more intense organizational work with the Indian National Congress, planning nationwide boycotts of schools, courts, and cloth imported from Britain. He urged Indians working as civil servants in the British-run government of India to resign. Gandhi traveled all around the country energizing the masses.

Large numbers of people responded as the campaign continued into early 1922. But again, some protests turned violent. In February of that year, protesters massacred twenty-two police. Gandhi promptly called a stop to the entire campaign.

Very soon thereafter, Gandhi was arrested, spending almost two years in jail. During the mid-1920s, the nationalist movement lost supporters and momentum. Gandhi himself focused on promoting *swaraj* at the grassroots, fostering local spinning for Indian cloth, nurturing better Muslim-Hindu relations, and working to improve the lives of the "untouchables."

8. I am especially indebted to the lengthy account of Gandhi's life in Peter Ackerman and Jack DuVall, *A Force More Powerful: A Century of Nonviolent Conflict* (New York: Palgrave, 2000), 61–111.

In 1927, another outrageous act by the British rulers reenergized the nationalist campaign and the Indian National Congress. The government had appointed a commission to deal with India's constitutional future, but did so without including even one Indian. Indians were furious. A reinvigorated congress begged Gandhi to lead a new campaign. At a meeting in December 1928, the congress, under Gandhi's leadership, gave the British viceroy one year to respond to their demand that India become a self-governing dominion within the British Empire.

Fortunately, a successful nonviolent campaign in Bardoli (a section of Gujarat), supported by Gandhi, added to his personal prestige and to wider acceptance of his nonviolent methods. This vigorous nonviolent campaign against a large hike in taxes on land persuaded the British officials to back down. Gandhi's popularity and respect took another leap forward.

In 1929, Gandhi worked hard to strengthen and expand the Indian National Congress in preparation for a national campaign if the viceroy, Lord Irwin, rejected their appeal of 1928. Lord Irwin did exactly that when Gandhi and other Indian leaders met with him. So in late December 1929, the Indian National Congress overwhelmingly adopted Gandhi's demand for full Indian independence. They also started planning a vast national campaign of noncooperation, but no one had yet developed the details of the action.

As Gandhi thought, prayed, and consulted at his ashram in Sabarmati, the idea of a national campaign of civil disobedience against the salt tax emerged. Since the nineteenth century, the British rulers had enjoyed a monopoly on the production of salt, and they imposed a tax on the sale of it. The tax hurt the poor the most. So Gandhi decided to urge Indians to break the law and make their own salt. When the viceroy ignored one last invitation from Gandhi to negotiate reform, Gandhi announced that the Salt Campaign would begin on March 12, 1930.

That day, Gandhi and about seventy trusted followers began their long march of two hundred forty miles to the sea at Dandi. There they planned to commit civil disobedience, making their own salt in defiance of the salt laws. As they walked through each village along the way, Gandhi gave a speech promoting the campaign of civil disobedience and urging local government officials to resign. The crowds began to swell—thirty thousand people at one place, fifty thousand at another. As he traveled, Gandhi gave interviews and wrote articles. The stories were front-page news in newspapers across the country and beyond. "Foreign journalists turned Gandhi into a household name in Europe and America."[9] *Time* named Gandhi "Man of the Year" in December 1930.

On April 6, Gandhi walked to the beach and picked up a handful of salt-laden dirt, thus signaling the beginning of civil disobedience. Everywhere Indians started breaking the law by boiling seawater to make their own salt. From Bengal in the east, to Madras in the south, to Bombay in the west, vast numbers of people broke the law. But still, the British rulers refused to arrest Gandhi, fearing to strengthen his campaign by making him a martyr. "To arrest Gandhi is to set fire to the whole of India," one nationalist newspaper observed.[10]

Gandhi decided to force the rulers' hand. He announced that he would lead a raid on the government's salt works. The authorities finally arrested Gandhi on May 4. So his wife and a seventy-six-year-old judge led the raid, and they too were arrested. Then a prominent woman poet, Sarojini Naidu, led the marches. The police blocked their way, and hundreds went to jail.

On May 21, Naidu urged nonviolence as she prepared to lead another attempt to enter the government's salt works. "You must not use violence under any circumstances," she said. "You will be beaten, but you must not resist; you must not even raise a hand to ward off blows."[11] As the demonstrators tried to climb over the barbed wire around the salt works, the police attacked the nonviolent marchers with steel-tipped clubs. "They went down like ten-pins," one foreign journalist reported.[12] When the police knocked down the first row of marchers, others promptly took their place. A contemporary eyewitness described the brutality: "From where I stood I heard the sickening whacks of the clubs on unprotected skulls. . . . Those struck down fell sprawling, unconscious or writhing in pain with fractured skulls or broken shoulders. In two or three minutes the ground was quilted with bodies. . . . The survivors without breaking ranks silently and doggedly marched on until struck down."[13] Day after day until June 6, the courageous marchers submitted to police brutality. The reports of a few courageous foreign journalists won support for the Indians around the world.

Around the country, local Indian National Congress leaders conducted many kinds of nonviolent campaigns. In the annals of nonviolent action, no

9. Ibid., 86.
10. Ibid., 88.
11. Quoted in ibid., 90.
12. Web Miller, *I Found No Peace: The Journal of a Foreign Correspondent* (New York: Simon & Schuster, 1963), 193.
13. Ibid.

episode is more astonishing than that of Badshah Khan and his nonviolent army of eighty thousand Muslim Pathans.[14] The Pathans lived in the strategic Khyber Pass, the northwest gateway to India from Afghanistan and Russia. The British who tried to subdue them considered the Pathans (or Pashtuns) the most savage, brutal warriors they had ever met. The Pathans' strict code of revenge obligated them to avenge the slightest insult. For a Pathan, the surest road to paradise was to die "with his rifle smoking."[15] India's future prime minister, Jawaharlal Nehru, commented that the Pathan male "loved his gun better than his child or brother."[16]

In fact, the Pathans are precisely the same people living in the same area (of present-day Afghanistan and northwest Pakistan) who today make up the core of the Taliban—the radical Muslims successfully fighting against the United States and its allies in Afghanistan.

When Badshah Khan persuaded the Pathans to adopt nonviolence, even Gandhi was amazed. "That such men," Gandhi exclaimed, "who would have killed a human being with no more thought than they would kill a sheep or a hen, should at the bidding of one man have laid down their arms and accepted non-violence as the superior weapon sounds almost like a fairy tale."[17]

But they did. Badshah Khan was a Pathan Muslim who became enthralled with Gandhi's vision of nonviolent struggle for freedom. Khan began to dream of "an army of nonviolent soldiers, directed and disciplined, with officers, cadres, uniforms, a flag."[18] Calling his volunteers the "Servants of God," Khan organized "the first professional nonviolent army."[19] They marched and drilled, wore a special uniform (a red shirt), and developed a careful organizational structure complete with officers—and even a bagpipe corps. They also worked in the villages, opened schools, and maintained order at public gatherings.

14. This section is based on Eknath Easwaran, *A Man to Match His Mountains: Badshah Khan, Nonviolent Soldier of Islam* (Petaluma, CA: Nilgiri Press, 1984). A second edition was published in 1999. See also Rajmohan Gandhi, *Ghaffar Khan, Nonviolent Badshah of the Pashtuns* (New Delhi: Viking, 2004); and Khan's autobiography, Khan Abdul Ghaffar Khan, *My Life and Struggle: Autobiography of Badshah Khan*, trans. Helen H. Bouman (New Delhi: Hind Pocket Books, 1969). See also the award-winning documentary film *The Frontier Gandhi: Badshah Khan, A Torch for Peace*, by T. C. McLuhan (2008).
15. Easwaran, *Badshah Khan*, 99.
16. Ibid., 20.
17. Ibid.
18. Ibid., 110.
19. Ibid., 111.

Badshah Khan's nonviolent army was ready when Gandhi launched the Salt Campaign.

Nowhere was the repression as bad as in Badshah Khan's home in the strategic northwest frontier. When he called his Pathan people to nonviolent resistance, Khan was quickly arrested. Nonviolent civil disobedience promptly broke out everywhere among the Pathans. Bayonets and bullets were the British response. On one bloody afternoon, they killed over two hundred unarmed protesters and wounded many more.

One incredible scene involved the Garhwal Rifles, crack Indian troops commanded by British officers. When they saw unarmed men, women, and children being slaughtered, they refused to obey orders to shoot. "You may blow us from your guns, if you like," they told their British commanders, "but we will not shoot our unarmed brethren."[20]

British brutality evoked massive support for the Pathans. In a very short time, Khan's nonviolent army swelled to eighty thousand volunteers. Fearing the Pathans' nonviolence even more than their former savagery, the British did everything to destroy the "Red Shirts" and provoke them to violence. They ordered them to strip naked in public and beat them into unconsciousness when they refused. After public humiliation, many were thrown into pools of human excrement. Everywhere, the British hunted Badshah Khan's nonviolent army like animals. But the proud Pathans remained firmly nonviolent.[21]

For the next decade and a half, Badshah Khan and his nonviolent Red Shirts played a key role in the battle for independence. Always they worked for peace and reconciliation. In 1946, when thousands died in Hindu-Muslim violence, ten thousand of Khan's Servants of God protected Hindu and Sikh minorities in the northwest frontier and eventually restored order in the large city of Peshawar.[22] When in 1947, Gandhi's campaign of nonviolent intervention finally wrested Indian independence from the British Empire, Badshah Khan's peaceful army of Pathan Red Shirts deserved a good deal of the credit.

This story of nonviolent direct action by Muslim Pathans with a long history of brutal violence (which continues in the Taliban today) is one of the most amazing chapters in the development of an alternative path to resolve social conflict. Khan's biographer is surely correct: "If Badshah Khan could raise a non-violent army of people so steeped in violence as the Pathans, there is no

20. Ibid., 123.
21. Ibid., 126–28.
22. Ibid., 175.

country on earth where it cannot be done."[23] Perhaps Gandhi's insistence that nonviolence is meant for the strong helps explain the Pathans' success. When Badshah Khan asked Gandhi why the Pathans grasped the idea of nonviolence more quickly than did the Hindus, Gandhi responded, "Nonviolence is not for cowards. It is for the brave, the courageous. And the Pathans are more brave and courageous than the Hindus."[24]

In the months immediately after Gandhi launched the Salt Campaign, boycotts and civil disobedience spread not only to Badshah Khan's area but also to many places across India. Indians in many locations disobeyed the salt laws. Farmers and others engaged in tax resistance. People boycotted British cloth imported from England, and the value of cloth imports plummeted by 50 percent. Local Indian officials resigned their government positions.

In some instances, when Indian soldiers refused to obey orders from their British officers to attack their fellow Indian protestors, the British temporally lost control. Gandhi and the Indian National Congress gained enormous prestige as their nonviolent campaign demonstrated the weakness of the British government in the face of massive civil disobedience.

But the British government did not collapse. It struck back hard, killing hundreds, battering thousands, and imprisoning tens of thousands. Those imprisoned included leaders of the Indian National Congress, such as Gandhi and Nehru, and also twenty thousand women—perhaps as many as sixty thousand people in all.[25] The British also seized and sold the land of people engaged in tax resistance.

The British rulers managed to keep the support of most of the Indian police and soldiers. Because of that, they were able to resist and arrest many demonstrators and hold them in jail. By September 1930, it was clear that the massive widespread boycotts, demonstrations, and civil disobedience had not made British India ungovernable.

In addition, many Indians were growing weary of the months-long campaign. Farmers were losing their land because of tax resistance; Indian business leaders were losing money because of the boycotts and demonstrations; and people everywhere were increasingly exhausted by the long campaign and began to lose enthusiasm. The leaders of the Indian National Congress were

23. Ibid., 189.
24. Ibid., 195.
25. Ackerman and DuVall, *Force More Powerful*, 96–98. For a different estimate, seventeen thousand women and one hundred thousand people overall, see Gene Sharp, *Waging Nonviolent Struggle: 20th Century Practice and 21st Century Potential* (Boston: Porter Sargent, 2005), 110.

in prison, and the organization was in disarray. More and more people urged Gandhi to seek a compromise.

Gandhi wrote to the British viceroy on February 14, 1931, requesting a meeting. On March 5, the two sides announced an agreement. The viceroy promised to release all the imprisoned demonstrators, allow banned organizations to operate again, permit local people to make their own salt, repeal repressive ordinances, and permit Indian officials to return to jobs from which they had resigned in protest.

Gandhi conceded even more. Without any promise of independence or agreement on the major economic issues, he agreed to end the protests and attend a conference in England in the fall of 1931 on the future of India. Gandhi apparently was excessively optimistic about the outcome of that meeting. But when it was over, India was no closer to independence than when it started.

By the time Gandhi returned from the London conference, the British rulers in India were already engaged in several repressive measures. Nehru was back in jail. In response, the Indian National Congress called for a new wave of civil disobedience on January 1, 1932. But popular enthusiasm was not there in the way it had been during the Salt Campaign, and the British cracked down hard. The congress did not call off this second round of civil disobedience for two years, but it was weak and never truly threatened British rule.[26]

For the second half of the 1930s, Gandhi devoted his energies to "constructive work: liberating untouchables and women, promoting village industries, reforming education and sanitation."[27] He was still the most important symbol of the struggle for independence, but only occasionally did he take a strong public political stance. The other leaders of the Indian National Congress, for their part, took advantage of political reforms, winning local elections and leading provincial governments with expanded authority. But the British were still clearly in control.

British rule also overcame a large, violent popular rebellion in 1942. But by the end of World War II, Britain was exhausted economically and militarily. The Indian National Congress was demanding independence. The British knew that to end dissent they must either agree to the demand for independence or invest energy and money that they did not have. On August 14, 1947, India and Pakistan became independent nations.

26. Ackerman and DuVall, *Force More Powerful*, 105.
27. Ibid., 109.

It is not accurate to say that Gandhi's campaign of nonviolent resistance decisively defeated the British and won immediate national independence. British rule continued for another sixteen years after 1930. But the Salt Campaign did play a huge role in India's eventual freedom. "Systematic nonviolent opposition to an unrepresentative entrenched government had never before been mustered on such a scale."[28] The great nonviolent campaign of 1930 did not promptly end British rule, but it did change the people of India in so fundamental a way that independence became inevitable. "The suffering of protestors did not change the mind of the British, but it did change the mind of Indians about the British. For tens of millions of Indians, *satyagraha* and its result changed cooperation with the [British] raj from a blessing into blasphemy. The old order, in which British control rested comfortably on Indian acquiescence, had been sundered."[29]

Gandhi's unprecedented national campaign of nonviolence made independence inevitable. In that sense, it did defeat the British Empire.

Gandhi's nonviolent action, however, did far more than help make India a free nation. It has also inspired countless nonviolent practitioners around the world: Martin Luther King Jr., Cesar Chavez, Dorothy Day, Cory Aquino, Lech Walesa. The list goes on and on. Gandhi himself even had a premonition of the future impact of his nonviolent action: "Things undreamt of are daily being seen, the impossible is ever becoming possible. We are constantly being astonished. . . . Impossible discoveries will be made in the field of nonviolence."[30] Thanks in part to Gandhi's example, they have.

28. Ibid., 110.
29. Ibid., 109.
30. August 25, 1940; quoted in Mohandas K. Gandhi, *All Men Are Brothers: Life and Thoughts of Mahatma Gandhi as Told in His Own Words*, ed. Krishna Kripalani (Ahmedabad: Navajivan, 1960), 80.

martin luther king jr. and gandhian nonviolence

The Battle against American Racism

The aftermath of nonviolence is the creation of the beloved community, while the aftermath of violence is tragic bitterness.

Dr. Martin Luther King Jr.[1]

In 1936, Gandhi uttered a prescient word to a visiting African American preacher and theologian, Dr. Howard Thurman. When Thurman told Gandhi that African Americans should use Gandhi's methods, Gandhi replied, "Well, if it comes true, it may be through the Negroes that the unadulterated message of nonviolence will be delivered to the world."[2]

American interest in nonviolence did not start with Gandhi, but the story of his successful nonviolent victory over the British Empire sparked much

---

1. James Melvin Washington, ed., *A Testament of Hope: The Essential Writings of Martin Luther King, Jr.* (New York: HarperOne, 1991), 8. I thank Lori Baynard for help in researching this chapter.

2. Quoted in Peter Ackerman and Jack DuVall, *A Force More Powerful: A Century of Nonviolent Conflict* (New York: Palgrave, 2000), 333. For a good, short overview of the role of nonviolence in the American civil rights movement of the 1950s and 1960s, see James C. Juhnke and Carol M. Hunter, *The Missing Peace: The Search for Nonviolent Alternatives in United States History* (Kitchener, ON: Pandora Press, 2001), chap. 11.

stronger interest, not least in the oppressed African American community.[3] A very small but growing number of Americans, both black and white, began to explore ways to use nonviolence to battle American racism, especially entrenched Southern segregation. The result was the amazingly successful nonviolent civil rights movement of the 1950s and 1960s. Many, many people played key roles, but Dr. Martin Luther King Jr. became by far the most powerful and visible leader.

The son of an influential preacher in Atlanta, King first encountered the life and teaching of Gandhi while a seminary student.[4] Before that, he thought that "love your enemies" worked only in personal relations. Racial groups and nations required a more realistic approach. But as King delved deeper into Gandhi's ideas, he came to see that "the Christian doctrine of love operating through the Gandhian method of nonviolence was one of the most potent weapons available to oppressed people in their struggle for freedom."[5] However, as he completed his doctoral dissertation on the liberal theologian Paul Tillich and began his first pastorate, at the age of twenty-five, at Dexter Baptist Church in Montgomery, Alabama, in September 1954, he had "a merely intellectual understanding" of nonviolence and "not the slightest idea" that he would encounter there a situation for nonviolence.[6] Montgomery soon changed that.

Montgomery was in the heart of the Old South, where segregation reigned supreme. It was not just that public facilities (water fountains, bathrooms, buses, restaurants, hotels) were segregated. Vigilantes and organized white groups threatened, tortured, and murdered "uppity niggers" who dared to challenge the racist system. All-white police forces, juries, and judges offered little hope of justice. Legal technicalities, death threats, and lynchings prevented most African Americans from registering to vote. The all-white southern Democratic Party exercised enormous influence in Washington, obstructing any effective national legislation against segregation.

Then on December 1, 1955, a tiny act of rebellion set in motion a vast, far-reaching revolution. That evening, Rosa Parks refused the bus driver's

3. See, for example, Charles Chatfield, "Nonviolent Social Movements in the United States: A Historical Overview," in *Nonviolent Social Movements: A Geographical Perspective*, ed. Stephen Zunes, Lester R. Kurtz, and Sarah Beth Asher (Oxford: Blackwell, 1999), 283–301.

4. For a discussion of Gandhi's influence on King, see David Cortright, *Gandhi and Beyond: Nonviolence for a New Political Age*, 2nd ed. (Boulder, CO: Paradigm, 2010), chaps. 2–3.

5. Martin Luther King Jr., "How My Mind Has Changed," *Christian Century*, April 27, 1960; reprinted in Washington, *Testament of Hope*, 38.

6. Ibid.

order to give up her seat to a white man.[7] (According to the law, whites rode in the front of public buses, blacks in the back, and if the white section was full, black riders had to give up their seats to whites.) Police soon arrested Parks and took her to jail. The black community responded to her arrest and conviction with a massive boycott of the city buses.

Dr. King was only twenty-six years old and had lived in Montgomery for slightly more than one year. The older, more prominent preachers hesitated to lead this dangerous venture, so they elected King president of the boycott movement (the Montgomery Improvement Association). Almost all African Americans in Montgomery boycotted the buses. They walked, carpooled, and took taxis, and the white-owned bus company started losing money.

The demands of the boycott were very modest: courteous treatment on the buses; "first come, first served" seating (whites could still sit in the front, and blacks would start filling seats from the back); and black bus drivers hired for black routes. But the white establishment was unwilling to negotiate.

The white response was ruthless: black taxi drivers were ticketed and arrested, black leaders were harassed by city officials, and King received threatening late-night phone calls. One night a caller growled, "Listen, nigger, we've taken all we want from you. Before next week you'll be sorry you ever came to Montgomery."[8] Overwhelmed, exhausted, and ready to give up, King sat down at his kitchen table and prayed aloud, "I am here taking a stand for what I believe is right. But now I am afraid. . . . I am at the end of my powers. . . . I can't face it alone."[9] Suddenly, he experienced the presence of God in a way he never had before. His fears quickly left as he heard an inner voice urging him to stand up for righteousness and assuring him that God would be at his side.

Three nights later, a bomb exploded in his house. An angry black crowd, ready to respond violently, quickly gathered. From the front porch of his bombed home, King pleaded for nonviolence: "Don't get your weapons. . . . We are not advocating violence. We want to love our enemies. . . . We must meet hate with love."[10]

---

7. For the previous training in nonviolence that Rosa Parks and others had received, see Juhnke and Hunter, *Missing Peace*, 217.

8. Quoted in Taylor Branch, *Parting the Waters: America in the King Years 1954–63* (New York: Simon & Schuster, 1988), 162.

9. Recounted in a sermon in *The Strength to Love*, printed in Washington, *Testament of Hope*, 509.

10. Quoted in Branch, *Parting the Waters*, 166.

A few months after the boycott succeeded, King explained in a speech at Berkeley, "From the beginning there was a philosophy undergirding the Montgomery boycott, the philosophy of nonviolent resistance."[11] "Christ furnished the spirit and motivation while Gandhi furnished the method."[12] King explained how black leaders used mass meetings and weekly training sessions to help the people understand the philosophy and practice of nonviolence. One must love even oppressors, not hate or humiliate them. In 1960, King acknowledged, "The experience of Montgomery did more to clarify my thinking on the question of nonviolence than all of the books I had read."[13]

As the weeks and months rolled on, the continuing bus boycott attracted national, even international, attention. Floods of reporters came to Montgomery. Their stories plus King's powerful speeches brought national attention and an influx of outside money. Especially after his arrest and conviction on trumped-up charges, King became more and more famous. The *New York Times* profiled him in its "Man in the News" section. Thousands of people flocked to hear King when he traveled to New York to speak.

On June 4, 1956, a panel of federal judges ruled in favor of a petition from the Montgomery boycott, which argued that segregation of state and city buses was unconstitutional. When, five months later on November 13, the US Supreme Court endorsed this decision, King and Montgomery's African American community celebrated. They had won. Celebrities from around the country called to congratulate Dr. King. King and other black preachers from Montgomery took a symbolic bus ride, sitting in the front, reveling in the polite welcome from the white bus driver.

The next January, King invited prominent black preachers from across the South to a conference in Atlanta on "nonviolent integration." White racists in Montgomery bombed four churches during the Atlanta conference, but the group proceeded to organize what was soon called the Southern Christian Leadership Conference (SCLC). With King as its president, the SCLC was destined to play a historic role in the nonviolent campaign against segregation.

Just a few weeks after the conference, King published in the *Christian Century* a ringing call for nonviolence in the struggle against American segregation and racism. King saw this struggle as part of the larger global demand for freedom and justice. Everywhere, he said, the oppressed had to decide whether

11. Washington, *Testament of Hope*, 12.
12. Ibid., 38.
13. Ibid.

to use violence or nonviolence in their battle for freedom. King was clear on which path was right. "The shores of history are white with the bleached bones of nations and communities" that chose violence.[14] The nonviolent alternative vigorously resists evil but seeks to win over, not defeat, the oppressor. "The aftermath of nonviolence is the creation of the beloved community, while the aftermath of violence is tragic bitterness."[15] We can persist in this costly love even for oppressors because we know "the universe is on the side of justice."[16]

King's leadership of the Montgomery bus boycott plus his phenomenal oratorical skill brought breathtaking fame and influence to this twenty-eight-year-old preacher. His face was on the cover of *Time* in February 1957. The *New York Times Magazine* ran a story of the Montgomery boycott largely focused on King. And he became the second African American to be on *Meet the Press*. King dreamed of using his vast new influence to lead a powerful nonviolent movement against segregation across the South.

But the next three years proved to be largely frustrating. In spite of King's giving two hundred speeches a year, meeting personally with President Eisenhower, and traveling to Ghana as the guest of President Nkrumah to celebrate the new nation's independence, the SCLC's ambitious plans for a massive voter-registration drive in the South largely fizzled. While King was in New York promoting his new book *Strive Toward Freedom*, a deranged woman jabbed a razor-sharp letter opener deep into his chest. It took hours for surgeons to remove the blade, which had grazed King's aorta. If he had sneezed, the blade would have punctured the aorta, and King would have died.

In the spring of 1959, Dr. King made a pilgrimage to India to deepen his understanding of Gandhi's vision and practice of nonviolence. "King wanted time to absorb Gandhism as a discipline that might help him escape a drift toward stagnation as a glorified after-dinner speaker."[17] He read material about Gandhi in preparation and then met with leading proponents of Gandhian nonviolence. Returning home, King was determined to reverse the SCLC's lack of success in the years since the Montgomery bus boycott. He dreamed of launching an "American Salt March."

Convinced that part of his more recent ineffectiveness was a failure to understand deeply and share broadly the philosophy of nonviolence, King

14. Ibid., 7.
15. Ibid., 8.
16. Ibid., 9.
17. Branch, *Parting the Waters*, 250.

organized the Institute on Nonviolent Resistance to Segregation in July 1959. Many of the leading American advocates of nonviolence led workshops. They dreamed of adapting Gandhian nonviolence for American Christians, but they were not clear on how precisely to do that.

King realized that he had to invest more energy in revitalizing the SCLC. That meant he must move back to Atlanta, where the SCLC had its headquarters. At the end of 1959, King relocated his family back to Atlanta and joined his father as co-pastor of historic Ebenezer Baptist Church.

Suddenly an effective nonviolent tactic emerged in early 1960. Sit-ins at segregated lunch counters sprouted in cities in the South. It started in Greensboro, North Carolina, when four black college freshmen spontaneously decided on February 1 to sit down at Woolworth's segregated lunch counter. Within days, hundreds of college students embraced the strategy.

In Nashville, Tennessee, James Lawson, a gifted student of nonviolence, had been conducting workshops on the history and practice of nonviolence. (Two years earlier, Dr. King had persuaded Lawson to move south to train people in nonviolence, and the Fellowship of Reconciliation, a national, largely pacifist organization, had helped with funding.) Lawson was training college students to prepare for a more activist confrontation than bus boycotts. They began planning a major sit-in in downtown Nashville for February 1960.

Before they began, however, word of the Greensboro sit-in hit the papers. The result in Nashville was hundreds of new students cramming into Lawson's training sessions. On February 13, more than one hundred well-dressed, highly disciplined black college students staged a sit-in at Woolworth's downtown lunch counter. Soon hundreds of students joined in. Initially, the police protected the students from taunting white vigilantes. But on February 27, the police suddenly disappeared, allowing white toughs to attack, punching and kicking the student demonstrators. Then the police returned and arrested the black nonviolent demonstrators. Outraged, the adult black community boycotted downtown stores, whose profits promptly plummeted. When white segregationists bombed the home of one of Nashville's most prominent black citizens, the students responded with a huge march to the downtown courthouse. In a dramatic confrontation on the courthouse steps with student leader Diane Nash, the mayor publicly agreed to desegregate the lunch counters. A new kind of activist nonviolence had scored a major victory.[18]

18. Ackerman and DuVall, *Force More Powerful*, 312–29.

Sit-ins quickly spread across many Southern cities. Already by the end of February, students were conducting sit-ins in thirty-one cities. By the end of April, the movement had spread to seventy-eight cities.

Dr. King had not initiated the student sit-ins. But when one of King's key colleagues, the Rev. Fred Shuttlesworth, witnessed the student demonstrations during the second week of sit-ins in North Carolina, he promptly advised King, "We must get with this."[19] The next week, King spoke at an evening rally in Durham, North Carolina, praising the student sit-ins. He was the only prominent leader of either race to endorse the sit-ins. King had quickly realized that the students had discovered the kind of new nonviolent strategy that he had been seeking. That night at Durham, King uttered a new call (radical for both black and white leaders) to "fill up the jails of the south."[20]

On April 15, about one hundred fifty students engaging in the sit-ins in nine different states came to a conference in Raleigh, North Carolina, to reflect on their activity. James Lawson and Dr. King were the two key speakers. Lawson gave a ringing speech on nonviolence grounded in love even for hostile enemies. Later King wowed the students with the same message. "Together, the two leaders inspired an enthusiasm for nonviolent activism such as neither had ever seen."[21] At the end of the conference, the students formed a new organization, the Student Nonviolent Coordinating Committee, and King provided the new organization a little office space at the SCLC's Atlanta headquarters. Privately, Lawson told King that he was ready to accept King's repeated invitation to join the SCLC and teach nonviolence to students all across the South.

In a way that no one could have foreseen, the sit-ins eventually played a decisive role in the presidential election of 1960. King had praised the student sit-ins, but he had not yet personally participated. He had never gone to jail as an act of nonviolent resistance. But in the fall of 1960, student leaders begged King to join them in a sit-in at segregated restaurants in downtown Atlanta. King hesitated. His father was adamantly opposed, but finally King agreed.

On October 19, the police arrested King and a number of students for trespassing. When King and the students refused bail, King spent his first night in prison. Two days later, at a press conference permitted by the jail authorities, King explained why he had joined the student sit-in: "I had to

19. Quoted in Branch, *Parting the Waters*, 273.
20. Quoted in ibid., 276.
21. Ibid., 291.

33

practice what I preached."[22] Within a couple days, the somewhat moderate white mayor worked out a deal to drop the charges against King. Before King could be released, however, the court received a bench warrant from nearby DeKalb County ordering King to be held on another charge. Six months before, a white DeKalb County policeman had stopped King when he noticed that King had a white woman in the car. When the officer discovered that King was still using his Alabama license even though he had been in Atlanta for more than three months, a judge gave King a twelve-month suspended sentence. Now DeKalb authorities argued that King's arrest in Atlanta violated the terms of his suspended sentence. At the trial a couple days later, the DeKalb judge revoked King's probation and sentenced him to four months of hard labor on a road gang.

State road gangs were dangerous places. They regularly included violent prisoners, such as murderers. People feared for King's life. Terror spread even more through the black community after the authorities under cover of night transferred a handcuffed and shackled King to a more distant maximum-security prison. King's wife, family, and friends were frantic. They called everywhere for help, including the Kennedy campaign for president.

The Kennedy campaign had carefully kept its distance from King's civil rights crusade because it wanted to carry majority-white Southern states. But Sargent Shriver managed to persuade Senator Kennedy to call Dr. King's wife, Coretta, to express sympathy at King's "lousy treatment." "I just wanted you to know that I was thinking about you and Dr. King,"[23] Kennedy told Coretta over the phone.

One other call was made. Robert Kennedy (Senator Kennedy's brother and campaign director) was annoyed that the DeKalb judge had (contrary to the law) refused to grant bail to King, who was charged only with a misdemeanor. Robert Kennedy made a personal call to the judge, who reversed himself and released King on a $2,000 bond.

Fortunately for the Kennedys, who were agonizing over a white backlash in the South if their actions received widespread publicity, the national press lost interest after King was released from jail. White America moved on to other issues. But the small civil rights office in the Kennedy campaign began to pick up signs of a major change in the black community. In 1956, 60 percent of African Americans had voted for President Eisenhower, a Republican. Now, Kennedy's civil rights office detected building support for Senator Kennedy, a Democrat.

22. Quoted in Branch, *Parting the Waters*, 352.
23. Ibid., 362.

A small circle in the Kennedy campaign concocted a daring plan. Without even telling the Kennedy brothers, they managed to print about two million copies of a pamphlet that described Senator Kennedy's sympathetic call to Coretta King. They made arrangements to distribute the pamphlet through the black church the Sunday before the election. Fearing attention in the white press, they did not run newspaper ads, even in the black press. The Sunday before the election, the "secret" pamphlet circulated very widely in the black community without the white press even noticing.

On election day, Kennedy won by a mere 112,881 votes nationally. The "Negro vote" had made the difference. In 1956, 40 percent of black voters went Democrat; in 1960 that number shifted to roughly 70 percent. "This 30 percent shift accounted for more votes than Kennedy's victory margins in a number of key states, including Michigan, New Jersey, Pennsylvania, Illinois and the Carolinas."[24] A postelection analysis of the campaign made it quite clear that the massive switch in the black vote had elected President Kennedy.

It was equally clear that the Kennedy calls on the King case, along with the daring, clandestine, last-minute massive distribution of the pamphlet reporting on those calls, had produced this huge switch in the black vote. Dr. King had significantly affected a presidential election. His stature and power increased immensely.

In May 1961, the Freedom Riders developed another way to use nonviolent confrontation to combat segregation.[25] The Congress for Racial Equality (CORE) decided to test a recent Supreme Court decision that outlawed segregation in interstate buses and terminals. As in the sit-ins, King did not initiate this effort but soon supported the Freedom Riders.

The first interracial group of Freedom Riders left Washington on May 4 with plans to travel on Greyhound and Trailways through seven Southern states to New Orleans. When they disembarked at the first stop in South Carolina, white thugs launched a brutal attack. Vigilantes firebombed one bus, and a white mob bludgeoned the riders in Birmingham, Alabama. Battered, the first Freedom Riders agreed to fly to New Orleans.

But students in Nashville promptly announced that they would go to Birmingham to continue the Freedom Ride. By this time the Freedom Riders had attracted droves of reporters and photographers doing stories for the national

24. Ibid., 374–75. See also John Hope Franklin, *From Slavery to Freedom: A History of Negro Americans*, 3rd ed. (New York: Random House, 1969), 626.
25. On the Freedom Riders, see Branch, *Parting the Waters*, 413–91.

and international press. Robert Kennedy, now the US attorney general, was also directly involved, trying both to protect the Freedom Riders and discourage further riders.

When the second group of Freedom Riders reached Montgomery, Alabama, on May 20, the police disappeared. A large white mob brutally attacked the riders with fists, baseball bats, and lead pipes. They smashed the cameras of many photographers. Someone with a lead pipe knocked unconscious a person from Attorney General Kennedy's office in Washington. Kennedy promptly sent in federal marshals to protect the Freedom Riders.

On May 21, King flew into Montgomery to preach at an evening rally in support of the Freedom Riders. Soon a huge, expanding crowd of angry white militants moved closer and closer to the church, packed full of increasingly terrified African Americans. King talked by telephone with Robert Kennedy, who promised that federal marshals were on their way. They finally arrived, and King began to preach after ten o'clock that evening.

For the next couple of days, the Freedom Riders were secluded with Dr. King in a house across the street from King's former home in Montgomery. The students tried hard to persuade King to join them on the bus, but he declined. Wednesday morning, as twelve Freedom Riders boarded the bus for Jackson, Mississippi, sixteen reporters joined them, and forty-two vehicles (mostly police cars) accompanied them on a seventy-mile-per-hour ride.

A few hours later, fourteen other Freedom Riders emerged to ride the Greyhound bus out of Montgomery. Again reporters and police accompanied them. Almost immediately, rumors spread that still another group of Freedom Riders was about to arrive from Atlanta. The group included prominent Northerners—distinguished white college professors and Yale chaplain William Sloane Coffin. As Coffin's group met with King in Ralph Abernathy's home, reports came in of many groups of students across the South planning to join the Freedom Riders.

Attorney General Kennedy grew increasingly angry that evening as he learned that the Freedom Riders whom he had helped protect were continuing their protest by refusing bail after they were arrested upon arrival in Jackson.

Angrily, Kennedy called King to demand an explanation for the students' refusal to accept bail. King explained that their conscience compelled them to protest unjust laws in this way.

On May 26, just three weeks after the first Freedom Riders left on the bus from Washington, King presided over a meeting of representatives of the

Freedom Riders. They formed the Freedom Ride Coordinating Committee, resolving to raise money, hire lawyers, and expand the Freedom Rides. They also requested that the attorney general ask the Interstate Commerce Commission to demand the desegregation of all interstate bus terminals. He did, and the Interstate Commerce Commission issued the mandate. By the end of 1961, most interstate bus terminals, even in the Deep South, were well on the way to integration.

Desperate to end the explosive Freedom Rides, Kennedy managed to persuade many of the leaders of the Freedom Ride Coordinating Committee, as well as the leaders of the major civil rights organizations, to focus on the Voter Education Project. Major foundations agreed to fund it. Southern leaders used less confrontation with continuing Freedom Riders, quietly throwing them in jail. National media attention moved elsewhere. But the daring Freedom Riders had provided another vivid demonstration of the power of nonviolent confrontation with injustice.

As King moved through 1962, however, things began to fall apart. A major effort in Albany, Mississippi, flopped. Much media attention disappeared. And the SCLC's finances were in trouble.

King began to make careful plans for a big campaign in Birmingham, Alabama. They would start with sit-ins against segregation, then organize a large boycott of downtown businesses, and eventually fill the jails. King's future depended upon success in Birmingham.

They launched the campaign on April 3, 1963, with a small sit-in at downtown lunch counters. But the campaign quickly bogged down. The black establishment—not to mention Attorney General Robert Kennedy—was largely opposed to the campaign. National media were hostile. Only small numbers of people were signing up to march and go to jail. After eight days of protests less than one hundred fifty people had been jailed. Northern and national news outlets were negative. Hopelessness pervaded King's cadre of leaders. King was torn between leaving Birmingham for a national speaking tour to replenish the SCLC's dangerously low finances and defying an injunction against parades and boycotts and going to jail.

King chose jail. On Good Friday, King led a march that grew to one thousand and landed him in solitary confinement. On April 13, King read, in a Birmingham newspaper smuggled into his cell, about a letter from white (liberal!) clergymen attacking King's campaign and urging him to be more patient. Using the edges of the newspaper, he started scribbling a response.

It was to become one of his most famous pieces, "Letter from Birmingham Jail."[26] After almost nine days in jail, King posted bond.

King and the other leaders decided to organize a mass protest march on May 2. But there were two problems. The injunction against marches would mean jail. And very few adults were stepping forward to volunteer for jail. Then they noticed that a growing crowd of students, indeed younger and younger students, was volunteering for their ongoing workshops on nonviolence. King struggled hard with whether he should allow children to face the danger of police brutality and jail. Knowing that failure in Birmingham was likely unless students joined the march, he reluctantly agreed.

On May 2, fifty teenagers marched out of 16th Street Baptist Church singing "We Shall Overcome." The police started loading them into police vans. Then came another fifty, and another, and another. One tough cop tried to persuade a group of elementary school children to stop marching, but they refused. He asked one little girl how old she was. "Six," she said as she walked boldly into the paddy wagon. By nightfall, six hundred children and youth were in jail.

The next day, more than one thousand children marched out of 16th Street Baptist Church. This time the blatantly racist police commissioner, Bull Connor, turned the fire hoses on the children as they marched. The powerful blasts of water knocked children over, tumbling some down the street. But still the children kept marching confidently out of the church. With the police overwhelmed, Connor unleashed his dog units on the children. One Associated Press photographer snapped a picture of a white policeman with his big dog's teeth sunk in the stomach of a young black man.

Pictures of Friday's violence flashed across the world.[27] National celebrities, including comedian Dick Gregory and folksinger Joan Baez plus more and more reporters, flew into Birmingham that weekend. On Monday, May 6, Dick Gregory led the first group of children out of the church. Over one thousand people marched that day, and one of King's lieutenants promised six thousand for Tuesday. When King addressed some five to ten thousand people in the Monday evening mass rally, he declared, "You are certainly making history."[28]

26. Reprinted in Washington, *Testament of Hope*, 289–302. In 2013, fifty years later, Christian Churches Together, noting that a clergy response to King's famous letter had never been issued, released "A Response to Dr. Martin Luther King Jr.'s 'Letter from Birmingham Jail'" (christianchurchestogether.org/wp-content/uploads/2013/08/CCT-Response-Letter-Birmingham-Jail.pdf).

27. For King's report on the power of these images, see Juhnke and Hunter, *Missing Peace*, 225.

28. Quoted in Branch, *Parting the Waters*, 773.

And he told the cheering crowd that 2,500 people were in jail. The next day, hundreds of black marchers flooded the downtown business district.

Members of the white business establishment realized that they had to negotiate with King. Painfully, they negotiated a compromise that produced substantial desegregation in downtown Birmingham. Nonviolent confrontation had won another huge victory.

Only when King left Birmingham to speak around the country did he begin to realize how sweeping was his success. Traffic was jammed for twenty blocks when he spoke to huge audiences in Cleveland. Fifty thousand came to hear him in Los Angeles for what was in effect the first integrated mass meeting. Mayor Daley gave him an official welcome in Chicago. In Detroit, the crowd was estimated to be more than one hundred twenty-five thousand. Magazines around the country printed King's "Letter from Birmingham Jail."

President Kennedy went on national television to say, "The events in Birmingham and elsewhere have so increased the cries for equality that no city or state or legislative body can prudently choose to ignore them. . . .We preach freedom around the world," the president noted, "but are we to say to the world . . . that this is the land of the free, except for Negroes, that we have no second-class citizens, except for Negroes?"[29]

King realized that the scenes of police brutality on national television and the scores of newspaper reports across the country and around the world had produced a sea of change in public opinion. At the same time, scores of local protests and white vigilante violence continued unabated. Racists murdered the prominent Mississippi leader of the NAACP, Medgar Evers. In the ten weeks after the success in Birmingham, over fourteen thousand arrests were made in racial demonstrations in 186 cities in the United States.

Dr. King and other prominent civil rights leaders laid plans for a huge March on Washington. They had little time to organize a march that they hoped would bring vast numbers of both black and white Americans to Washington. On the morning of the march, "twenty-one charter trains pulled into Washington and buses poured south through the Baltimore tunnel at the rate of one hundred per hour."[30] Most of the marchers, a crowd of some two hundred fifty thousand, were African Americans, but tens of thousands of whites also participated.

National television broadcasted live the glorious event at the Lincoln Memorial. Dr. King was the last of many famous leaders who addressed the crowd.

29. Quoted in ibid., 824.
30. Ibid., 876.

Toward the end, he departed from his prepared speech and wowed the huge crowd with his never-to-be-forgotten words, "I have a dream."

I have a dream that one day on the red hills of Georgia, sons of former slaves and sons of former slave-owners will all be able to sit down together at the table of brotherhood. . . . I have a dream my four little children will one day live in a nation where they will not be judged by the color of their skin but by [the] content of their character.[31]

President Kennedy watched King on television at the White House—the first time he had listened to a complete speech by King. "He's damn good," the president commented to his aides. Most African Americans and a growing number of whites now recognized King as a national spokesman. One year later, King received the Nobel Peace Prize.

Only a few months after the March on Washington, President Kennedy was assassinated in Dallas. When he died, his civil rights bill was stuck in Congress. That would change with the new president, Lyndon Johnson.

President Johnson promptly told the nation that the best way to honor the slain president would be to pass his civil rights bill. Civil rights groups, labor groups, and churches mobilized widespread support. On July 2, 1964, President Johnson signed the historic Civil Rights Act. It banned discrimination in public accommodation, employment, unions, and publicly funded programs and established the Equal Employment Opportunity Commission.[32] The nation had taken another important step away from its tragically racist past.

The 1964 Civil Rights Act, however, offered very little help against the numerous legal and other measures in many Southern states that prevented most African Americans from registering to vote. The Student Nonviolent Coordinating Committee (SNCC) began a voter registration drive in Selma, Alabama, in 1963, but it had made little progress by the end of 1964. Blacks were a majority in Dallas County, where the city of Selma was located, but only 320 of 15,115 blacks of voting age had managed to register.[33] Dallas County opened the voter registration office on only two days a month, and white registrars regularly ruled that black applicants (even accomplished black schoolteachers) had failed the (legal) literacy test. County sheriff James Clark harassed those who tried to register.

31. Washington, *Testament of Hope*, 219.
32. Thomas R. Brooks, *Walls Come Tumbling Down: A History of the Civil Rights Movement, 1940–1970* (Englewood Cliffs, NJ: Prentice Hall, 1974), 235.
33. Ibid., 252.

Soon after accepting the Nobel Peace Prize on December 10, 1964, King came to Selma to announce that his organization (the SCLC) would throw its power and prestige into the campaign for black voter registration in the city and county. "We will seek to arouse the federal government by marching by the thousands to the place of registration."[34] If necessary, King would demand federal registrars and federal marshals to protect those seeking to register.

On January 19, 1965, King defied a local ban, leading a march to the court-house. When Sheriff Clark grabbed Amelia Boynton (a well-known woman in the march), arresting her and about sixty others, the story quickly became headline news in the *New York Times* and *Washington Post*. As part of the black elite, black schoolteachers usually avoided radical protest. But the sheriff's abuse and arrest of Boynton so outraged them that more than one hundred black teachers marched to the courthouse on January 20 to protest. On the steps, the sheriff poked the teachers with his nightstick. The effect was to unite the black community in support of the voter registration drive.[35]

On February 1, King purposely defied a local ordinance about marches and was arrested. When news of his arrest spread, five hundred schoolchildren quickly marched to the courthouse, and they too were arrested. The next day, three hundred more children went to jail. On February 10, the sheriff and his deputies used cattle prods and billy clubs to force about 165 demonstrating children to walk fast or run two miles on the way to jail. Each night, national television news flashed across the nation the images of white police abusing black children. President Johnson met with Dr. King, and his office announced that the president would send a voting rights bill to Congress.

The marches continued in the next several weeks. So did police harassment and white vigilante attacks. Dozens were beaten. Jimmy Lee Jackson died after being battered and shot by police while trying to protect his eighty-two-year-old grandfather, who had been beaten by a white mob. After weeks of marching and brutality, the black community began to grow weary.

King responded by proposing a huge march from Selma to Montgomery (the capital of Alabama). On March 7, five hundred African Americans marched out of Selma down the road to Montgomery. At the Edmund Pettus Bridge, near the edge of Selma, the marchers were met by state police and Sheriff Clark's deputies, some on horseback. The police attacked with tear gas and

---

34. Quoted in ibid., 253.
35. Juan Williams, *Eyes on the Prize: America's Civil Rights Years, 1954–1965*, 15th anniversary ed. (New York: Penguin Books, 2002), 259–60.

nightsticks. They fractured John Lewis's skull and sent dozens to the hospital. Again, widespread national television and newspaper coverage followed.

King promptly issued a call for prominent national clergy to join him in a new march. Sympathizing leaders from across the nation quickly flew into Selma. On March 10, about four hundred fifty whites joined a thousand African Americans in a march across the Edmund Pettus Bridge. That night, white racists clubbed three white ministers who had come for the march, and one of the ministers, James Reeb from Massachusetts, later died. White America was outraged—far more, alas, by the death of this one white person than by the long, long string of blacks killed by white racists. Thousands participated in sympathy marches around the nation. More than four thousand religious leaders rushed to Washington to demand voter rights legislation.

On March 15, President Johnson presented a new voter registration bill to Congress as an estimated seventy million Americans watched on television. In perhaps his best speech, Johnson declared, "Every American citizen must have an equal right to vote."[36] And he concluded with the words of one of the civil rights movement's theme songs: "We *shall* overcome."[37] A tear slipped down Dr. King's cheek as he watched on television as President Johnson ended his speech.

On March 21, after President Johnson had federalized the Alabama National Guard to protect the marchers, Dr. King finally began the successful Selma-to-Montgomery march. It took five days to reach the capital. As they moved toward the steps of the state capitol in Montgomery (the very place where Jefferson Davis was sworn in as president of the Confederate States of America during the Civil War), King led twenty-five thousand people, including virtually all the nation's black dignitaries, accompanied by many white leaders. As segregationist Alabama governor George Wallace peeked out from behind venetian blinds in his office at the state capitol, national television spread Dr. King's words across the nation as he addressed the crowd:

> My people, listen. The battle is in our hands. . . . I know some of you are asking today, "How long will it take?" . . . How long? Not long, because the arm of the moral universe is long but it bends toward justice.[38]

On August 6, President Johnson signed into law the historic 1965 Voting Rights Act as Rosa Parks, Dr. King, and many other civil rights leaders stood

36. Quoted in Brooks, *Walls Come Tumbling Down*, 257.
37. Quoted in ibid.
38. Quoted in ibid., 258.

in the President's Room of the capitol rotunda and watched. The legislation's tough provisions quickly removed many of the legal and informal barriers to black voter registration. Within a year, nine thousand blacks had registered to vote in Dallas County, Alabama, and the people voted Sheriff Clark out of office.[39] When the bill passed in 1965, there were only 475 elected black officials in the whole nation; five years later, there were about 2,240.[40] Nonviolent protest was changing America.

Unfortunately, the civil rights coalition began to fall apart after the successful events of 1965. Riots erupted in American cities. Black radicals denounced the participation of whites in the campaign against segregation. And white liberals turned much of their attention to the war in Vietnam.

In the summer of 1965, Watts, a large black section of Los Angeles, exploded in riots that killed thirty-four people, injured over a thousand, and landed over three thousand in jail. Far worse riots erupted in scores of cities across the country in 1966 and 1967. King opposed the violence but seemed powerless to prevent or stop it. Black power advocates took over SNCC and CORE, driving out white members and rejecting King's nonviolence. When King spoke out against the war in Vietnam (first in 1965 and then more strongly in 1967), both mainstream white Americans and most black establishment leaders condemned him. President Johnson was furious.

In 1966, King tried to take his nonviolent campaign to the North. He rented an apartment in Chicago and began an "End the Slums" campaign. The tactics he had used so effectively in the South failed to produce the same results in the North. Chicago's Mayor Daley was wily enough to avoid confrontation, and Chicago's black community refused to unite around King's efforts. Even fewer blacks followed King as he tried to lead marches into segregated white neighborhoods. In August, King completed an agreement with Mayor Daley that included some significant promises: open housing and bank loans for homebuyers without racial consideration. Some, however, criticized the agreement as a sellout with little substance.

Devastating riots in the summer of 1967 further discouraged Dr. King. Urban blacks seemed to be rejecting his call for nonviolence. As King searched for a way to channel black rage in a fruitful, nonviolent direction, he decided to call another march on Washington. He began to plan for the Poor People's March in the spring of 1968. In the previous few years, King had thought

39. Ibid., 286.
40. Ibid., 293.

more and more about economic issues. He spoke more clearly about the way economic injustice contributed to the plight of African Americans. And he tried to broaden his appeal to poor people of all races. But prominent black leaders strongly questioned the wisdom of the proposed Poor People's March on Washington, in light of the growing white backlash because of the riots and the fact that 1968 involved a presidential election. Plans for the march bogged down. Little enthusiasm emerged. Even King himself was uncertain.

Suddenly, a riveting diversion appeared. A racist action in January 1968 by the sanitation department in the city of Memphis, Tennessee, led over a thousand black sanitation workers there to go on strike. They demanded that the city recognize their union for the first time and improve their pay. When the police broke up a sit-in with clubs and mace, King agreed to come to support the garbage workers, more than 90 percent of whom were black.

The strike reflected King's growing concern with economic injustice. It also brought together again the old civil rights coalition of labor and African Americans. King led a march on March 28 that ended in tragedy. Drunken disorder, looting, and arson led to vicious, indiscriminate police brutality. Police killed one teenager, clubbed dozens, and arrested hundreds. King was deeply dismayed by the violence but clung to his belief that he could lead a nonviolent march.

He called another march for April 8, giving time to bring in civil rights and labor leaders. The Thursday before, King spent the day in room 306 of the Lorraine Hotel in Memphis planning for the upcoming march. Just before leaving for dinner, he stepped out on the balcony, joking with his colleagues. A lone assassin was waiting in a nearby window, and his deadly bullet ended the life of America's greatest advocate of nonviolence. King was only thirty-nine years old.

Dr. King's nonviolent civil rights campaign did not end racism or poverty, but it profoundly changed America. It provoked national legislation that largely ended legal segregation and led to the election of thousands of black officials. It opened doors in education and employment that over the next decades offered new opportunities to African Americans. And it changed the thinking of many Americans, both blacks and whites. Many blacks developed a new pride, and many whites came to better understand and oppose the evil of racism. Thanks to the nonviolent work of Dr. King, America slowly became a better nation.

King contributed immensely to our understanding of nonviolence. Perhaps this is most clear in the way he combined power and love, national political influence and grassroots organizing. He saw clearly how organizing nonviolent protest among poor African Americans in the rural South could be used—thanks to the attention of the national media that such action provoked—to pressure powerful politicians in Washington to act. King's work was a living implementation of his famous statement about power and love: "One of the greatest problems of history is that the concepts of love and power are usually contrasted as polar opposites. Love is identified with a resignation of power and power with a denial of love. . . . What is needed is a realization that power without love is reckless and abusive, and that love without power is sentimental and anemic."[41] King's practice of activist nonviolence is a powerful illustration of how to combine them.

King's nonviolent civil rights campaign also deepened global understanding and appreciation of nonviolence. It demonstrated the way television's powerful depiction of violence against nonviolent protestors could move the hearts and transform the thinking of tens of millions of uninvolved citizens. And its success "conferred on nonviolent action a new aura of effectiveness that it had never before possessed."[42] Thanks to the way mass media conveyed the stories and images of King's nonviolent campaign all around the world, Dr. King helped fulfill Gandhi's dream that African Americans would deliver the message of nonviolence to the world.

41. "Where Do We Go from Here?" in Washington, *Testament of Hope*, 577–78, quoted in Cortright, *Gandhi and Beyond*, 192.
42. Ackerman and DuVall, *Force More Powerful*, 332.

4

nonviolent intervention
in guerrilla warfare

You take risks for peace just as you take risks for war.

Sharon Hostetler[1]

I was scared on the morning of January 11, 1985. Along with about twenty other Witness for Peace volunteers, I was riding a dusty bus down a twisting road in a remote guerrilla-infested part of northern Nicaragua. As we wound our way down the hillside into the valley toward the small town of San Juan de Limay, we knew that a thousand US-funded Contras lay hidden in the surrounding hills.

The Contras had announced their intention to capture the encircled town. Frequent ambushes and attacks on surrounding villages, farmhouses, and cooperatives had occurred. Nancy Donovan, an American Maryknoll sister from the town, had been kidnapped and then released three days earlier.[2] In the previous month, the Contras had captured and tortured many civilians. Thirty-three had died. The Contras' attacks had closed all roads to the town for a month.

Our bus was the first outside vehicle to try to break that blockade. As we slowly navigated the twisting roads down the side of the hills and then drove

1. Quoted in Witness for Peace Documentation Project, *Kidnapped by the Contras: The Peace Flotilla on the Rio San Juan, Nicaragua, August 1985* (Santa Cruz, CA: Witness for Peace Documentation Project, 1985), 9. I thank Rebecca Hall for help in revising this chapter.

2. Reed Brody, *Contra Terror in Nicaragua: Report of a Fact-Finding Mission: September 1984–January 1985* (Cambridge, MA: South End Press, 1985), 87–90.

47

past burnt tractors destroyed by the Contras, I prayed hard that there would be no sudden burst of gunfire, no surprise ambush. There wasn't. We arrived safely in the town. (It would have been bad politics to use US-supplied weapons to kill American Christians.)

I was relieved, and the townspeople were overjoyed. Later we were told that the people of San Juan de Limay slept more securely that night than they had in weeks. They knew that an attack was highly unlikely while American Christians were present.[3]

My little personal pilgrimage of fear and faith is one tiny part of a much larger story. From the beginning of the movement in 1983 until 1991, over four thousand volunteers, typically in teams of twenty, traveled to war zones in Nicaragua as part of Witness for Peace.[4] One team rode a rusty fishing boat to rendezvous with a huge US warship. Edén Pastora's Contras kidnapped another team while they were sailing up the Rio San Juan, which flows between Nicaragua and Costa Rica. Others faced more mundane hardships, such as coping with upset digestive systems that demanded hasty, frequent treks to unfamiliar toilets.

What prompted so many comfortable American Christians to risk disease, injury, and even death in a nonviolent challenge to the guerrillas invading Nicaragua?

▤ A History of Outside Intervention

The story begins early in the twentieth century.[5] In 1912, the United States sent the Marines to invade Nicaragua and effect regime change. They would stay for most of the next two decades,[6] leaving the country in the hands of Anastasio Somoza García, the head of the US-created National Guard.[7] While the Somoza family and those closest to them grabbed huge amounts of land and

---

3. For a longer account of that trip, see Ronald J. Sider, "Why Me, Lord? Reluctant Reflections on the Trip to Nicaragua," *The Other Side*, May 1985, 20–25.

4. Edward Griffin-Nolan, *Witness for Peace: A Story of Resistance* (Louisville: Westminster John Knox, 1991), 10.

5. I thank Dr. Arnold Snyder for granting me permission to make generous use of an unpublished paper, "Witness for Peace in Nicaragua," which he wrote in early 1985. From February 15 to December 15, 1984, Arnold was the coordinator of Witness for Peace in Nicaragua.

6. Mauricio Solaún, *U.S. Intervention and Regime Change in Nicaragua* (Lincoln: University of Nebraska Press, 2005), 24.

7. Morris H. Morley, *Washington, Somoza, and the Sandinistas: State and Regime in U.S. Policy toward Nicaragua, 1969–1981* (New York: Cambridge University Press, 1994), 36.

wealth, the rest of the country suffered. Over two hundred thousand *campesinos*, at one point almost a third of the population,[8] were left without land or any means to survive in a primarily agricultural economy.[9] The majority of Nicaraguans prior to the 1979 revolution faced appalling living conditions.[10]

Although most individual Americans were not directly responsible for the poverty and agony in Nicaragua, certainly, the foreign and economic policy of the United States as a whole was partly to blame. "Dependency" is the word that prominent Cornell University historian Walter LaFeber used to describe the relationship in this period of Nicaragua (and Central America generally) to the United States.[11] It was a dependency that tied Central American economies to a few export crops sold to the United States and led to wealth for a ruling elite and poverty and malnutrition for the rest. Such dependency was also directly linked to political and military intervention. In 1954, in Guatemala, for example, "the CIA organized, armed, and trained a rebel force that overthrew the democratically elected government of Jacobo Arbenz Guzman after it had nationalized land belonging to the U.S.-based United Fruit Company."[12] As demonstrated in the cases of Nicaragua and Guatemala, US foreign policy in Central America focused "on the notion of violence as the ultimate arbiter of power and guarantor of basic U.S. interests—political, economic, and strategic."[13]

In the late 1970s, at the cost of perhaps as many as fifty thousand lives, a broad coalition of Nicaraguan people joined in a popular insurrection to overthrow the corrupt Somoza dictatorship. To the bitter end, some powerful US interests continued to support the brutal dictator. As late as June 21, 1979, Secretary of State Cyrus Vance called on the Organization of American States to send a "peacekeeping force" to Somoza's aid.[14] Some days earlier, one hundred thirty US congressional representatives had demanded the restoration of direct military aid to the dictator. The liberal alternatives to Somoza and the guerrillas within Nicaragua could not compete with the powerful "Somoza lobby" in Washington. Thus, the final victory on July 19, 1979, was directed

8. Ibid., 51–52.
9. Walter LaFeber, *Inevitable Revolutions: The United States in Central America*, 2nd ed. (New York: W. W. Norton, 1993), 226.
10. Morley, *Washington, Somoza*, 54.
11. LaFeber, *Inevitable Revolutions*, 112.
12. Roger Peace, "Winning Hearts and Minds: The Debate over U.S. Intervention in Nicaragua in the 1980s," *Peace & Change* 35, no. 1 (2010): 4.
13. Morley, *Washington, Somoza*, 3.
14. Ibid., 188.

and led by the leftist guerrilla movement, the Sandinista Front for National Liberation (FSLN). On that day, Nicaragua embarked on its socialist political venture, vowing to redistribute the land among the people, educate and provide health care for the masses, and establish a mixed economy to be run, it was claimed, in the interests of Nicaraguans rather than foreign investors.

Regardless of how one views the Sandinista government's rule during the 1980s in Nicaragua (I give it a very mixed review),[15] it is undeniable that the Nicaraguan revolution brought both immediate benefits and new hope for a brighter future to the poorest segments of the population. Anthony Quainton, the US ambassador to Nicaragua in the earlier years of the Reagan administration, admitted on a number of occasions that the Sandinista government had in fact brought about significant improvement in land distribution, health, nutrition, and education for the Nicaraguan population as a whole. The new government distributed land to over one hundred fifty thousand families. It built health clinics and other essential infrastructure. "Within a year 100,000 student volunteers went out into the countryside and reduced the country's illiteracy rate from over 50 percent to 13 percent."[16] The FSLN kept many of the promises that it had made to the Nicaraguan people.

From the beginning, however, the Reagan administration was bitterly opposed to the Sandinista government. And there were reasons for concern. The FSLN had engaged in anti-American rhetoric—understandable, considering the effect that US intervention had already had in Nicaragua. The group's alleged involvement in sending arms to the revolutionary movement in El Salvador had already prompted the Carter administration to withhold some aid.[17] Promised elections were not held for five years, and there were Marxist-Leninists in the Sandinista coalition along with nationalists and Catholics. Actions designed to undercut the independence of other centers of power, such as independent trade unions, occurred. All these were valid reasons for anxiety. But they hardly justified the simplistic charge that the Sandinista party

15. See Sider, "Why Me, Lord?" For a highly critical view of the Sandinistas, see Humberto Belli, *Breaking Faith: The Sandinista Revolution and Its Impact on Freedom and Christian Faith in Nicaragua* (Westchester, IL: Crossway Books, 1985). For a positive evaluation, see James B. McGinnis, *Solidarity with the People of Nicaragua* (Maryknoll, NY: Orbis Books, 1985), 5–25. See also Mario Vargas Llosa, "Nicaragua," *New York Times Magazine*, April 28, 1985, 37.

16. Peter Costantini, "An American Tragedy," *New Internationalist* 324 (June 2000): 34.

17. Peace, "Winning Hearts and Minds," 5; William M. Leogrande, "Making the Economy Scream: US Economic Sanctions Against Sandinista Nicaragua," *Third World Quarterly* 17, no. 2 (1996): 330.

was a monolithic Marxist-Leninist group determined to destroy the church and impose a Soviet-style totalitarian society. Undoubtedly, some Sandinista members wanted that. Others most certainly did not.

Instead of following a balanced policy of protesting violations of human rights and democratic freedoms, the US government launched a secret war in late 1981.[18] The United States trained and financed a counterrevolutionary movement (the Contras) led by former officers of Somoza's private army. The stated aim of this covert operation was to stop the supposed flow of arms from Nicaragua to El Salvador and to destabilize the Sandinista government. Later, however, when the Contra army numbered over ten thousand fighters and the United States offered no convincing evidence of substantial arms flow to El Salvador, the administration admitted that it had embarked on an effort to "overthrow" the Sandinista government and to make it "say uncle."[19]

The result was enormous suffering and massacre in Nicaragua. Civilian casualties included "approximately 30,000 Nicaraguans killed, thousands more maimed and wounded, 350,000 internally displaced."[20] Many independent reporters and eyewitnesses detailed widespread attacks on civilians.

Contrary to the Just War tradition's prohibition against targeting civilians, the Contras almost daily kidnapped, tortured, mutilated, and killed noncombatants. During my trip to San Juan de Limay in January 1985, I listened to the local medical doctor describe how the Contras had broken the fingers and mutilated and dismembered the bodies of the thirty-three people they had killed the previous month near that one small town. The son of the woman who was to be our cook was so badly tortured and mutilated that his father could identify him only because of his belt.[21] Independent human rights organizations, such as Americas Watch and Amnesty International, consistently reported similar Contra atrocities against civilians.[22]

Many American citizens were outraged at the expenditure of their tax dollars to support this carnage.

18. Francis A. Boyle, "Determining U.S. Responsibility for Contra Operations under International Law," *American Journal of International Law* 81, no. 1 (1987): 87.

19. "On Making 'Em Say Uncle," *New York Times*, February 23, 1985.

20. Peace, "Winning Hearts and Minds," 8.

21. Sider, "Why Me, Lord?," 22.

22. See Amnesty International, *Nicaragua: The Human Rights Record* (London: Amnesty International, 1986), 32ff.; Americas Watch, *Human Rights in Nicaragua: 1985–1986* (New York: Americas Watch, 1986), 86.

▨ Witness for Peace Begins

In July 1983, an interdenominational group of one hundred fifty US citizens took a dramatic new step of nonviolent intervention in guerrilla warfare. They traveled to the Nicaragua-Honduras border to be present with the people suffering attacks and to pray and keep vigil for peace. While present in the beleaguered border town of Jalapa, the delegation witnessed the terrible effects of the war on the population. They also brought hope and temporary safety. One grateful Jalapa resident told the group, "At least tonight they won't shell us, because you are here."[23]

An idea began to germinate among the vigilers. If their mere presence could provide security from attacks by the Contras, why not establish a "permanent presence" of US citizens to stand nonviolently with the Nicaraguan people?

Before the group left Nicaragua, plans emerged for a permanent presence in Nicaragua, originally envisaged as hundreds of volunteers stationed along the border. Local activists from two religious groups within Nicaragua issued a formal invitation and agreed to act as sponsors. The Evangelical Committee for Aid and Development (CEPAD), an evangelical Protestant development agency,[24] and the Antonio Valdivieso Ecumenical Center, an agency promoting religious and social research, issued a formal invitation and agreed to act as sponsors. Unfortunately, the government of Honduras rejected a similar request to operate there too. But the Nicaraguan government gave preliminary approval, including the important provision that the project would neither support nor oppose any Nicaraguan political party.[25]

The new organization was called Witness for Peace (WFP). Its history is a story of transition from Spirit-inspired dream to dusty reality. The first four volunteers left the United States for Nicaragua in October 1983. The earliest focus of WFP was the town of Jalapa in northern Nicaragua. (At that time the Contras hoped to capture the town, establish a provisional government, and seek aid from friendly countries.) WFP's initial goal was to establish a team of ten to twenty witnesses who would commit themselves to a six-month stay at the Nicaraguan border. Periodically, short-term

23. Quoted in Snyder, "Witness for Peace," 5.
24. Hector Perla Jr., "Si Nicaragua Venció, El Salvador Vencerá: Central American Agency in the Creation of the U.S.–Central American Peace and Solidarity Movement," *Latin American Research Review* 43, no. 2 (2008): 151–52.
25. Clare Weber, *Visions of Solidarity: U.S. Peace Activists in Nicaragua from War to Women's Activism and Globalization* (Lanham, MD: Lexington Books, 2006), 46.

teams, staying in Nicaragua for only one or two weeks, would join them. It was hoped that the permanent presence along the border would number at least fifty people at all times—a far cry from several hundred, but in itself a considerable undertaking.

In December 1983, the first short-term team arrived for a two-week stay. From the start, the visits of the short-term teams were conceived as educational opportunities while also being opportunities to promote peace in the war zones. The two weeks spent in Nicaragua included interviews with both opponents and supporters of the Sandinista revolution.

As 1984 unfolded, the organization grew, both in Nicaragua and in the United States. Eventually, a manageable operation emerged, comprising a steering committee, a small full-time staff, plus many volunteers in both countries. At the heart of the operation was a team of fifteen to twenty long-term volunteers in Nicaragua, and three delegations of short-term volunteers visiting Nicaragua every month. That basic pattern was to continue throughout the decade. By 1991, over four thousand WFP volunteers had visited Nicaragua.[26]

Goals and Strategy

WFP's fundamental goal was to end the US-funded guerrilla warfare in Nicaragua. The method was nonviolent direct action. WFP's official statement of purpose pledged "to plumb the depths of the religious nonviolent tradition and continually to envision and experiment with creative, powerful nonviolent actions." Boldly, they declared themselves ready "to take risks in the struggle for peace comparable to the risks people take in war."[27]

The initial strategy in Jalapa was "deterrence through interpositioning." The Contras planned to seize the town; WFP hoped that the mere presence of US citizens in Jalapa would be enough to deter them. The Contras knew that it would be politically costly to wound or kill praying American citizens.

This strategy, however, worked only for a short time because the Contras' strategy soon changed. Aborting their effort to seize a major town, the Contras began attacking isolated farms, cooperatives, and government-funded

26. Christian Smith, *Resisting Reagan: The U.S. Central American Peace Movement* (Chicago: University of Chicago Press, 1996), 78.
27. Cited in Witness for Peace Documentation Project, *Kidnapped by the Contras*, 40.

projects, such as schools and clinics, in order to destroy the social and economic infrastructure of the country. They targeted key civilian workers and community leaders (especially teachers, doctors, and agricultural specialists) for abduction, torture, and assassination. It was impossible for a few dozen WFP volunteers to stand between even a tiny fraction of the Nicaraguan people and ten thousand guerrillas engaged in hit-and-run terrorist attacks on constantly shifting targets across northern Nicaragua. Interpositioning, however, was not entirely abandoned. It happened dramatically in the case of the encounter with the US warship. Arnold Snyder, who led WFP's Nicaraguan team for a year, thinks that it would have worked in San Juan de Limay in late 1984 and early 1985 if there had been enough volunteers.[28] Overall, however, deterrence through interpositioning does not fit the tactics of guerrilla warfare.

WFP therefore redirected its efforts toward visiting places recently attacked in order to document and publicize the targeting of civilians. This redirection was shaped in part by the assault of the town of Ocotal on June 1, 1984. Instead of attacking the town's army base, the Contras focused exclusively on civilian and economic targets. They destroyed the country's largest lumber mill, offices of the electric company, grain storage silos, and many other vital economic plants and facilities.[29] WFP volunteers arrived the next day to help with cleanup and reconstruction and to publicize the atrocities. One WFP volunteer discovered a CIA-written manual designed to teach Nicaraguans how to destabilize and sabotage their government and economy.[30] Publishing evidence of this CIA manual helped galvanize American public opinion against funding the Contras.

After Ocotal, the central strategy of WFP focused on shifting US public opinion against the war in Nicaragua by documenting and publicizing the ongoing atrocities. WFP published frequent news briefs based on eyewitness testimony gathered by volunteers and also a bimonthly newsletter. A regularly updated telephone hotline in the United States provided a steady flow of direct information from WFP staff in Managua. Every month, three teams of short-term volunteers returned to the United States to speak to churches and write or stimulate articles for church and secular media. WFP itself estimated that by 1986 the organization had reached a hundred million

28. Snyder, "Witness for Peace," 15.
29. Brody, *Contra Terror*, 55–56.
30. Ibid., 58.

Americans.[31] That undoubtedly made a difference in shifting US public opinion against the war.

The media in the United States exist not to educate but rather to increase audience ratings and widen circulation in order to garner advertising. The courage and suffering of the Nicaraguan people, the violence, mutilations, and assassinations that their country endured on a daily basis, were simply not considered newsworthy for a US audience, and so they went largely unnoticed. The kidnapping of an American nun, however, or a shrimp boat carrying American citizens making contact with a US Navy frigate were headline material. The efforts of a few thousand US citizen volunteers were able to command the sort of media coverage that the little country of Nicaragua was generally denied.

Not surprisingly, WFP's two most dramatic episodes—the encounter with a US warship and the kidnapping along the Rio San Juan—attracted the most attention.

■ Challenging a US Warship

On November 6, 1984, President Ronald Reagan won a second term as president in a landslide victory. That same evening, his government announced that US warships were tracking a Soviet freighter bound for Nicaragua's Corinto harbor.[32] On board, it was claimed, were crates similar to those used to transport Soviet MiG fighter jets. Fears of war skyrocketed as the US government implied that it would not tolerate the alleged Soviet MiGs, which would "upset the delicate balance of power in the region."[33]

On November 7, the Soviet freighter bearing the mysterious crates approached the Nicaraguan harbor of Corinto. It was already within Nicaraguan territorial waters, just seven miles from the coast, when two US Navy frigates gave chase. When a Nicaraguan Coast Guard cutter went to meet the Soviet ship, one of the US frigates gave chase, coming within five miles of the coast. An unmarked C-130 aircraft overflew the port, drawing antiaircraft fire from onshore batteries. Although the Nicaraguan government repeatedly denied

31. Estimates published by WFP in a 1986 promotional letter.
32. Nikolas Stürchler, *The Threat of Force in International Law* (Cambridge: Cambridge University Press, 2007), 196.
33. "US Concerned over Possible MIG Deliveries to Nicaragua," *Christian Science Monitor*, August 20, 1984 (http://www.csmonitor.com/1984/0820/082028.html).

the presence of MiG fighter aircraft on the Soviet freighter (and the US government was later shown to have been perfectly aware that no MiGs were on the ship),[34] fears of invasion mounted.[35] The government of Nicaragua called the country to mobilize for defense. It announced that student production brigades, in all numbering twenty thousand young people, would abandon their project of picking coffee and cotton in order to mobilize for the defense of Managua. Managua would be defended "barrio by barrio" if the United States decided to invade. In the international arena, Nicaragua called for an emergency meeting of the United Nations Security Council.[36] In Nicaraguan cities, people hurriedly began digging community air-raid shelters, and the government armed neighborhood militia.[37]

It was in this charged atmosphere that twelve long-term WFP volunteers gathered together in Managua on November 8 to share a noon meal, reflect on Scripture, pray, and plan. Their feelings are best expressed by Arnold Snyder:

> We shared a feeling that an evil force beyond all human control was propelling events toward a terrible and bloody conclusion. The time of sharing and prayer drew us together and strengthened us; the presence of the Holy Spirit was unmistakable in the coming of hope and the banishing of fear. We were moved from helplessness to a time of planning for action, trying to conceive of ways in which we could most effectively stand up to be counted as opposing the further violence our government seemed bent on imposing on the people of Nicaragua.
>
> The most outlandish idea to surface was also the most inspired: that we rent a flotilla of boats and place ourselves between the US frigates and [the] town and harbor of Corinto.[38]

"Wetness for Peace," as it was quickly dubbed, demanded speed. Two WFP short-term delegations in different parts of Nicaragua had to be assembled, and government permission had to be given for them to enter the war zone. The teams rushed to notify the press, assemble food, find transportation, and rent a boat—all in one and a half days.

At noon on Saturday, eighty US citizens, accompanied by twenty international journalists, converged on Corinto. Their "peace flotilla" was modest

---

34. Griffin-Nolan, *Witness for Peace*, 126.
35. Stürchler, *Threat of Force*, 198.
36. Ibid., 199.
37. Griffin-Nolan, *Witness for Peace*, 125.
38. Snyder, "Witness for Peace," 19–20. In this section I am relying on Snyder's eyewitness account.

in the extreme. One rusty old shrimp boat, the *Subtavia*, would sail forth to challenge the US Navy frigate with a message of peace.

Snyder's words capture the mood of the nonviolent marines:

> Those of us gathered for worship in the Baptist church of Corinto continued to feel the dark threat of war around us, but there was also an unmistakable presence of God's peace in the midst of the storm, expressed by the songs that began spontaneously as we waited for the service to begin. As we have so often had to note in our work in Witness for Peace, God strengthens us in special and unexpected ways when we leave our private fears and join together for a common purpose.[39]

Following a moving service and prayer of commissioning, the group marched through the town to the boat, carrying banners and singing songs of hope and victory. Forty people clambered aboard, and the trusty *Subtavia* pulled away from the dock in a cloud of diesel smoke. Slowly it moved toward international waters and an uncertain encounter. Those left on shore prayed together in the ruins of the fuel storage tanks destroyed by the CIA attack on Corinto in October 1983.

After two hours, a small dot appeared on the horizon. As the third hour passed, the forbidding outline of a US warship loomed ever larger. As the sun began to sink over the horizon, the little shrimp boat sailed within half a mile of the huge ship, awesome with its constantly moving radar antennae and its artillery and missile batteries now visible. Just as the *Subtavia* came within hailing distance, the warship began to move. The little shrimper increased its speed to close the distance, but the warship suddenly turned toward the open sea and sped away.

As the navy ship began to move away, the Rev. Stuart Taylor of the long-term team grabbed a loudspeaker and shouted to the US sailors on the departing warship, "Why are you here? Why are you threatening the people of Nicaragua? Go away! Leave us and these people in peace!"[40] But by this time the great ship was well out of earshot. David had come to speak to Goliath without so much as a sling in hand, but the giant would have none of it.

The nonviolent marines in the tiny shrimp boat were disappointed. They had hoped to speak to the American sailors on board the ship, but not a single person on the frigate was available the entire time. The final appeal had to be directed toward a huge, mute machine.

39. Ibid., 21.
40. Griffin-Nolan, *Witness for Peace*, 125.

The rendezvous was a success even though the WFP volunteers could not communicate directly the message of peace. It was filmed, recorded, and reported to millions around the world from the United States and Canada to Europe, Latin America, Africa, and Asia. The image of the great warship retreating from the unarmed, rusty tub conveyed its own message. At the farewell service on Thanksgiving Day, after many days of maintaining a permanent vigil on the beach of Corinto, Baptist pastor Ernesto Cordova reminded the WFP volunteers, "The little ship did not have firepower, but it had the power of love, the power of justice, the power of God. And the weakness of God is stronger than the power of men." One courageous act of nonviolent interpositioning had played its small part in nudging leaders and national public opinion away from violent conflict. By Thanksgiving the threats of attack and fears of invasion had subsided.

■ Kidnapped by the Contras

Twenty-one months later, WFP volunteers again captured news headlines around the world. Traveling in the first nonmilitary vessel to enter one section of the Rio San Juan beyond El Castillo for over two years, fifty-six people with WFP were kidnapped by the Contras.[41]

In the preceding months, tensions had risen along the Rio San Juan, which flows between Costa Rica and Nicaragua. The Contras were launching regular raids into Nicaragua and then retreating across the border into Costa Rica. On May 31, 1985, two members of the Costa Rican Civil Guard were murdered near the river. The Sandinistas blamed the Contras, and the Contras blamed the Sandinistas. Many feared that some new incident could provide a pretext for US intervention.

WFP decided to sail a peace flotilla down the dangerous section of the river. A delegation of twenty-nine WFP volunteers and eighteen members of the press were ready to embark on August 6, 1985.

The day before, however, Edén Pastora, leader of the Contras operating from Costa Rica, issued a press release announcing that he had ordered his men to fire on "wolves in sheep's clothing."[42] At its press conference, WFP responded with firmness: "For centuries, Christian theologians have justified the risking of human

41. For the following story, see Witness for Peace Documentation Project, *Kidnapped by the Contras*.

42. Stephen Kinzer, "29 U.S. Activists Reportedly Freed in Nicaragua," *New York Times*, August 9, 1985 (http://www.nytimes.com/1985/08/09/world/29-us-activists-reportedly-freed-in-nicaragua.html).

life to wage war. In Nicaragua today, we are called to take risks for peace."[43] Sharon Hostetler, joint coordinator of WFP in Nicaragua, said during an interview with CBS, "We hope to God, like all the Nicaraguans, that none of us will be killed. We are willing to risk danger. . . . We pray and reflect on the fact that the call to peace is not easy. You take risks for peace just as you take risks for war."[44]

Flying a large WFP banner, the delegation sailed from El Castillo on August 6. The journey downstream was peaceful. But the next morning, on the return voyage, trouble erupted. Shots rang across the bow, and everyone hit the deck. Guerrillas ordered the boat to the Costa Rican shore and identified themselves as members of ARDE (Pastora's Contra organization).

The next thirty hours were terrifying. At the command of their armed kidnappers, the entire delegation, including an elderly woman and an eighty-year-old man, stumbled uphill through difficult jungle terrain. Sandals fell off in deep mud. Too exhausted to trudge farther, they were finally allowed to rest in a thatched hut one and a half miles from the river.[45]

Toward evening, the guerrillas decided to let the group return to the boat. People slipped and fell on the muddy downhill path, rendered more treacherous by the day-long rain. They got lost and separated from each other, finally reaching the boat only after dark. But William, the guerrilla leader, was furious, partly because of embarrassment at losing his way. Enraged, he ordered them to march up the hill to the hut again in the darkness.

The old woman collapsed on the ground, sobbing. Her feet were bleeding. Totally exhausted, she had no energy to obey the orders and march another one and a half miles. That was the most terrifying moment of the entire episode. Many feared that the guerrillas would shoot the old woman. She feared that others would die because of her.

William grudgingly agreed to allow everyone on board for the night, provided they kept the lights out and made no noise. The next afternoon, all were released. With song and prayer, they gratefully finished the return voyage.

No peace treaties were signed because of the short voyage of this peace flotilla. But radio, television, and newspapers around the world broadcast a new chapter in the amazing story of nonviolent resistance.

43. Quoted in Witness for Peace Documentation Project, *Kidnapped by the Contras*, 9.
44. Ibid., 6.
45. Stephen Kinzer, "Reporters Say Pastora Rebels Held 29 in Nicaragua," *New York Times*, August 11, 1985 (http://www.nytimes.com/1985/08/11/world/reporters-say-pastora-rebels-held-29-in-nicaragua.html).

▨ Evaluating Witness for Peace

How successful was WFP in stemming the tide of conflict in Nicaragua? In 1984, Congress passed a law effectively prohibiting further aid to the Contras, a testament to the strength of public opinion against the war. A year later, however, Reagan imposed a trade embargo against Nicaragua, perpetuating economic violence against the country, while continuing to fund the Contras illegally in what became known as the Iran-Contra Affair.[46] He continued to explore other options for expressing his support, among them one last aid package, which Congress voted down in 1988.[47] US opposition to the Nicaraguan government ended only in 1990, when Violeta Chamorro won the presidential election over FSLN President Daniel Ortega.[48] In the end, attempts to change US policy toward Nicaragua never truly won out over Reagan's anticommunist agenda.

There is no doubt, however, that Witness for Peace played a significant role in the complicated history of US-Nicaraguan relations during the Reagan era. Occasionally, the presence of WFP deterred attack. Documentation and publication of civilian casualties had an influence on US policy. And WFP forged another courageous model of nonviolent direct action.

Deterrence of Contra attack was very modest but not irrelevant. The presence (and publicity about the presence) of WFP in Jalapa was probably one factor in the Contras' abandonment of their effort to capture that town. The Contras did not attack San Juan de Limay while my delegation was there. The US warship clearly did not want to deal with a shrimp boat full of praying American Christians accompanied by international journalists.

Because of intercepted radio messages describing WFP vehicles and activities, WFP was aware that the Contras were informed about WFP activities and reported on their movements. Only one town was attacked while WFP volunteers were present.

Had they wished to do so, the Contras could easily have ambushed WFP delegates many times as they drove the isolated roads into the war zones. Since the Contras clearly did not wish to kill US citizens, this translated into

46. Leogrande, "Making the Economy Scream," 338.
47. "Wrong from the Start; Reagan's Contra War, Reagan's Failure," *New York Times*, February 7, 1988 (http://www.nytimes.com/1988/02/07/opinion/wrong-from-the-start-reagan -s-contra-war-reagan-s-failure.html).
48. Leogrande, "Making the Economy Scream," 343.

a measure of protection for the Nicaraguan people while WFP volunteers were present. A highly placed Nicaraguan government official, when asked if WFP's nonviolent presence deterred attack, answered unequivocally, "Yes, it helps. Because the one thing that is feared by the Reagan government is that U.S. citizens might die. . . . So yes, it matters that nonviolent Christians are present as a barrier."[49]

Gilberto Aguirre, executive director of CEPAD, the evangelical agency in Nicaragua that worked closely with WFP, has said the same thing: "You have to extend and increase Witness for Peace work. We have seen that the impact of your work is very great, not only in the USA, but with the Contras. You could save a lot of lives."[50]

On balance, one must conclude that the deterrent effect of WFP was at best only a modest nuisance for the Contras. More important than WFP's attempt at deterrence was its growing impact on US public opinion and indirectly on US public policy through the documentation and publication of civilian casualties. The aim was to change a policy, not simply to be willing to risk death by interpositioning oneself between warring factions. If no one had been willing to take such a risk, of course, there would have been nothing to tell. But because they did, they had stories to publicize.

And they did just that. "In time, Witness for Peace was mailing its newsletter to forty thousand readers and its recruitment and fund-raising letters to more than one million contacts a year. Witness for Peace organized more than 1,000 local media and congressional contacts in 380 cities and 49 states."[51] WFP estimated that fifty-one million people heard over a thousand radio and television interviews of returning delegations. Four hundred thousand individuals heard over eight thousand in-person presentations to local church and community groups. Over sixty million Americans saw or read national media coverage of the kidnapped delegation on the Rio San Juan. Probably a hundred million Americans in all were reached.[52]

Reaching that many Americans even very infrequently undoubtedly helped shape US public opinion. WFP deserves some of the credit for the fact that a majority of Americans grew to oppose US support for the Contras and persuaded Congress to deny funding to them from 1984 to 1986 and again

49. Quoted in Snyder, "Witness for Peace," 36.
50. Quoted in Witness for Peace Documentation Project, *Kidnapped by the Contras*, 47.
51. Smith, *Resisting Reagan*, 78.
52. Estimates published by WFP in a 1986 promotional letter.

in 1988. That one of the most popular presidents in American history was unable to rally majority support for one of his top foreign-policy objectives is due in part to WFP.

Finally, WFP has had an intangible but important long-term impact. Even its modest success has opened the eyes of untold thousands to a nonviolent alternative for resisting violence. The influence of thousands of returning volunteers excited about the potential of nonviolent direct action worked its way through American churches like yeast in dough. Nor was the impact limited to the United States. News of this effort spread to many countries. Perhaps the comment of a (nonpacifist) Baptist leader in Nicaragua typifies the educational impact of WFP in many places: "I didn't understand nonviolence at first. I came to understand nonviolent action for peace by the testimony of the witnesses [WFP volunteers] in a place where the people were being violated by force of arms."[53]

WFP is one subplot in a living, growing story of courageous pioneers seeking alternatives to lethal violence.[54] WFP's part of that developing story demonstrates that nonviolent resistance to guerrilla warfare is possible.[55] The Philippine People's Revolution, to which we turn in the next chapter, shows that nonviolent revolution is also realistic.

53. Quoted in Snyder, "Witness for Peace," 38.

54. A complete evaluation of WFP would go way beyond this brief sketch. Among other things, I believe that WFP was too hesitant to criticize Sandinista violations of human rights and democratic freedoms. WFP, however, challenged the Sandinista government a number of times. For example, in meetings with Sandinista officials, including President Ortega, representatives of WFP criticized aspects of government policy, including mistreatment of Miskito people, failure to provide for conscientious objectors in the draft law, incommunicado detention of prisoners, and President Ortega's trip to the Soviet Union.

When President Ortega suspended certain civil liberties in October 1985, the WFP November-December newsletter said, "We oppose the decision to suspend civil liberties. . . . We are deeply saddened by developments in Nicaragua restricting human rights."

In 1985 and 1986, WFP loaned a staff person, Mary Dutcher, to the Washington Office on Latin America. Using WFP resources, she produced two widely publicized reports both entitled "Nicaragua: Violations of the Laws of War by Both Sides." These reports criticized human rights violations by both the Contras and the Nicaraguan government.

In the summer of 1985, when WFP delegates were kidnapped by the Contras, a WFP spokesman, Dennis Marker, criticized several specific Sandinista practices during a nationally televised interview on the McNeil-Lehrer Report.

55. For two other treatments of WFP, see Joyce Hollyday, "The Long Road to Jalapa," and Jim Wallis, "A Venture of Faith and Prayer," in *The Rise of Christian Conscience: The Emergence of a Dramatic Renewal Movement in the Church Today*, ed. Jim Wallis (New York: Harper & Row, 1987), 30–41, 42–46.

5

wheelchairs versus tanks

I have decided to pursue my freedom struggle through the path of
nonviolence. . . . I refuse to believe that it is necessary for a nation to
build its foundation on the bones of its youth.

Benigno Aquino[1]

The most stunning nonviolent victory since those of Mahatma Gandhi and Martin Luther King Jr. occurred in the Philippines in early 1986. Praying nuns, nursing mothers, and old women in wheelchairs turned back bayonets and tanks. In four breathtaking days in late February, Filipino "people power" toppled President Ferdinand Marcos, one of the world's most durable dictators.

■ Marcos and His Opponents

The story, of course, began much earlier. Marcos won the presidential election in 1965. In 1972, he declared martial law to "eliminate the threat of violent overthrow of the government."[2] This was not lifted until 1981. Even then, extralegal powers enabled him to continue his repressive rule.

1. Quoted in Douglas J. Elwood, *Philippine Revolution, 1986: Model of Nonviolent Change* (Quezon City: New Day, 1986), 19. I thank David Fuller for help in researching this chapter.
2. Stanley Karnow, *In Our Image: America's Empire in the Philippines* (New York: Ballantine Books, 1989), 359.

Marcos used dictatorial powers to amass great wealth for himself, close friends, and cooperative foreign companies.[3] His wife, Imelda Marcos, reportedly had three thousand pairs of shoes and "squandered $12 million on jewelry in a single day in Geneva."[4] To promote his development policy based on export crops, he ruthlessly suppressed workers who demanded decent wages and land reform. (Toward the end of his rule, the average wage for a sugarcane cutter working thirteen to fourteen hours a day was $7.00 a week.) Both Amnesty International and the International Commission of Jurists documented thousands of political prisoners in Marcos's jails. Electric shock torture, water torture, extended solitary confinement, and beatings were common. Poorly trained soldiers led by corrupt officers terrorized civilians, "often looting or acting on behalf of local landowners and officials seeking revenge against rivals. They coined a euphemism, *salvaging*, to signify the arbitrary detention of villagers, many of whom disappeared after being held for interrogation."[5] Such measures propped up a system whereby a tiny portion of the population received a huge percentage of the nation's total personal income.[6]

While Marcos and company stashed billions in Swiss banks, the majority of the people suffered grinding poverty. Three quarters of the people lived below the poverty line. Seventy-seven percent of all children under the age of six suffered from malnutrition.

Not surprisingly, a Marxist guerrilla movement gained increasing acceptance. A tiny group when Marcos declared martial law in 1972, the Marxist-led New People's Army had grown into a strong national movement by the mid-1980s. Many prominent people felt that civil war was inevitable. It might take ten years of bloody battle, they guessed, but no other course seemed viable.

But the assassination of Senator Benigno Aquino, on August 21, 1982, ignited a fire that brought revolution by different methods.[7] Aquino held the

3. For much of the following data, see Ricki Ross, "Land and Hunger: Philippines," *Bread for the World Background Paper*, no. 55, July 1981.

4. Karnow, *In Our Image*, 373.

5. Ibid., 386.

6. According to Virginia Baron, "The Philippine Example," *Fellowship* 53, no. 3 (1987): 4.

7. My sources for this chapter include the following: Monina Allarey Mercado, ed., *People Power: The Philippine Revolution of 1986; An Eyewitness History* (Manila: James B. Reuter, S.J., Foundation, 1986) (this magnificent book of eyewitness accounts and splendid pictures also contains short synopses of developments and valuable historical notes [pp. 308–14] on which I have relied for many of the historical details); several articles in the March 1987 issues of *Fellowship* 53, no. 3 (1987); Peggy Rosenthal, "Nonviolence in the Philippines: The Precarious Road," *Commonwealth*, June 20, 1986, 364–67; Elwood, *Philippine Revolution*; Bel Magalit, "The Church and the Barricades," *Transformation* 3, no. 2 (1986): 1–2; Peter

double honor of being Marcos's most prominent political opponent and longest-held (1972–80) political prisoner. Reading Jesus and Gandhi in prison, this conventional, self-serving politician experienced a renewal of personal faith and a transforming commitment to the poor and nonviolence.[8]

Released in 1980 to obtain heart surgery in the United States, Aquino prepared himself for the right moment to return home to challenge Marcos's repressive dictatorship. The nonviolent tactics that he intended to use were abundantly clear in a statement made to the subcommittee on Asian and Pacific Affairs of the US House of Representatives on June 23, 1983:

> To gather empirical data and firsthand information, I traveled to the Middle East, Southeast Asia, and to Central America. I interviewed the leaders of the most "successful revolutions" and talked to both the victors and the vanquished, the relatives of the victims and the survivors. I have concluded that revolution and violence exact the highest price in terms of human values and human lives in the struggle for freedom. In the end there are really no victors, only victims. . . .
>
> I have decided to pursue my freedom struggle through the path of nonviolence, fully cognizant that this may be the longer and more arduous road. . . .
>
> I have chosen to return to the silence of my solitary confinement and from there to work for a peaceful solution to our problems rather than go back triumphant to the blare of trumpets and cymbals seeking to drown the wailing and sad lamentations of mothers whose sons and daughters have been sacrificed to the gods of violent revolution. Can the killers of today be the leaders of tomorrow? Must we destroy in order to build? I refuse to believe that it is necessary for a nation to build its foundation on the bones of its youth.[9]

But Aquino was not to return to his prison cell when he stepped off the plane at Manila International Airport on August 21, 1983. Instead, he dropped dead in a hail of bullets in an assassination almost certainly approved by President Marcos.

■ The Beginnings of Nonviolent Opposition

The country erupted in outrage. Spontaneously, a huge, nonviolent demonstration occurred. Day and night, millions moved past Aquino's coffin in

---

Ackerman and Jack DuVall, *A Force More Powerful: A Century of Nonviolent Conflict* (New York: Palgrave, 2000), chap. 10.

8. Hildegard Goss-Mayr, "When Prayer and Revolution Became People Power," *Fellowship* 53, no. 3 (1987): 9.

9. Quoted in Elwood, *Philippine Revolution*, 19.

grief and silent defiance. Two million people marched peacefully in an eleven-hour funeral procession that persisted through sunshine and rain, thunder and lightning.[10] They responded enthusiastically when Aquino's mother and widow begged them to continue the struggle nonviolently. Two key symbols of the opposition to Marcos emerged: yellow, the color of the chrysanthemums that covered his casket, and the letter *L* "to signify Laban, the opposition political party."[11]

This emotional outpouring did not immediately alter political reality. Marcos was still the dictator. The growing Marxist guerilla movement (NPA) increasingly appeared to many as the only alternative as Marcos continued to crack down on opponents.

To be sure, there were a few courageous voices promoting a nonviolent alternative. As early as the 1960s, some poor communities organized nonviolent struggles and won small but significant victories. Since the early 1970s, Francisco Claver, bishop on the desperately poor, guerrilla-infested island of Mindanao, had been promoting nonviolent liberation of the poor. Marcos's army called him a Marxist. The Marxist guerrillas claimed that he supported the army. Bishop Claver quietly continued forming Christian communities committed to a nonviolent search for justice in his diocese. He also promoted the study of nonviolent social change among a small circle of Catholic bishops.[12]

Then, in February 1984, a short visit by two veteran nonviolent trainers crystallized more widespread interest in nonviolent alternatives. Hildegard and Jean Goss-Mayr had worked for decades promoting nonviolence in Europe and Latin America. Both Archbishop Dom Helder Camara of Brazil and the Nobel Prize winner Adolfo Pérez Esquivel of Argentina have traced their commitment to nonviolence to personal encounters with the Goss-Mayrs.[13] As the couple traveled through the Philippines in February 1984, they concluded that the hour was late for any nonviolent efforts. But they also sensed a widespread yearning for some realistic alternative to the agony of civil war.

10. Mercado, *People Power*, 10, 304.
11. Karnow, *In Our Image*, 405.
12. Goss-Mayr, "Prayer and Revolution," 8; Rosenthal, "Nonviolence in the Philippines," 366. For earlier examples of nonviolence, see Esther Epp-Tiessen, "Militarization and Non-Violence in the Philippines," *The Ploughshares Monitor* 7, no. 2 (1986), 3; Richard L. Schwenk, *Onward, Christians! Protestants in the Philippine Revolution* (Quezon City: New Day, 1986), 37.
13. Rosenthal, "Nonviolence in the Philippines," 364.

On the last day of their visit, Butz Aquino (brother of the assassinated Benigno Aquino) met privately with them. Aquino was an active leader in the ongoing protests against the dictatorship. Privately with the Goss-Mayrs, he confided his personal wrestling with the option of armed revolution:

> A few days ago the arms merchants visited us and said to us, "Do you think that with a few demonstrations you will be able to overthrow this regime? Don't you think you need better weapons than that? We offer them to you. Make up your mind." . . . You see it is providential that you have come at this point of time, because ever since this visit I am unable to sleep. Do I have the right to throw our country into major civil war? What is my responsibility as a Christian politician in this situation? Is there really such a thing as nonviolent combat against an unjust system like that of Marcos?[14]

In response, the Goss-Mayrs challenged him to decide for himself. They warned that vigorous preparation for nonviolent resistance is essential: "Nonviolence is not something you do spontaneously and without preparation."[15] The couple volunteered to return to do seminars if invited.

The invitation came within weeks. In the summer of 1984, the Goss-Mayrs returned for six weeks of seminars on nonviolence. They held sessions for leaders among the political opposition (including Butz Aquino), labor unions, peasants, students, and the church. Bishop Claver organized a three-day seminar for twenty Catholic bishops. Everywhere, the Goss-Mayrs advocated a twofold approach to nonviolence: nonviolent opposition to the structural violence in Marcos's economic and political system, and abandonment of the inner violence in one's own heart.

> The seed of the violence was in the structures, of course, and in the dictator. But wasn't it also in ourselves? It's very easy to say that Marcos is evil. But unless we each tear the dictator out of our own heart, nothing will change. Another group will come into power and will act similarly to those whom they replaced. So we discovered Marcos within ourselves.[16]

AKKAPKA, a new Philippine organization committed to nonviolence (formed in July 1984), emerged from these seminars. AKKAPKA is the acronym for Movement for Peace and Justice. It also means "I embrace you" in Tagalog, the national language of the Philippines. Led by the Jesuit priest José

---

14. Quoted in ibid., 365. See Hildegard Goss-Mayr's account in "Prayer and Revolution," 9.
15. Quoted in Rosenthal, "Nonviolence in the Philippines," 365.
16. Goss-Mayr, "Prayer and Revolution," 9.

Blanco, AKKAPKA held forty seminars on nonviolent social change in thirty provinces around the country in its first year.[17]

The numbers seriously interested in using nonviolent methods grew rapidly in late 1984 and 1985. Three weeks of seminars in Protestant circles by the American ethicist Richard Deats swelled their ranks. Even so, those involved were hardly ready for the surprise of November 3, 1985.

■ Marcos's Announcement and AKKAPKA's Initiatives

On that day, Marcos suddenly announced presidential elections for February 7, 1986. In the words of one analyst, "Marcos was sure he would be given a new mandate to continue in office, either by winning the elections or simply by having them rigged."[18] While the ideological left decided to boycott the elections, AKKAPKA quickly devoted all its energy toward trying to guarantee a fair election. They focused on three activities: encouraging the people to vote, preparing poll watchers, and organizing prayer tents.[19]

People intimidated by years of violent governmental repression needed to be encouraged to cast fear aside, reject government bribes, and vote according to their consciences. Regularly, in previous elections, armed thugs had intimidated voters and stolen ballots. So AKKAPKA joined other religious and civic organizations to help train half a million men and women, young and old, clergy and laity, to defend the ballot boxes nonviolently, even if attacked by armed soldiers or thugs.

AKKAPKA set up prayer tents in ten highly populated areas. One was located in the heart of Manila's banking community. Day and night, from mid-January 1986 to the end of the crisis, people came to these tents to fast and pray. Hildegard Goss-Mayr, who saw the tents in operation in early 1986, has underlined their importance:

> We cannot emphasize enough the deep spirituality that gave the people the strength to stand against the tanks later on. People prayed every day, for all those who suffered in the process of changing regimes, even for the military, even for Marcos. . . . It makes a great difference in a revolutionary process where people

17. Ibid., 10.
18. Joshua Paulson, "People Power against the Philippine Dictator—1986," in Gene Sharp, *Waging Nonviolent Struggle: 20th Century Practice and 21st Century Potential* (Boston: Porter Sargent, 2005), 239.
19. Goss-Mayr, "Prayer and Revolution," 10.

are highly emotional whether you promote hatred and revenge or help the people stand firmly for justice without becoming like the oppressor. You want to love your enemy, to liberate rather than destroy him.[20]

Almost immediately after Marcos announced the snap election, more and more people began to call on Cory Aquino, widow of the assassinated Benigno, to challenge Marcos at the polls. Unwilling at first, she reluctantly agreed, announcing her candidacy on December 5, 1985, just two months before the election. In the short, intense campaign that followed, she discovered massive popular support. Clearly, she was on her way to a decisive electoral victory.

Marcos, however, used vast, unparalleled fraud to steal the election. According to the Catholic Bishops' Conference of the Philippines, there was widespread buying of votes, intimidation of voters, fraudulent tabulation of returns, harassment, terrorism, and murder.[21] In metropolitan Manila alone, six hundred thousand people could not vote because Marcos's agents had scrambled the voting lists.

Tens of thousands of nonviolent poll watchers with the National Citizens' Movement for Free Elections (NAMFREL) courageously placed their bodies in the midst of all this corruption and violence. (NAMFREL had emerged as an independent organization in the 1984 parliamentary elections to conduct a quick, independent vote count and prevent some of the worst dishonesty.) Strong international support strengthened their hand in the 1986 presidential elections. NAMFREL deployed its thirty thousand volunteers at the most critical polling stations. Six hundred nuns, nicknamed the NAMFREL Marines, went to the most problematic locations. During the day of voting and the subsequent vote count, these nonviolent volunteers risked death many times. Twenty-four hours a day, they formed human chains and literally tied themselves to ballot boxes so that the boxes could not be stolen.[22]

NAMFREL's quick count showed Cory Aquino with a substantial lead. But the official tabulation placed Marcos ahead. On February 9, thirty young computer workers involved in the official vote count left their posts to protest the deliberate posting of dishonest returns.[23] That daring act removed any

20. Ibid.
21. See the bishop's official declaration, quoted in Mercado, *People Power*, 77.
22. Ibid., 43, 67, 68, 71.
23. Kurt Schock, *Unarmed Insurrections: People Power Movements in Nondemocracies*, (Minneapolis: University of Minnesota Press, 2004), 77.

credibility still enjoyed by the official returns. In spite of that, the parliament (Batasan) prepared to declare Marcos the winner.

■ The Bishops Speak Out

At this desperate moment, the Catholic Bishops' Conference of the Philippines issued one of the more daring political pronouncements of modern times by an official church body. On February 13, the bishops denounced the elections as fraudulent. They declared that Marcos's government could not command the people's allegiance because it lacked all moral foundation, and they called on the faithful to resist this evil with peaceful nonviolence.

"We are not going to effect the change we seek by doing nothing, by sheer apathy," the bishops insisted. In their pronouncement, read from pulpits all across the country, the bishops dared to propose nonviolent resistance:

> Neither do we advocate a bloody, violent means of righting this wrong. If we did, we would be sanctioning the enormous sin of fratricidal strife. Killing to achieve justice is not within the purview of our Christian vision in our present context.
>
> The way indicated to us now is the way of nonviolent struggle for justice.
>
> This means active resistance of evil by peaceful means—in the manner of Christ. . . .
>
> We therefore ask every loyal member of the Church, every community of the faithful, to form their judgment about the February 7 polls. And if in faith they see things as we the bishops do, we must come together and discern what appropriate actions to take that will be according to the mind of Christ. . . .
>
> These last few days have given us shining examples of the nonviolent struggle for justice we advocate here. . . .
>
> Now is the time to speak up. Now is the time to repair the wrong. . . . But we insist: Our acting must always be according to the Gospel of Christ, that is, in a peaceful, nonviolent way.[24]

Hildegard Goss-Mayr believes that this declaration by the bishops was the first occasion, at least in modern times, when a conference of Catholic bishops publicly called on the faithful to engage in nonviolent civil disobedience to overthrow an unjust system.[25] Cardinal Jaime Lachica Sin,

24. Quoted in Mercado, *People Power*, 77–78.
25. Rosenthal, "Nonviolence in the Philippines," 367.

the archbishop of Manila, called it "the strongest statement any group of bishops has produced anywhere since the days of Henry VIII [in the early sixteenth century]."[26]

Though a small minority in a majority Catholic country, a handful of Filipino evangelicals connected with the Institute for Studies in Asian Church and Culture (ISACC) led by Melba Maggay also joined the call for nonviolent resistance. On February 20, 1986, an evangelical radio ministry, Far East Broadcasting Company (FEBC), began to broadcast programs about civil disobedience. Unfortunately, the Philippine Council of Evangelical Churches (PCEC) called for Filipinos to "submit to authority" and support the official election results, which favored Marcos.[27]

As the bishops' statement reverberated around the Philippines, Cory Aquino was meeting with three hundred fifty key advisers to plan a campaign of nonviolent resistance. The Goss-Mayrs joined Cory Aquino, Cardinal Sin, and others to devise scenarios and develop an extended, non-violent campaign of marches and boycotts designed to overthrow Marcos. A crowd of one million cheering supporters wildly applauded as Cory Aquino launched her campaign of civil disobedience on February 16. The tide had turned.[28]

Marcos, however, was determined to stay in power. He announced his intention to meet force with force. The struggle would be long and tough.

■ "People Power"

Surprise struck again on Saturday evening, February 22. Juan Ponce Enrile (Marcos's minister of defense) and General Fidel Ramos unexpectedly rebelled. Denouncing the fraudulent elections in a news conference, they declared Cory Aquino the rightful president, and at 9:00 p.m., with only two hundred armed defenders, they barricaded themselves inside their camps in the middle of metropolitan Manila. The two hundred soldiers were at the mercy of Marcos's army of two hundred fifty thousand. The president could destroy them at will.

26. Quoted in Elwood, *Philippine Revolution*, 5.
27. David S. Lim, "Consolidating Democracy: Filipino Evangelicals between People Power Events, 1986–2001," in *Evangelical Christianity and Democracy in Asia*, ed. David H. Lumsdaine (Oxford: Oxford University Press, 2009), 255.
28. Rosenthal, "Nonviolence in the Philippines," 367; Mercado, *People Power*, 67.

At that moment, Butz Aquino and Cardinal Sin unleashed "people power." Late on Sunday night, Butz Aquino called cause-oriented groups to fill the streets outside Enrile's and Ramos's camps. "We will surround the camps and protect them with our bodies," he announced boldly.[29]

Cardinal Sin went on the radio Saturday evening and urged the people to surround the camps. "Go to Camp Aguinaldo and show your solidarity" with Ramos and Enrile, "our two good friends," the cardinal pleaded.[30] Within hours, thousands of men, women, and children ringed the gates of the camps, blocking any potential movement by Marcos's army. Marcos would have to kill civilians if he chose to attack.

Before he went on the radio, Cardinal Sin called three orders of nuns, saying to each, "Right now get out from your cells and go to the chapel to pray. . . . And fast until I tell you to stop. We are in battle."[31] No troops attacked the rebels on Saturday night.

By Sunday morning, the streets around the camps were overflowing with people. Families came with children and picnic baskets. In spite of the danger, the mood was festive. Some groups even held worship services.[32] All over the city, taxi and truck drivers spontaneously volunteered to shuttle people to the scene of action. Ramos and Enrile went on the air to beg for more civilians to flood the streets to act as a buffer between them and Marcos's soldiers. They fully expected an attack. According to a professor at the Philippine Military Academy, it was this surge of "people power" that made the difference. "It was the first time in history," Lieutenant Colonel Eduardo Purificacion said, "that so many civilians went to protect the military."[33]

The nonviolent soldiers of this "classless revolution" came from every walk of life.[34] Wealthy bankers, top executives, and businesspeople drove their cars to the camps. The poor walked. Men and women, children and grandparents, priests and nuns, flooded the streets. Pregnant women and women with babies in their arms came ready to defy advancing tanks.

Sunday afternoon at 3:00 p.m. the tanks came. A large force of marines with tanks and armored personnel carriers headed for Enrile and Ramos's

29. Quoted in Mercado, *People Power*, 106.
30. Quoted in ibid., 105.
31. Quoted in ibid.
32. Lim, "Consolidating Democracy," 256.
33. Quoted in Mercado, *People Power*, 120.
34. Ibid., 1, 109, 122; Elwood, *Philippine Revolution*, 14; Mark Thompson, *Democratic Revolutions: Asia and Eastern Europe* (New York: Routledge, 2004), 22.

little band of rebels. Rumbling through the streets, the huge machines stopped only a kilometer from Ramos's headquarters, blocked by thousands of bodies ready to die rather than let them continue.

Amado L. Lacuesta Jr., one of the hundreds of thousands of civilians in the streets, offers a powerful eyewitness account of the people's raw courage.[35] As he squeezed his way through the densely packed street, he finally got close to where General Tadiar of the marines was negotiating with the civilians who surrounded his tanks and armored personnel carriers (APCs). The sea of people were praying, some holding small statues of the Virgin Mary. General Tadiar demanded that the people let him through, but they refused. Just then, Butz Aquino arrived, clambered up on the APC, and explained how people power could avoid bloodshed.

As the soldiers pushed Aquino off the huge machine, its engines roared. Weeping and praying, the people expected to be crushed. At the very front were three nuns, kneeling in prayer an arm's length from the throbbing motors. The metal mountain jerked forward once, twice, then stopped. The crowed cheered wildly. As a military helicopter made a low sweep, the people offered cigarettes to the soldiers, who looked away with a mixture of disdain and uncertainty. Again the engines roared, and the machine jerked forward. Men pushed against the advancing metal wall as the nuns continued to kneel in prayer. Row after row of densely packed bodies stood ready to be pulverized by tons of metal. But again the towering monster halted. This time, after more hesitation, the APC swiveled and retreated to the deafening roar of thousands of relieved, cheering voices.

Cardinal Sin tells the story of bedridden, eighty-one-year-old Mrs. Monzon, owner of Arellano University. Everywhere she went, she used a wheelchair. But Mrs. Monzon insisted on joining the people in the streets in front of the camps. When the tanks came, she wheeled in front of the advancing war vehicles. Armed with a crucifix, she called out to the soldiers, "Stop. I am an old woman. You can kill me, but you shouldn't kill your fellow Filipinos." Overcome, a soldier jumped off the tank and embraced the bold nonviolent resister. "I cannot kill you," he told her, "you are just like my mother." She stayed in the street all night in her wheelchair.[36]

The marines finally withdrew without firing a shot.

Monday brought more high drama. At dawn, three thousand marines succeeded in dispersing part of the crowd with tear gas. But seven helicopter gunships with sufficient firepower to obliterate both Enrile and Ramos's

35. Cited in Mercado, *People Power*, 125–27.
36. Cited in ibid., 127.

rebel troops and the surrounding crowds landed peacefully and defected. At 9:00 a.m. Marcos appeared defiantly on television for a few minutes and then disappeared as rebel soldiers seized Channel 4 TV.

Romeo Lavella Jr., who lived near Channel 4, tells what he saw just after rebels seized the station.[37] Hearing scattered gunshots, he rushed into the streets, where swarms of people stood between two groups of heavily armed soldiers. The pro-Marcos loyalists had more than twice as many men as the rebels who had just seized the station.

As sporadic gunfire erupted, a pickup truck carrying a priest praying loudly slowly inched forward. As the priest prayed the rosary and sang the Ave Maria, the people did the same. In the truck were statues of the crucified Christ and the Virgin Mary. Awed, the soldiers stopped shooting. As another priest and civilians helped negotiate an agreement between the soldiers, the priest and people continued to pray and sing. Channel 4, meanwhile, stayed in the hands of the people.

Hundreds of thousands jammed the streets in front of the camps on Monday. From Cardinal Sin's four auxiliary bishops to unknown slum dwellers, the people defied the guns and tanks.

Another striking encounter occurred in front of the Polymedic Hospital near the camps. Several trucks with gun-wielding soldiers and two APCs slipped past the crowd by displaying yellow streamers (Cory Aquino's campaign color). A moment later, however, the crowd discovered their mistake, and people rushed to seal the street. Middle-aged women prayed loudly as helicopters hovered overhead. As the people stood their ground, the massive machines halted. Nobody would retreat. L. P. Flores's eyewitness account of the soldiers' reactions reveals the mystery of "people power":

> The people pressed their bodies against the armor. Their faces were pleading but they were clothed in nothing but raw courage. In that decisive and tense moment, the soldiers atop the armored carriers pointed their guns of every make at the crowd but their faces betrayed agony. And I knew then, as the crowd, too, must have discerned: the soldiers did not have the heart to pull the trigger on civilians armed only with their convictions. The pact had been sealed. There was tacit agreement: "we keep this street corner, you retreat." And true enough, the armored carriers rolled back and applause echoed.
>
> The face of that soldier struggling in agony for the decision to shoot or not, on the verge of tears, will forever remain in my memory.[38]

37. Cited in ibid., 203–4.
38. Quoted in ibid., 207.

74

Dozens, indeed hundreds, of similar personal struggles ended with soldiers accepting flowers and embracing civilians. The battle was over. By Monday afternoon, a majority of the armed forces had abandoned Marcos. On Tuesday morning, Marcos stubbornly went through an inaugural ceremony, but his power had evaporated. Late that evening he fled. Cory Aquino was president.

■ Evaluating a Nonviolent Success

It would be naive, of course, to suppose that unarmed civilians in the streets singlehandedly overthrew Marcos. International pressure (including President Reagan's belated decision to abandon Marcos) and the revolt of the army were clearly important. According to an editorial in the *Philippine Daily Inquirer*, however, it was massive nonviolent resistance that made the difference.

> When the revolution now popularly called People Power began, it was triggered by two Filipinos—Juan Ponce Enrile and Fidel Ramos. But neither of them would have survived if the people had not put themselves between the attackers and the leaders of the revolt.
>
> People all over the world then saw the unbelievable.
>
> Filipinos charging at giant tanks with Volkswagens. Nuns and priests meeting armored cars with Rosaries and prayers. Little children giving grim soldiers flowers and urging them not to fight for Marcos. People linking arms and blocking tanks, daring them to crush their fellow Filipinos, which they did not.[39]

Reading through the many eyewitness accounts in Monina Allarey Mercado's *People Power: The Philippine Revolution of 1986*, one is amazed by the centrality of prayer and religious devotion. Sister Teresa was one of the Carmelite nuns ordered to fast and pray by Cardinal Sin. "We never forgot even for an instant that we were doing battle. We daily called God in prayer to assist us all: Those outside and we inside."[40] The radio accounts of the struggle in the streets, Sister Teresa reported, shaped their prayers.

Praying nuns and nonviolent resisters armed only with religious symbols had functioned as an effective deterrent:

> People were willing to die but not to kill. And I thought that even if some soldiers were willing to shoot the people, they were not willing to shoot the crucifixes.

39. Editorial in the *Philippine Daily Inquirer*, February 27, 1986, quoted in Mercado, *People Power*, 246.
40. Quoted in ibid., 254.

Many of them come from the provinces where they were raised to fear God. They could never shoot at people who were praying. They could have shot people who were throwing stones, as they did during the rallies. But this was the first time that they were confronted with prayers. They did not know how to react. I think this was crucial to the whole nonviolence stance.

The people were there to defend the camp. They were not aggressors. We cannot pray and be violent at the same time. The religious character of the revolution made the revolution very unique. If you took away the religious flavor of the revolution, you would have removed the essence of it.[41]

Professor Randolf David, director of Third World Studies at the University of the Philippines, concluded in amazement, "I have been a student of revolutions, but this is the first time I have seen an assault led by the Virgin Mary."[42] Another observer stated simply, "Marcos had the guns, but Cory had the nuns!"[43]

Undoubtedly, the previous training in nonviolence had played a genuine role, although the convergence of the masses to protect the rebel soldiers was essentially a spontaneous emotional response rather than the result of careful organizing. Not surprisingly, nonviolent leaders such as Father Jose Blanco, the founder of AKKAPKA, believe that the Philippine revolution points the way for the rest of the world:

What does God wish us to proclaim to the world through our nonviolent revolution? Simply this: the political problems of people can be solved without recourse to arms or violence.

The world's problems are best solved if we respect the humanity, the dignity of every human person concerned. The desire to be violent or to use violence can be tamed and diminished, if we show love, care, joy to those who are unjust and wish to be violent. Violence addresses the aggressor. Nonviolence searches out and addresses the humanity in the enemy or oppressor. When that common humanity is touched, then the other is helped to recognize the human person within and ceases to be inhuman, unjust, and violent.

One does not have to be a Christian to reach out to the humanity in the other.[44]

41. Vincent T. Paterno, quoted in ibid., 257.
42. Melba Maggay, "People Power Revisited," in *Following Jesus: Journeys in Radical Discipleship; Essays in Honor of Ronald J. Sider*, ed. Paul Alexander and Al Tizon (Oxford: Regnum Books International, 2013), 128.
43. Quoted in Douglas J. Elwood, ed., *Toward a Theology of People Power: Reflections on the Philippine February Phenomenon* (Quezon City: New Day, 1988), 1.
44. From his epilogue in Mercado, *People Power*, 306. See Gene Sharp's more cautious but similar comments in "Philippines Taught Us Lessons of Nonviolence," *Los Angeles Times*,

Such optimism needs tempering. One successful nonviolent revolution does not banish war. Nor dare one overlook the special circumstances that helped nonviolence succeed in this unique situation. Furthermore, simply overthrowing Marcos did not instantly create economic justice in the Philippines. Widespread poverty and injustice continued in the following decades, even as democratic processes took root and grew stronger, slowly promoting greater economic justice.

The People Power revolution of 1986 not only ousted a brutal dictator but also gave the world a new term. Worldwide, the term "people power" is now used to describe peaceful mass protest movements.[45]

The amazing fact about the People Power revolution of 1986 is that the Filipino people did depose a powerful dictator with virtually no bloodshed. Precisely in a context where many had concluded that the only viable path was years of bloody revolution, nonviolence produced a stunning victory. Nonviolent revolution works.

April 4, 1986 (articles.latimes.com/1986-04-04/local/me-24516_1_nonviolent-resistance). After the victory, AKKAPKA continued promoting nonviolent social change in the Philippines. See Richard Deats, "Fragile Democracy in the Philippines," *Fellowship*, October-November 1987, 14–16.

45. Thompson, *Democratic Revolutions*, 18; see also Schock, *Unarmed Insurrections*, esp. chap. 3. In the Philippines "people power" occurred two more times. See Lim, "Consolidating Democracy," 252.

defeating the soviet empire

For four decades after the end of World War II, two nuclear-armed superpowers dominated global life: the communist Soviet Union and the democratic West led by the United States. Soviet leaders willingly used overwhelming military power to crush dissidents, including those in their Eastern European satellites who tried to abandon Communism. Everyone knew that any violent rebellion against the Soviet Union would fail miserably.

But nonviolent action accomplished what violent resistance could not. Between 1989 and 1991, overwhelmingly nonviolent movements successfully defied and dismantled "one of the world's greatest military superpowers."[1] Nonviolent protest and resistance overthrew Communist dictators in Poland, East Germany, Czechoslovakia, and the Baltic states and played an important role in the collapse of the Soviet Union itself.

It would be false to claim that nonviolent action was the only factor in this historic change. Economic factors were also crucial. When Mikhail Gorbachev became head of the Communist Party in the Soviet Union in 1985, he realized that important changes were necessary to correct severe economic problems. His response was *perestroika* (modest movement toward a partially free market system) and *glasnost* (much more freedom of speech

1. Lee Smithey and Lester R. Kurtz, "'We Have Bare Hands': Nonviolent Social Movements in the Soviet Bloc," in *Nonviolent Social Movements: A Geographical Perspective*, ed. Stephen Zunes, Lester R. Kurtz, and Sarah Beth Asher (Oxford: Blackwell, 1999), 121.

and some acceptance of a more democratic political system). Gorbachev's visit to China shortly before the massacre of nonviolent student protestors in Tiananmen Square on June 4, 1989, and his reflection on that violence probably contributed to his opposition to repeating the violent repression that the Soviet Union had inflicted earlier on Hungary (1956) and Czechoslovakia (1968). On October 28, 1989, a spokesman for the Soviet foreign ministry declared that the Soviet Union had no right to interfere in the political affairs of Communist Eastern Europe.[2] Gorbachev's changes in the Soviet Union undoubtedly created some space for nonviolent protest in the soviet satellite states in Eastern Europe.

But ruthless Communist dictators commanding strong armies and pervasive secret police ruled all of these countries. They had no intention of giving up their power. Their long history of frequently suppressing dissent with over-powering force made resistance seem useless.

However, in country after country in Eastern Europe in 1989, nonviolent movements succeeded in overthrowing these Communist dictators. Quiet, often underground resistance and the slow emergence of unofficial parallel institutions independent of the Communist rulers developed slowly over a couple of decades. Then suddenly, in 1989, they burst into the open. After an initial defeat in 1980–81, the Solidarity movement forced the Communist leaders of Poland to negotiate and eventually accept a new government led by Solidarity in August 1989. Powerful nonviolent protests forced the Hungarian Communist leaders to accept constitutional amendments on October 18, 1989, that embraced democracy. Massive demonstrations in East Germany in the autumn of 1989 led to the fall of the Berlin Wall on November 9, and the collapse of Communism shortly thereafter. As nonviolent resisters in Czechoslovakia prepared for action in late 1989, they noted "that nonviolent resistance against communist regimes had been successful in Poland after ten years, in Hungary after ten months and in East Germany after ten weeks"; they concluded—rightly, it turned out—that it would take "only ten days" in Czechoslovakia.[3]

Developments in the Soviet Union were far too complex to summarize here. But it is significant that nonviolent resistance played a critical role in defeating one final attempt of Communist leaders to reverse all of the reforms unleashed by Gorbachev.

2. Ibid., 119.
3. Ibid., 100.

Hardliners (including many of the top leaders under Gorbachev) launched a coup d'état on August 18, 1991. They imprisoned Gorbachev at his vacation home and announced a new government on August 19. But Gorbachev's program of decentralization had already given great power to the individual republics that made up the Soviet Union. Boris Yeltsin was the elected leader of the largest, the Russian Republic, with his headquarters in the Russian White House in Moscow. About noon on August 19, Yeltsin climbed up on one of the tanks sent by the leaders of the coup to surround the White House and arrest him. He denounced the coup, persuaded many soldiers to disobey orders, and rallied the people. By nightfall, more than ten thousand unarmed civilians had surrounded the White House to protect it. The troops disobeyed orders to shoot at Yeltsin's unarmed defenders, and the coup failed. Nonviolence had played a key role in defeating a final attempt of Communist hardliners to prevent the collapse of Soviet Communism.[4]

Starting in the late 1980s, the Baltic republics of Latvia, Lithuania, and Estonia also provided a stunning example of nonviolent resistance—indeed, even nonviolent national self-defense.[5] Because of a deal made between Hitler and Stalin, these three nations had been under Soviet control since the 1930s. The people longed for independence. On August 23, 1989, two million people in the three countries formed a human chain linking their three capital cities to demand independence from the Soviet Union.

In elections on March 18, 1990, pro-independence candidates swept to power in Latvia and two months later declared Latvia independent. Expecting military attack by Soviet forces, the Latvians organized what was probably the first clear plan for national defense through nonviolent resistance. On January 11, 1991, Soviet troops killed and wounded peaceful civilians in Lithuania. Two days later, half a million Latvians gathered in Riga, the capital, to protest the violence in neighboring Lithuania and underline their intention to defend Latvia's independence nonviolently. Tensions remained high, and Soviet troops remained in Riga. In fact, on August 19, 1991, when the Soviet hardliners attempted a coup in the Soviet Union, the Soviet army also took over Riga. But that coup collapsed, as noted earlier, thanks to nonviolent resistance in Moscow. The Soviet Union was disintegrating, and the Baltic republics were free. "The Soviet empire was defeated not by foreign invaders or a military

4. See Gene Sharp, *Waging Nonviolent Struggle: 20th Century Practice and 21st Century Potential* (Boston: Porter Sargent, 2005), 287–98.
5. See ibid., 277–85.

coup, but rather by a series of nonviolent popular insurgencies."[6] To understand more clearly how nonviolent action was so decisive in defeating one of
the strongest and most vicious military empires of the twentieth century, I
explore in the next two chapters two examples in detail: the ten-year campaign
in Poland and the ten-week struggle in East Germany.

6. Smithey and Kurtz, "'We Have Bare Hands,'" 96.

solidarity

A Trade Union and the Pope versus Communist Dictators

A wall cannot be demolished with butts of the head. We must move slowly, step by step, otherwise the wall remains untouched and we break our heads.

Lech Walesa[1]

Solidarity[2] is the amazing story of how daring Polish shipyard builders defied their Communist rulers, developed the first independent trade union in the Communist world, and eventually played a key role in the collapse of Communism in Eastern Europe and the Soviet Union.[3] And, after

1. Quoted in Michael Dobbs, Dessa Trevisan, and K. S. Karol, *Poland, Solidarity, Walesa* (New York: McGraw-Hill, 1981), 104.
2. I thank my Ayres Scholar, Stefanie Israel, for her excellent research on this chapter.
3. Roman Laba, *The Roots of Solidarity: A Political Sociology of Poland's Working-Class Democratization* (Princeton, NJ: Princeton University Press, 1991), 182; James DeFronzo, *Revolutions and Revolutionary Movements* (Boulder, CO: Westview Press, 1991), 54–55; Michael Meyer, *The Year That Changed the World: The Untold Story Behind the Fall of the Berlin Wall* (New York: Scribner, 2009), 48. Archie Brown observes, "The example of Solidarity, which began as an independent trade union and then became a mass political movement, was not followed by any other country in the world" (*The Rise and Fall of Communism* [New York: HarperCollins, 2009], 437), but the success of Solidarity exposed the weakening grip of the Soviets and gave an

the failure of violent methods in 1970, they did it with nonviolent protest. The Polish Solidarity movement is stunning evidence that nonviolent forms of resistance and protest can be successful even under a totalitarian regime. Solidarity's victory did not occur overnight, but it demonstrated that courageous workers united by a common cause and conviction ultimately wielded more power than ruthless Communist dictators.

■ Poland under Soviet Control

Poland has suffered a long, painful history of invasion, occupation, and control by foreign powers. During World War II, it endured brutal German and Soviet invasions. Poles initially resisted Nazi invasion violently in the famous Warsaw Uprising. But Hitler's armies prevailed after two months, and Hitler ordered the destruction of Warsaw, killing two hundred thousand people. Soon after World War II ended, Stalin's army and pro-Soviet Polish Marxists established harsh Communist rule.[4] They implemented Stalinism based on the Soviet model. Poland underwent industrialization and collectivization under a totalitarian regime marked by bureaucracy, suppression of individual freedom, and terror.[5]

Economic reforms initially created high growth rates in the 1950s. When growth rates started to taper off in the 1960s, the party tried to correct the problem by increasing investment in the agricultural sector. However, the party invested mainly in unproductive state farms, in an effort to drive out private farmers. In 1969, the harvest failed. In 1970, the party discontinued importing grain for feedstock. Food supplies dropped drastically, creating a national crisis.[6]

The regime responded by increasing food prices without raising wages. Workers, who already spent nearly half of their income on food, were enraged.[7]

■ An (Unsuccessful) Violent Protest (1970)

The party-dominated "official" unions did nothing about the situation, but workers at the Lenin shipyard launched a strike. A young electrician, Lech

---

example of what was possible. See also the detailed analyses in Peter Ackerman and Jack DuVall, *A Force More Powerful: A Century of Nonviolent Conflict* (New York: Palgrave, 2000), 113–74.

4. Dobbs, Trevisan, and Karol, *Poland*, 19–24.

5. Ibid., 26–27.

6. Laba, *Roots of Solidarity*, 15.

7. Ibid., 18–19.

Walesa, was one of the leaders. Without central organization, the strike caught on and spread quickly. Workers gathered in front of the shipyard director's building and used the PA system to announce their demands: cancellation of the price increases, reform of the pay system, and "'resignation' of the ruling regime."[8]

After an hour with no response, they headed downtown to the Communist Party headquarters to announce their strike to the whole town. About one thousand workers marched out of the shipyard heading toward downtown Gdansk, armed with tools and clubs in case the militia should attack them. On the way, others joined them.[9]

When the crowd, now swelled to three thousand, approached party headquarters at 4:00 p.m., they met a motorized militia demanding that they disperse. When the workers disobeyed and pushed toward the headquarters, the police obeyed orders to use their nightsticks. Angry workers responded by throwing stones at the police. Police reinforcements soon arrived, attacking the crowds with clubs and gas grenades. The people then attempted to burn the headquarters. The riot spread, and workers engaged in acts of sabotage by destroying anything that symbolized state power or status and privilege.[10]

The following day, the workers declared a general strike, and people from other factories joined those in the streets. The crowd grew to fifteen thousand. Fired on by police, the strikers set fire to the party headquarters. Local security forces retreated, but only to await the arrival of the army. The strike spread to the nearby city of Gdynia.[11]

By the next day, thirty-five thousand well-armed troops had arrived ready to squelch the rebellion with force. They shot and killed as many as two to three hundred strikers and wounded more than a thousand in several cities.[12] The workers' revolt collapsed.

The workers' action in 1970 demonstrated that striking citizens had real power. But the workers also learned a painful lesson: the Communist rulers would not hesitate to employ violence against them, and in a battle of force the police and army would surely win. Rocks and tools could not compete

8. Ibid., 21–23.
9. Ibid., 23.
10. Ibid., 26–28.
11. Ibid., 30–39.
12. See the differing estimates in Gale Stokes, *The Walls Came Tumbling Down: The Collapse of Communism in Eastern Europe* (New York: Oxford University Press, 1993), 17; Michael D. Kennedy, *Professionals, Power, and Solidarity in Poland: A Critical Sociology of Soviet-Type Society* (Cambridge: Cambridge University Press, 1991), 35.

with guns and tanks. This realization helped nurture a new, more patient, nonviolent movement.[13]

Church, Workers, and Intellectuals Unite

The Communist Party named a new leader in an effort to neutralize the discontent. His economic reforms led to improved living conditions in the early 1970s, but in June 1976, in an effort to stave off impending economic difficulties, the government raised food prices. Workers promptly went on strike across the nation. The government fired thousands of workers, arrested at least two thousand, and beat untold numbers. But the government also promptly reversed the price increases.[14]

One result of the brief 1976 strike was that dissident Polish intellectuals decided to support the cause of the workers. The Committee for Defense of Workers (KOR) was formed. KOR defended imprisoned workers, began circulating underground workers' newspapers, and helped with underground efforts to organize free trade unions,[15] effectively raising consciousness among the proletariat.[16]

The Roman Catholic Church also spoke out in defense of workers. In September 1976, Cardinal Wyszynski (the primate of Poland) insisted, "It is the clergy's duty to defend the workers' interests against hasty and ill-considered government measures. . . . It was painful that workers should have to struggle for their rights against a workers' government."[17]

For years, another Polish Catholic leader, Cardinal Wojtyla, had been engaged in church renewal, energizing church-based movements independent of the state. In 1978, the world's Catholic cardinals stunned almost everyone by naming Cardinal Wojtyla as the new pope. Pope John Paul II's visit to his homeland in June 1979 attracted millions of Poles. In his many speeches at

13. Alain Touraine et al., *Solidarity: The Analysis of a Social Movement; Poland 1980–1981*, trans. David Denby (Cambridge: Cambridge University Press, 1983), 186; George Weigel, *The Final Revolution: The Resistance Church and the Collapse of Communism* (New York: Oxford University Press, 1992), 53; Ackerman and DuVall, *Force More Powerful*, 119–21.

14. Kennedy, *Professionals*, 38, 40; Stokes, *Walls Came Tumbling Down*, 26; Laba, *Roots of Solidarity*, 104.

15. Touraine et al., *Solidarity*, 35–36; Kennedy, *Professionals*, 41.

16. Timothy Garton Ash, *The Polish Revolution: Solidarity* (New Haven: Yale University Press, 2002), 27.

17. Ibid., 22–23.

historic religious and national sites, he defended the right to dignity for individuals and workers.[18] His words evoked a deeply emotional response with his listeners as he appealed to their religious and national identity. He inspired new hope that there was a morally legitimate way to defend human dignity: "The antipoliticians [e.g., KOR] had begun the process of creating a civil society in which such a moral change could occur, but John Paul II's visit to Poland suddenly jolted millions of Poles to their first awareness that this was indeed a proper sphere in which to begin a hopeless enterprise."[19]

The workers, the intellectuals, and the church united behind a common cause in a way never before seen in Polish Communist history or the Soviet bloc. They launched underground publishing houses and held unauthorized university lectures. The church often provided a safe place for opponents of the government to meet. Millions of Polish Catholics attended Mass each Sunday. The police spied on, arrested, and beat activists, but they failed to prevent a growing underground movement of resistance. This alliance soon grew into Solidarity.[20]

In 1976, Lech Walesa's fiery tirades against official unions finally got him fired. For the next few years, Walesa was fired from one job after another. Courageously and persistently, however, he spread the vision of independent trade unions, surviving with support from the church.[21]

◼ Formation of Solidarity (1980)

In August 1980, another wave of strikes broke out. The workers of the Lenin shipyard called in Lech Walesa to help lead them. In a sit-down strike on August 15 they demanded a pay raise. To their surprise, the authorities granted the pay raise the same day. But rather than accept it, some of the workers insisted on continuing the strike until other local workers' demands were met. The following day, they formed the Inter-Factory Strike Committee, with 388 enterprises represented. The committee of nineteen delegates drafted a list of demands, the first of which was for a free trade union—something that did not exist anywhere in the Communist world.[22]

18. Stokes, *Walls Came Tumbling Down*, 33.
19. Ibid., 34.
20. Ash, *Polish Revolution*, 27.
21. Ackerman and DuVall, *Force More Powerful*, 137.
22. Touraine et al., *Solidarity*, 37.

The following week, intellectuals extended their support and acted as political advisers to the Inter-Factory Strike Committee. Workers across Poland continued to mobilize and go on strike. The Catholic Church expressed support but called for moderation.[23] From his powerful pulpit in Rome, Pope John Paul II spoke out on behalf of the strikers, declaring their demands to be legitimate. The Polish bishops cited teaching from the Second Vatican Council in support of strikers, declaring that workers had the right to organize.[24]

As strikes spread to other parts of the country, the authorities at the Lenin shipyards tried to complete a deal there. They almost succeeded, but at the last minute the workers there decided to stay on strike until the authorities dealt with other strikers. "We must continue the strike out of solidarity until everyone has won," Lech Walesa announced.[25] Delegates from many striking enterprises came to the Lenin shipyards, joining the Inter-Factory Strike Committee (MKS). Its central demand was free trade unions. More and more striking workers joined MKS. Strikes spread to more and more areas of Poland.

The government had to negotiate. When Deputy Prime Minister Mieczyslaw Jagielski met with Walesa and his colleagues, he offered to reform the official trade union. But the workers insisted on their own independent union. In Warsaw, the Politburo debated whether to accept a deal or use armed repression. To relieve some of their concerns, Walesa said that the striking workers were "not fighting against the socialist system" and would accept the "leading role" of the Communist Party.[26] On Sunday, August 31, the government and the workers reached an agreement. Workers all over Poland would for the first time have a right to form their own free unions.

In the August 31 agreement, the government recognized the MKS as the representative of workers in the whole Gdansk-Gdynia region. The workers named their new union "Solidarity" and chose Walesa as their new chairman.

When the official media published the August 31 agreement, Polish workers everywhere discovered their new right to organize freely. All across Poland workers rushed to organize. On September 17, delegates from across the country met in Gdansk to form a National Coordinating Commission to guide the regional unions. They called the movement "Solidarity." Already by September

23. Ibid., 37–39.
24. George Weigel, *Witness to Hope: The Biography of Pope John Paul II* (New York: Harper Perennial, 2005), 402.
25. Ackerman and DuVall, *Force More Powerful*, 144.
26. Ibid., 151.

17, it had three million members. By December, the number skyrocketed to ten million. Most Polish workers now belonged to an independent union. "Nothing like it had ever happened before in any communist-ruled society."[27]

Most Poles were euphoric. But Walesa wisely cautioned workers that they would have to continue the struggle until the agreement was implemented.[28] Repeatedly, in the fall of 1980, the government clashed with Solidarity, breaking promises and harassing workers.

The authorities had good reason to be worried. A million farmers had organized their own union, Rural Solidarity. University students established their own free union. Every regional branch of Solidarity published its own free newspaper.

Conflict between Solidarity and the government intensified in 1981. Walesa and some other Solidarity leaders tried to minimize direct confrontation with the government, fearing that it would lead to a violent response, even a Soviet invasion.[29] But not even the Polish Communist leaders controlled the fate of Poland. In April 1981, top Soviet leaders from Moscow summoned the Polish leaders to a secret rendezvous just inside the Soviet border. They demanded a crackdown. "The Polish leaders stalled, but the question was not whether but when."[30] Final plans for the crackdown were in place by mid-September.

By mid-December, all the troops were in position. On December 12–13, they struck, arresting thousands of Solidarity leaders, intellectuals, and activists. Tanks smashed through walls and gates to expel remaining strikers inside the shipyards. The authorities justified the violent takeover by falsely claiming that Solidarity had planned to use violence to take over the country.[31] They banned public meetings, forbade strikes, "suspended" Solidarity, and censored all mail and telephone communications. By the end of December, the government was in complete control—at least on the surface.

In the early years of martial law, there was a great deal of disagreement over what approach the underground remnants of Solidarity should take in continuing the struggle. Jacek Kuron, a prominent intellectual in the movement who had previously promoted nonviolent struggle, wrote a letter from prison suggesting that, given the circumstances, he would support collective violent action on behalf of the people.[32] Zbigniew Bujak, who avoided arrest

27. Ibid., 152.
28. Touraine et al., *Solidarity*, 39–41.
29. Stokes, *Walls Came Tumbling Down*, 39–42.
30. Ackerman and DuVall, *Force More Powerful*, 160.
31. Ash, *Polish Revolution*, 300.
32. Stokes, *Walls Came Tumbling Down*, 105.

and became a key leader in underground Solidarity, disagreed with Kuron and instead argued that "local groups and social circles in the community should organize . . . to build a system of social structures independent of the state."[33]

Bujak and others who agreed with his approach created the Temporary Coordinating Committee (TKK) to organize underground union activity. Other underground organizations formed. Solidarity soon began to put out numerous underground newspapers, reaching over one million Poles by 1984.[34]

Pope John Paul II pointedly expressed his solidarity with the Polish people in his visit to Poland in 1983. He publicly declared that he spoke for those "who are acutely tasting the bitterness of disappointment, humiliation, suffering, of being deprived of their freedom, of being wronged, of having their dignity trampled upon." When the government responded with promises of returning to "appropriate humanitarian and legal solutions," the pope insisted that meant honoring the agreement made with Solidarity in August 1980.[35]

On their way to an open-air Mass, thousands of Poles passed the riot police (who were armed with guns) chanting, "We forgive you." Hundreds of thousands of Poles showed up at the Mass, while many millions more watched on television. The visit of the courageous Polish pope served to help resurrect Solidarity and restore hope to continue the struggle nonviolently.[36]

The pope had insisted that he would not visit unless he was allowed to meet with Walesa. Wojciech Jaruzelski, the top Communist leader, did not want to allow it, but the meeting finally took place. The act of the meeting itself sent the message that Solidarity was still alive and had the backing of the pope.[37] That same year, Walesa received the Nobel Peace Prize.

Solidarity's activities remained clandestine. Activists who struggled to keep Solidarity alive in its underground form paid a price. Slowly, however, Jaruzelski began to permit some pluralism by allowing for allegedly "self-governing" unions in an attempt to win over workers. But most workers did not join, nor did intellectuals buy into the party's attempt to look as if it were implementing the values of Solidarity.[38] Jaruzelski even released Walesa from prison in November 1982.

33. Ibid., 105–6.

34. Ibid., 106–7.

35. Jonathan Kwitny, *Man of the Century: The Life and Times of Pope John Paul II* (New York: Henry Holt, 1997), 476–77.

36. Ibid., 477–78.

37. Stanislaw Dziwisz, *A Life with Karol: My Forty-Year Friendship with the Man Who Became Pope*, trans. Adrian J. Walker (New York: Doubleday, 2008), 150–55.

38. Ash, *Polish Revolution*, 367–68.

The economic recovery that Jaruzelski had hoped to achieve under martial law did not take place. Solidarity put out a report documenting the economic crisis. The West would not offer aid as long as the regime refused to negotiate with Solidarity.[39]

Meanwhile, Jaruzelski began to imagine himself as a Polish Gorbachev, introducing reform. In an attempt to demonstrate his tolerance of pluralism, he released all political prisoners in August and September 1986, including key Solidarity leaders. Shortly after the amnesty was announced, Walesa formed the Solidarity Provisional Council (TRS). Although Solidarity was still not legal, the TRS was out in the open, unlike its underground counterpart, the TKK. Some regional councils came out in the open by joining Walesa's organization, but others remained underground with the TKK, making Solidarity very decentralized at this point.[40] Walesa later merged these organizations to form the National Executive Commission (KKW), which was tolerated, although it remained illegal.[41] Solidarity was not a powerful union with millions of members; rather, it was a "small but still-prestigious political front."[42]

When the party responded to another economic crisis with price increases in 1988, workers went on strike in the spring and again in August. The strikes forced the party to negotiate. On August 31, a key Communist leader met with Walesa and agreed to roundtable negotiations that would include Solidarity. The strikes were called off when the party promised to make Solidarity a legal entity once again.[43]

Roundtable Negotiations and Electoral Victory

Hardliners in the Communist Party delayed negotiations for several months. But on February 6, 1989, twenty-six party representatives met with twenty-nine delegates from Solidarity, plus observers from the church, in a roundtable to discuss the future of Poland. By April 6, they had reached a historic agreement: free unions, expanded freedom of the press, an independent court, even free parliamentary elections.[44]

39. Ibid., 368–69.
40. Stokes, *Walls Came Tumbling Down*, 115.
41. Ash, *Polish Revolution*, 369.
42. Ackerman and DuVall, *Force More Powerful*, 170.
43. Ash, *Polish Revolution*, 370–71.
44. Ackerman and DuVall, *Force More Powerful*, 170–71.

Everyone made compromises. In order to gain official union status, Solidarity agreed that the majority of the seats in parliament would go to the Communist Party and only a minority would be open to free election to be held in two months.[45]

Solidarity was officially registered as a union on April 18, 1989, in keeping with the roundtable agreements. On election day, Solidarity candidates were overwhelmingly victorious, winning all but one of the contested seats in both houses. In the ensuing months, a coalition government was formed, and on August 24, 1989, Tadeusz Mazowiecki became prime minister in a Solidarity-led coalition government. He was "the first non-Communist prime minister of an East European state in almost forty years."[46]

To the world's surprise, Gorbachev shrugged, and the Soviet Union did not invade. Poland was free to continue down the path of democracy. Other Eastern bloc countries, encouraged by Poland's example and the Soviet Union's new policies of *glasnost* and *perestroika*, soon followed suit.

Solidarity succeeded for many reasons: the incredible courage of hundreds of thousands of Polish workers; the brave support of the Catholic Church and a brilliant Polish pope; the cooperation of intellectuals and workers; the patience to build underground alternative structures when public resistance was largely impossible; Gorbachev's reforms in the Soviet Union. Perhaps most important was the firm resolve after the failure of violent rebellion in 1970 to use nonviolent methods. This decision was partly pragmatic, partly principled. As George Weigel says, "The bad guys had all the guns, and the good guys knew it."[47]

Lech Walesa, however, seemed to go beyond mere pragmatism in his response to a question after receiving the Nobel Peace Prize:

Question: You've chosen the course of nonviolence. Isn't this a form of weakness, of your inability to achieve freedom or independence by other means?

Walesa: It's the course chosen by the majority of Poles, and the majority of people worldwide. And it's probably thanks to nonviolence that I am where I am now. I'm a man who believes in dialogue and agreement. I strongly believe that the twenty-first century will not be a century of violence. We've already tried and tested every form of violence, and not once in the entire course of human history has anything good or lasting come from it.[48]

45. Stokes, *Walls Came Tumbling Down*, 124–26.
46. Ibid., 130.
47. Weigel, *Final Revolution*, 53.
48. Lech Walesa, *A Way of Hope* (New York: Henry Holt, 1987), 287.

In 1991, Pope John Paul II wrote in praise of the nonviolent means success-fully employed by Solidarity:

The protests which led to the collapse of Marxism tenaciously insisted on try-ing every avenue of negotiation, dialogue and witness to the truth, appealing to the conscience of the adversary and seeking to awaken in him a sense of shared human dignity.

It seemed that the European order resulting from the Second World War and sanctioned by the Yalta Agreements could only be overturned by another war. Instead, it [was] overcome by the nonviolent commitment of people who, while always refusing to yield to the force of power, succeeded time after time in find-ing effective ways of bearing witness to the truth. This disarmed the adversary, since violence always needs to justify itself through deceit, and to appear, how-ever falsely, to be defending a right or responding to a threat posed by others.[49]

In Poland, nonviolent action defied and defeated ruthless Communist dictators.

49. Quoted in Weigel, *Final Revolution*, 53.

the revolution of the candles

The Nonviolent Overthrow of East German Communists

Only without violence do we achieve peace and justice.

East German church leaders

At the end of World War II, the victors divided Germany into zones ruled by the Allies.[1] Rather quickly, West Germany emerged as an independent democratic nation, and within a decade it enjoyed a flourishing economy. The eastern zone, controlled by the Soviet Union, became a Soviet satellite ruled by the Communist Party. By the later 1950s, the lack

1. For more on this chapter's subject, see Jörg Swoboda, *The Revolution of the Candles: Christians in the Revolution of the German Democratic Republic*, ed. Richard V. Pierard, trans. Edwin P. Arnold (Macon, GA: Mercer University Press, 1996); Barbara von der Heydt, *Candles Behind the Wall: Heroes of the Peaceful Revolution That Shattered Communism* (Grand Rapids: Eerdmans, 1993); Bud Bultman, *Revolution by Candlelight: The Real Story behind the Changes in Eastern Europe* (Portland, OR: Multnomah, 1991); Wendy R. Tyndale, *Protestants in Communist East Germany: In the Storm of the World* (Burlington, VT: Ashgate, 2010); Andrew Curry, "Before the Fall," *Wilson Quarterly* 33, no. 4 (2009): 16–25; Mahmood Monshipouri and John W. Arnold, "The Christians in Socialism—and After: The Church in East Germany," *Journal of Church and State* 38 (1996): 751–73; Stephen Zunes, Lester R. Kurtz, and Sarah Beth Asher, eds., *Nonviolent Social Movements: A Geographical Perspective* (Oxford: Blackwell, 1999); Timothy Carter Ash, *We the People: The Revolution of '89 Witnessed in Warsaw, Budapest, Berlin and Prague* (Cambridge: Granta Books, 1990). I thank Howard Pinder for his research for this chapter.

of economic opportunity and absence of freedom moved thousands of East Germans, especially the young and the educated, to leave for the West. To stem the economic hemorrhaging from this loss of skilled workers, the East German government built the infamous Berlin Wall in August 1961 to stop the flow of people from the Communist section of Berlin to freedom in West Berlin.

A vast, ruthless secret police (the Stasi) infiltrated every part of East German society, crushing any dissent from official Communist ideology and practice. (The Stasi was actually larger than Hitler's Gestapo, even though East Germany's population was only one-fifth the size of Hitler's Germany.) The church, however, enjoyed some freedom to think and assemble apart from the control of the Communist Party and its secret police.

Slowly, in the 1980s, small, largely secret protest groups focusing on human rights, peace, and care of the environment emerged, usually in connection with the churches. As the only organization in East Germany that the Communist state did not manage and control, the churches offered modestly "safe" places for people to meet.[2] Most important of all were the prayer services in the churches "that managed to imbue the whole protest movement with a deeply rooted ethic of nonviolence that was the condition of every action taken."[3]

In 1982, Christian Führer, pastor of St. Nicholas Church in Leipzig (the second-largest city in East Germany), started regular "Peace Prayers" (*Friedensgebete*). After a prayer service, groups stayed in the church to discuss issues such as the environment and nuclear disarmament. But the Stasi spied on, harassed, and not infrequently arrested and imprisoned these groups. Attending the prayer meetings could mean the end of a person's career or being blackballed from university. For some time, the numbers attending the Monday Peace Prayers dwindled to as few as ten people. But Pastor Führer persevered, and prayer services for peace sprang up in other places.

In late 1987, tension increased between the churches and the state in East Germany. When a large assembly of Christians frankly described the depressing condition of everyday life, the Communist authorities warned the church leaders that they were "playing with fire."[4] The state launched a vigorous attack on church newspapers.

Then on May 7, 1989, an independent citizens' group electrified the nation with a report of widespread fraud in the recent East German elections. The

2. Tyndale, *Protestants in Communist East Germany*, 105–9.
3. Ibid., 110.
4. Swoboda, *Revolution of the Candles*, 31.

churches had provided important support to citizens' groups that had been able to monitor some of the vote counting. When these groups reported substantial fraud, the church launched an official protest.[5] As the report spread, furious citizens began mass demonstrations.

The fury over voter fraud was only one of the many complicating factors for the East German Communist rulers desperate to maintain control of a disintegrating situation in the summer of 1989. Vast numbers of East Germans began to flee the country. When the Hungarian government took down the barbed-wire fence along the border with democratic Austria, tens of thousands of East Germans traveled to Hungary and then on to the West via Austria. Several thousand sought refugee status in the West German embassy in Prague, the capital of Czechoslovakia. And by the end of the summer, one hundred twenty thousand East Germans had applied for official visas to emigrate to the West, even though that regularly provoked severe penalties. At an annual meeting in September, the East German Church Federation adopted a position paper on the current situation, calling for a free press, a democratic multiparty system, freedom of travel, and economic reforms.[6] The numbers at Pastor Führer's Monday Peace Prayers ballooned to hundreds, then thousands.

The Stasi cracked down. In Dresden, the police drove armored cars into a large crowd and arrested hundreds. Larger and larger antigovernment demonstrations in the next three days produced more and more arrests. By October 7, over one thousand three hundred people were in prison enduring severe mistreatment.[7] Widespread police violence also happened in other cities, including Leipzig.

At the same time, peaceful protests blossomed all over the country. Regularly, they started with prayer services for peace in the churches, where speakers urged the crowds to remain nonviolent. Then they moved into the streets. No one knew when the police would unleash overwhelming force.

The situation was extremely dangerous as Pastor Führer contemplated leading the October 9 prayer for peace in his church in Leipzig. Three days before, the official party newspaper ran a threatening story under the headline "Hostility to the State Will No Longer Be Tolerated." It threatened further use of force to stop "these counterrevolutionary actions."[8] Rumors of troop

5. Curry, "Before the Fall."
6. Swoboda, *Revolution of the Candles*, 36.
7. Tyndale, *Protestants in Communist East Germany*, 5.
8. Swoboda, *Revolution of the Candles*, 38–39.

movements flew around. Pastor Führer knew that the Communist leaders in charge of East German internal security had praised the Chinese Communists for their violent crackdown in Tiananmen Square in June.[9] The authorities had brought ten thousand additional Stasi police into the city and given the order to "use all means available against terror and every act of violence."[10] Pastor Führer received calls that Monday afternoon warning him to cancel the prayer service.[11]

That same afternoon, six people met privately in a desperate search for a way to avoid bloody conflict. A theology professor who regularly attended Führer's prayer services, a famous orchestra conductor, and a political satirist met with three Communist Party secretaries and hammered out an appeal to everyone to remain peaceful. The party secretaries promised that the police would act peacefully if the protestors did the same. The professors rushed the statements to Pastor Führer's church and other churches holding prayer services just in time for the appeal to be read to everyone. It was also broadcast on radio and loudspeakers in the city.[12]

After the prayer service at St. Nicholas, several thousand people walked out of the church with lighted candles, ready for the kind of peaceful candlelit march that they had been doing after each prayer service for almost a month. Outside in the streets, they saw both thousands of armed police and tens of thousands of people ready to join their march through the city. Seventy thousand people marched around Leipzig that evening.[13] That they were unarmed was visible from the fact that they held a candle in one hand and shielded it from the breeze with the other. Heavily armed police lined the streets as the people marched.

Seventy thousand demonstrators moved through Leipzig's streets without offering a single provocation to the armed guards who were waiting for the order to shoot at them. No one hurled a stone through a window in frustration at the mute and fearful years. No one shouted defiantly at the massive display of police and military power. No one so much as knocked off a policeman's cap. The only fires that were lit were candles. Forty years of frustration, repression, and pent-up resentment were not expressed in any way that gave the armed forces reason to shoot. The order to open fire on the demonstrators never came.[14]

9. Bultman, *Revolution by Candlelight*, 177.
10. Von der Heydt, *Candles Behind the Wall*, 175.
11. Bultman, *Revolution by Candlelight*, 178.
12. Ibid., 179–86; Swoboda, *Revolution of the Candles*, 44.
13. Tyndale, *Protestants in Communist East Germany*, 1.
14. Von der Heydt, *Candles Behind the Wall*, 186.

Later, Pastor Führer reflected on the amazing evening:

> Nonviolence is clearly the spirit of Jesus. With these people who grew up with
> pictures of class enemies, and whose parents grew up with the Nazis and vio-
> lence and racial hatred, you can prove it didn't come from here. . . . And the few
> Christians that there are in this unchristian country—they didn't do it either. . . .
> That was the spirit of God at work.[15]

In retrospect, October 9 was the crucial turning point. The next Sunday,
almost all worship services in East Germany mentioned the amazing developments of October 9 in sermons, announcements, and prayers. In a pastoral
letter, the bishop of Thuringia called for a free press, elections by secret ballot, and freedom to travel. And he urged everyone to "stand firm on the basic
principle of nonviolence."[16]

A week after October 9, prayer services followed by demonstrations happened all over the country. "Everywhere people holding candles streamed out
of their churches to fill the streets."[17] In Leipzig, one hundred fifty thousand
people marched, shouting the name of Gorbachev and demanding freedom to
travel and democratic elections. A week later, three hundred thousand paraded
through Leipzig carrying countless candles.[18]

On October 17, the Communist Party forced Erich Honecker, longtime
general secretary of the party and head of state, to step down. The party then
named Egon Krenz as general secretary, and soon thereafter he became head
of state and chairman of the National Defense Council. Frustrated and upset
that the popular demand to separate the party and the state had been ignored,
hundreds of thousands continued their peaceful protests. Three hundred thousand again marched in Leipzig on October 30 after the Monday evening prayer
services. On November 4, over half a million people—the largest mass rally
ever in East Germany—marched in Berlin.

On November 8, the entire top leadership (the Politburo) of the Communist
Party resigned. A new prime minister known for his promotion of reform was
selected. The next evening, the dam finally burst.

During an internationally televised press conference, a Politburo spokesman declared that "one may apply for travel to foreign countries without the

15. Ibid., 187.
16. Swoboda, *Revolution of the Candles*, 49.
17. Tyndale, *Protestants in Communist East Germany*, 8.
18. Swoboda, *Revolution of the Candles*, 51–52, 59.

need to show special reason."[19] Tens of thousands of East Germans promptly headed for the checkpoints at the Berlin Wall and other borders with West Germany. By 10:00 p.m., the border guards simply moved out of the way as tens of thousands from East Germany streamed into West Berlin. The whole world watched that night as East and West Berliners hugged one another in amazement and others pulled pieces from the hated Berlin Wall.

The next day, the leaders of the church met to reflect on the astonishing developments. They thanked everyone "who contributed to the nonviolent nature of the demonstrations since October 9" and urged everyone to continue nonviolently. "Only without violence," they declared, "do we achieve peace and justice; only without violence do we preserve the life that has been entrusted to us."[20]

After the fall of the Berlin Wall, events moved at breakneck speed. Prominent church leaders helped to moderate high-level negotiations on political change. They also urged all citizens to avoid the trap of "hate-filled, revengeful thinking" and thereby protect what the nation had achieved in a "peaceful revolution."[21] On December 19, West German Chancellor Helmut Kohl came to East Germany for talks with the prime minister. Within a year, East Germany became part of one reunited Germany.

Massive nonviolent protest had achieved what would have been totally impossible through violence.

19. Ibid., 70.
20. Ibid., 71.
21. Ibid., 75.

recent victories of a growing movement

S cholars of nonviolent action report that the past three decades have witnessed a large upsurge in the use of nonviolent resistance to injustice, oppression, and authoritarian governments. In the last two decades of the twentieth century, "primarily nonviolent 'people power' movements have overthrown authoritarian regimes in nearly two dozen countries."[1]

Increasingly, nonviolent campaigns have used the growing literature on nonviolent action to design effective strategies. In Serbia, for example, a well-organized group opposed to the dictatorship of President Slobodan Milošević published manuals using Gene Sharp's scholarly studies and organized widespread training in nonviolent action. Their efforts from 1997 to 2000 eventually led to the massive peaceful demonstrations and strikes that forced Milošević to give up power.[2]

In part III, we will explore in some detail three recent examples of nonviolent action: the successful nonviolent campaign of Liberian women against a vicious dictator; the largely nonviolent toppling of long-standing dictators in Tunisia and Egypt during the "Arab Spring" of 2011; and the emergence of small but growing organizations training peacemaker teams to intervene nonviolently in situations of violent conflict.

1. Stephen Zunes, Lester R. Kurtz, and Sarah Beth Asher, eds., *Nonviolent Social Movements: A Geographical Perspective* (Oxford: Blackwell, 1999), 2.
2. See Gene Sharp, *Waging Nonviolent Struggle: 20th Century Practice and 21st Century Potential* (Boston: Porter Sargent, 2005), chap. 27.

8

"gather the women to pray for peace"

Liberian Women Overthrow a Dictator

[Mass Action for Peace] was prompted by emotion—by women's exhaustion and desperation—but there was nothing spontaneous about it; . . . we planned every move we made.

Leymah Gbowee[1]

T he women of Liberia were tired. They were tired of decades of conflict and civil war. They were tired of the military coups and the frequent violence that had become the norm under dictators and warlords. As one Liberian woman put it, "[Violence] happened so long it seemed like a way of life."[2]

After several years of civil war between various factions struggling for control of the country's natural resources, warlord Charles Taylor became president in 1997.[3] He quickly took complete control of the country's finances,

---

1. Leymah Gbowee, *Mighty Be Our Powers: How Sisterhood, Prayer, and Sex Changed a Nation at War* (New York: Beast Books, 2011), 138–39. I thank Rachel Lesher for help with the research on this chapter.

2. Deddeh Kwekwe, "Violence against Women in Liberia: A Situation Report," *Women's World* 39/40 (2006): 26.

3. Kevin Conley, "The Rabble Rousers," O, *The Oprah Magazine*, December 2008 (http://www.oprah.com/omagazine/Leymah-Gbowee-and-Abigail-Disney-Shoot-for-Peace-in-Liberia).

using vast amounts for himself and further impoverishing the people. Many of Liberia's citizens could not even afford a cup of rice.

Taylor also created his own private army, known as the Anti-Terrorism Unit (ATU), headed by his son Chuckie. The ATU kidnapped and forced many young boys to be child soldiers. Stories spread quickly of cells behind the executive mansion where women were raped and Taylor's opponents were tortured or killed. Taylor's reign became one of the most notorious examples of a brutal disregard for the rule of law, human rights, and justice.

Many Liberian women became widows and single parents. Many witnessed the death of their children and husbands firsthand. Women themselves endured vicious treatment. In the late 1990s, pregnant women were commonly cut open as a form of sport; others were raped, forced into marriage with Taylor's fighters, or forced to become sex slaves.[4] A survey by the World Health Organization in 2005 reported that 90 percent of Liberian women had suffered physical or sexual violence during the course of the country's civil war.[5]

Etweda Cooper, an educated Liberian woman who helped organize the early peace efforts, described how the dire situation in which children were dying, people were starving, and husbands were being killed moved women to become peace activists. "[Women] had become heads of household and we were carrying the burden of taking care of the family. . . . We decided we are the survivors; we are also peacemakers. . . . We make up the bulk of the population so why should we be ignored? So we added our voices to the peace process."[6]

Leymah Gbowee, a native Liberian and a future winner of the Nobel Peace Prize, spent her teenage years surrounded by the bloody civil war. At the age of seventeen, she learned of a United Nations Children's Fund (UNICEF) program that trained people to become social workers to work with others traumatized by war. Gbowee joined the program, and after graduating she worked with women in a trauma healing and reconciliation program.[7]

In 1999, Gbowee was introduced to a network of women who were working for social justice in West Africa. Gbowee recalls, "The women were at our physical, psychological, and spiritual limits. But we discovered a new source of strength: each other." Together, Liberian women, including Gbowee, formed

4. Kwekwe, "Violence against Women," 26.
5. Ibid.
6. Robert M. Press, "'Guided by the Hand of God': Liberian Women Peacemakers and Civil War," *Review of Faith & International Affairs* (Spring 2010): 24.
7. "Pray the Devil Back to Hell," *Bill Moyers Journal*, June 19, 2009 (http://www.pbs.org /moyers/journal/06192009/profile.html).

WIPNET, the Women in Peacebuilding Network, with the broad goal of elevating women to enable them to play key roles alongside men in peacebuilding.[8] Gbowee still remembers vividly the emotional electricity of that first meeting:

> How to describe the excitement of that first meeting of the Women in Peacebuilding Network . . . The energy in those rooms! Just being in a gathering of so many women was empowering. The fun, the jokes, the happiness. You forgot that you didn't have food at home. We were full of excitement and plans. . . . No one else in Africa was doing this: focusing only on women and only on building peace. . . . The potential power of this movement was immense. . . .
>
> WIPNET brought everything together for me: You can't cure trauma when violence is ongoing, so the primary effort must be working for peace. You can't negotiate lasting peace without bringing women into the effort, but women can't become peacemakers without releasing the pain that keeps them from feeling their own strength. Emotional release isn't enough in itself to create change, but WIPNET channeled that new energy into political action.[9]

The group of women involved in WIPNET realized that women must become more active in peacemaking. But they also knew that the widespread discrimination against women in West African society made that very difficult. They also knew that "women also suffered from lack of awareness and skills in peacemaking and also lacked the confidence, exposure and opportunity to get involved."[10]

Gbowee was chosen to be the coordinator of WIPNET's chapter in Liberia. The group focused first on educating its own leaders about issues in local politics, then on directing the world's attention to the need for women to play a role in ending war, and finally on training women to speak out and teach others about issues of war and peace. The group's hope was that one day every region would have a female activist who spoke to and educated her community.[11]

■ A "Crazy Dream"

By 2003, Gbowee was a thirty-one-year-old single mother of four after fleeing her abusive husband. Sick of the constant state of violence in her country, she

8. "WIPNET," *The Global Network of Women Peacebuilders* (http://www.gnwp.org/members /wipnet).
9. Gbowee, *Mighty Be Our Powers*, 112–14.
10. Ibid.
11. Ibid., 117.

began each day on her knees praying that the fighting would stop. One night she had a vision: "I didn't know where I was. Everything was dark. I couldn't see a face, but I heard a voice, and it was talking to me—commanding me: 'Gather the women to pray for peace!'"[12] She told a friend that she couldn't believe God would call her: "I was a single parent and in my church I couldn't excel to any position of authority because I was not married. I felt I was the wrong person for God to be speaking to. . . . I was doing everything wrong. I felt if God had to be speaking to someone, it had to be the perfect person. . . . I was terrified."[13]

Later, Gbowee called that moment "the start of everything." She began to pray for inspiration as she traveled and spoke to church groups across the country: "God, what message do you want the people to hear?" Weeks later at a church meeting, she shared her vision and proposed to other Christian women that they should join together to protest the violence. She invited all women to participate, calling on mothers, grandmothers, aunts, and sisters.[14] At that meeting, a Muslim woman, Asatu, stood up and told the group how impressed she was with their efforts. "We're all serving the same God," Asatu went on to say, "and I want to promise you all today that I'm going to move it forward with the Muslim women. . . . We will all work together to bring peace to Liberia."[15]

Gbowee recalls that moment as a stunning one that reached across old divides in Liberia caused by both tribal and religious differences. Christian and Muslim women had never worked together, so Asatu's proposal was one that no one had imagined before. Although some Christians said that working with Muslims would dilute the women's faith, Gbowee promptly committed herself to an interfaith effort. The group began to use the motto "Does the bullet know a Christian from a Muslim?" to espouse the heart of their work toward peace for all citizens of Liberia.

The women gathered to pray every Tuesday. But prayers without action did not feel like enough; the situation in the country grew worse and worse as civil war spread in opposition to Charles Taylor, who was fighting to protect his power at all costs. The cities lay in ruins without water or lights, and

12. Ibid., 122.
13. Leymah Gwobee, interview by Charlie Rose, *Charlie Rose Show*, MSNBC, October 17, 2011.
14. Gbowee, *Mighty Be Our Powers*, 124.
15. Abigail Disney, producer, and Gini Reticker, director, *Pray the Devil Back to Hell*, Fork Films, DVD, 2008.

radio and television stations were shut down. "We lived in a closed, guarded box," Gbowee writes, "and the most ordinary acts could bring down a terrible punishment."[16]

Led by Gbowee, Asatu, and WIPNET, women from all over the country began to mobilize an interfaith protest movement modeled after the action of the biblical character Esther, who interceded for her country in front of the king.[17] Together, the women dreamed of boldly confronting dictator Charles Taylor and demanding an end to the war. They visited mosques, markets, and churches, enlisting more women and always giving the message "Liberian women, awake for peace!" The women went out in pairs, and sometimes if certain women were not getting along, they were temporarily paired to compel cooperation.

The women passed out flyers that read, "We are tired! We are tired of our children being killed! We are tired of being raped! Women, wake up—you have a voice in the peace process!" They also handed out simple drawings explaining their message to women who could not read.[18] Flyers were hung on market stalls and street poles and were distributed to women at the market. They especially targeted areas where women gathered.

It was not an easy process. Women had suffered for so long that they had come to a place where they "look down, not ahead," Gbowee writes. Yet the women began to take notice and respond positively to the new, empowering way that Gbowee and her friends spoke to them.[19] The Christian and Muslim women of WIPNET released a statement called "Vision of Peace" to the press: "We envision peace. A peaceful coexistence that fosters equality, collective ownership and full participation of particularly women in all decision-making processes for conflict prevention, promotion of human security and socioeconomic development."[20]

The women also formed a pact to withhold all sexual activity from their husbands and partners until a peaceful solution was reached. The Liberian women believed that if they withheld sex, their partners might also begin to pray for peace and support an end to the war. As Gbowee later admitted, "The [sex] strike lasted, on and off, for a few months. It had little or no practical effect, but it was extremely valuable in getting us media attention."[21]

---

16. Gbowee, *Mighty Be Our Powers*, 126.
17. Disney and Reticker, *Pray the Devil Back to Hell*.
18. Gbowee, *Mighty Be Our Powers*, 127.
19. Ibid.
20. Ibid., 129.
21. Ibid., 147.

▪ "The Women of Liberia Want Peace Now!"

Presidential elections were set to take place in 2003, but with the growing conflict between Taylor and anti-Taylor rebel groups, such as Liberians United for Reconciliation and Democracy (LURD) and Movement for Democracy in Liberia (MODEL), a peaceful election seemed unlikely. International pressure for peace talks and a ceasefire between Taylor and rebel groups increased, but neither group would agree to sit down with the other.

The women of Liberia responded with what became a classic demonstration of the power of nonviolent protest. They were well on their way to providing a textbook case for Gene Sharp, the expert on nonviolence. "Nonviolent action," Sharp has said, "is a technique by which people who reject passivity and submission, and who see struggle as essential, can wage their conflict without violence. Nonviolent action is not an attempt to avoid or ignore conflict. It is one response to the problem of how to act effectively in politics, especially how to wield power effectively."[22]

The women of WIPNET saw the unwillingness of the men in power to sit down together as an opportunity to "wield their power" and speak out. The women released a single statement to the radio stations, "The women of Liberia want peace now!" with all of their names signed after it. This move placed the women at the center of attention, with new interest in their work from the media and women across Liberia. WIPNET began to hold meetings every night, sometimes in rooms so packed that not everyone who wanted to attend could fit inside. The women made plans for another public statement, this time as a physical assembly of women from across the country.

The women planned their first protest along the route that Charles Taylor traveled twice a day on his way to and from parliament. The women created nonpartisan posters, emphasizing peace and not politics, to hold as they protested. Again using Esther of the Bible as their model, the women chose the simplicity of plain clothing to signify their humble but wholehearted commitment to saving their people.[23] They wore plain white clothes to signify their commitment to peace, wore no makeup or jewelry, and wrapped their hair in simple scarves.

22. United Nations, "International Day of Non-Violence: 2 October" (http://www.un.org/en/events/nonviolenceday/background.shtml).
23. Disney and Reticker, *Pray the Devil Back to Hell.*

Charles Taylor had banned street marches, warning Liberians not to embarrass his administration. Yet the women planned to do exactly that in deliberate provocation—one "so dramatic and public it would make the demands of Liberia's women impossible to ignore."[24] The Women of Liberia Mass Action for Peace held their first protest on April 1, 2003. Led by Leymah Gbowee, more than two thousand women participated in the protest.[25] They prayed, sang, sat, danced, and held posters declaring "The women of Liberia want peace now!"

Over two thousand five hundred women showed up each day for the next week to stage a nonviolent protest against the dictator's role in the violence plaguing their country. The women used all of the nonviolent strategies they could enlist: protest, picketing, media, community organization, public statements, and prayer vigils. For twelve hours a day the women chanted and sang, "We want peace, no more war!"[26] As Charles Taylor's motorcade drove by each day, the women stood by the roadside with a huge banner repeating their message: "The women of Liberia want peace now!"

Gbowee was clearly the leader and spokesperson of the movement, but she was surrounded by a leadership team of Muslim and Christian women who were responsible for the day-to-day activities of the protest. Each night, the women of WIPNET met together and spent hours discussing the progress and the setbacks of the day. These daily evaluations shaped the next day's strategies. As Gbowee has said, the movement was "prompted by emotion—by women's exhaustion and desperation—but there was nothing spontaneous about it; managing a huge daily public protest was a complicated task and we planned every move we made."[27]

A Visit with the President

Leymah Gbowee and the other leaders issued a statement giving Charles Taylor three days to respond to their movement. "We will continue to sit in the sun

24. Gbowee, *Mighty Be Our Powers*, 136.
25. Kylin Navarro, "Women of Liberia Mass Action for Peace," *The Lokashakti Encyclopedia of Nonviolence, Peace & Social Justice*, 2003. Reprinted with permission from Swarthmore College's Global Nonviolent Action Database (http://www.lokashakti.org/encyclopedia/groups/725-women-of-liberia-mass-action-for-peace).
26. Gbowee, *Mighty Be Our Powers*, 144.
27. Ibid., 138–39.

and in the rain until we hear from the president!" the women chanted. After three days passed without word from Taylor, the women notified the press that Taylor's time was up, and they moved to the parliament building, filling the parking lot so that no one could come or go. For three days, the women stood in pouring rain in front of the parliament and refused to move until the president responded to them.

On April 11, the Women of Liberia Mass Action for Peace issued a position statement on the Liberian crisis.[28] They simply demanded peace:

> We want peace, no more war.
> Our children are dying—we want peace.
> We are tired of suffering—we want peace.
> We are tired of running—we want peace.

Finally, after the women marched and protested for more than a week, the parliamentary speaker came to where the group was sitting in the field to announce that Charles Taylor would see them in his executive mansion.

By 6:00 a.m. on April 23, 2003, more than two thousand women stood outside Taylor's executive mansion to hear Gbowee make their case to the president and the president of the senate (the only female government official present). Standing in front of Charles Taylor, who was wearing a military suit and dark glasses, Gbowee remembers feeling a strong need to say something to him that would convey the anguish of the death and pain that he had caused. She boldly stated their position with these words:

> The women of Liberia, including the IDPs [internally displaced persons], we are tired of war. We are tired of running. We are tired of begging for bulgur wheat. We are tired of our children being raped. We are now taking this stand, to secure the future of our children. Because we believe, as custodians of society, tomorrow our children will ask us, "Mama, what was your role during the crisis?" And we will have an answer.[29]

A group of the city's religious leaders who were also at the president's mansion that day partnered with the women to issue a list of clear, nonpartisan demands. First, the government and the rebels had to declare an unconditional ceasefire. Second, the government and the rebels had to meet together to talk. And third, an intervention force had to be sent to Liberia.

28. Navarro, "Women of Liberia."
29. Gbowee, *Mighty Be Our Powers*, 141.

The president listened to Gbowee without expression. When he finally spoke, he told the women that he was sick that day, but "no group of people could get me out of bed but the women of Liberia, who I consider to be my mothers."[30] President Taylor said he would attend peace talks with the rebels, but he challenged the women to demand the same of the rebels.

At the end of April, the leaders of LURD agreed to meet with Taylor for peace talks. The peace talks began in Sierra Leone, but soon they fell apart. Finally, a group backed by the United Nations succeeded in scheduling peace talks between Taylor and the rebels for June 4 in Ghana. When the women heard the news, everyone broke into song. "The Christian women sang Muslim songs. The Muslims sang hymns," Gbowee recalls.[31]

Barricading the Peace Talks

On June 4, 2003, peace talks began in Accra, Ghana, between rebels from LURD and MODEL and government leaders, including the president. The presidents of South Africa, Nigeria, Ivory Coast, and Sierra Leone, along with a delegation of leaders from the United States, also attended the talks. General Abubakar, former president of Nigeria, mediated the talks. Small donations from the community allowed a group of seven women from Women of Liberia Mass Action for Peace to travel to Ghana to gather, sing, and hold signs on the lawn in front of the building where the meetings were held.

Early in these peace talks, a United Nations war crimes tribunal informed Charles Taylor that he had been secretly indicted on charges of war crimes, prompting Taylor to flee back to Liberia to escape arrest.[32] Panic hit the people of Liberia. Soon after, war broke out again in Monrovia, and the peace talks were postponed. Taylor's men drove through the streets, shouting that if the president were arrested, they would kill everyone and burn everything.

Violence in Monrovia peaked on July 21, after a missile hit the American embassy compound, where many Liberians had taken shelter from the unrest. Forces from the rebel group LURD entered the city, and soon seven displaced persons camps were under rebel control. General Abubakar tried to convince the fighters to stop, and talks were scheduled to reconvene. They did, but little

30. Ibid.
31. Ibid., 153.
32. Navarro, "Women of Liberia."

progress occurred in the next month, and the violence in Liberia continued. Gbowee and the other women approached their breaking point. Gbowee recalls thinking, "How could I have been so stupid as to think a handful of women could stop a war? *You fooled me, God.*"[33]

The group of women in Ghana continued to sit outside the negotiating room with their signs and sent for reinforcements. Finally, in desperation, they went to the doors of the building where talks were taking place and sat down, linking arms, around the building. They refused to let any of the delegates leave until a peace agreement was reached.[34]

When security guards arrived to arrest the women, Gbowee threatened to undress right there, and she began to do so. She thought, "If you think you can humiliate me with an arrest, watch me humiliate myself more than you could have dreamed."[35] But her action also threatened to humiliate them, because in Africa it is a curse to see a mother naked, a type of spiritual emasculation.[36] The women refused to move until the delegates attended all meetings, took the sessions seriously, and refrained from jeering and insulting the women as they passed by. If a peace agreement was not signed within two weeks, the women promised to barricade the hall again.

Three weeks later, on August 17, 2003, after receiving strong pressure from the international community, which threatened to cut off international funding if an agreement was not reached, the Comprehensive Peace Agreement was signed, ending decades of war in Liberia. There were three main points of the agreement: first, Charles Taylor would resign from the presidency and go into exile; second, a transitional government would be formed to oversee democratic elections; and third, a United Nations peacekeeping force would be dispatched to Monrovia. The new transitional president, Gyude Bryant, attributed the success to the women of WIPNET. "Something great happened," he told the women, "and we can say it happened because of you all."[37]

Charles Taylor was exiled to Nigeria, and in May 2012 an international tribunal sentenced him to fifty years in prison for eleven counts of war crimes and crimes against humanity, including murder, rape, torture, and the use of

33. Gbowee, *Mighty Be Our Powers*, 160.
34. Navarro, "Women of Liberia."
35. Gbowee, *Mighty Be Our Powers*, 161–62.
36. Eliza Griswold, "Firebrand for Peace," *Newsweek*, September 26, 2011, 13.
37. Gbowee, *Mighty Be Our Powers*, 164.

child soldiers.[38] Taylor's son was sentenced to ninety-seven years of jail time in the United States for crimes against humanity committed in Liberia.[39]

■ A New Liberia

When the women returned to Liberia, they held celebrations in the field where the protests had been held. People came to shake their hands and thank them. Children followed them, chanting, "We want peace—no more war!"[40] All around the women, though, was a country in a desperate state of destruction. Two hundred thousand people had died. One in three Liberians had been displaced. More than 75 percent of the country's physical infrastructure had been destroyed.

The women knew that their work did not end with the signing of the peace treaty. "Our actions were the foundation of a movement, not its end product," Gbowee declared.[41] The women of Liberia were determined that the conditions of the peace agreement be implemented. WIPNET and the Liberian Women's Initiative organized a two-day retreat for eighty women leaders from across Liberia to examine the Comprehensive Peace Agreement and set benchmark goals for its implementation.[42] The meeting also determined to equip the women leaders to engage with United Nations mission teams in Liberia and hold them accountable to a timetable.

On August 4, 2004, international United Nations peacemaking forces finally entered Liberia. At first the women found themselves shut out of the disarmament process. But when the process bogged down, women activists were invited into the process of disarmament, demobilization, and reintegration of soldiers into the community.[43] Under leadership from the United Nations Mis-

38. Marlise Simons and J. David Goodman, "Ex-Liberian Leader Gets 50 Years for War Crimes," *New York Times*, May 30, 2012, A1.

39. "Taylor's Son Jailed for 97 Years," *BBC News*, January 9, 2009 (http://news.bbc.co.uk/2/hi/americas/7820069.stm). Taylor has filed an appeal of the conviction on grounds that trial judges made dozens of factual and legal errors.

40. Gbowee, *Mighty Be Our Powers*, 167.

41. Ibid., 168.

42. The Liberian Women's Initiative (LWI) was one of the first women's groups to protest the war in Liberia, beginning as early as 1994. Several of the women instrumental in WIPNET's protest movement in Liberia, including Asatu and Etweda Cooper, were members of the LWI.

43. Dorina Bekoe and Christina Parajon, "Women's Role in Liberia's Reconstruction," *United States Institute of Peace*, May 1, 2007 (http://www.usip.org/publications/women-s-role-liberia-s-reconstruction).

sion in Liberia (UNMIL) team and local women, by December 2005, hundreds of individuals had turned in their weapons for cash. In some communities, women traveled to disarmament camps to meet and directly confront fighters to persuade them to give up their arms and turn them in to the women, who then gave them to the United Nations team.[44]

The Women of Liberia Mass Action for Peace also spoke out for the reintegration of soldiers into society. As one leader said, "Peace is a process, not an event. We must accept combatants into our midst. How can we move on if we don't forgive?"[45] Although it would be painful and difficult, the women encouraged their fellow citizens to move forward in the peace process by accepting soldiers back into their communities and helping them find productive work. Gbowee later wrote,

> Organizations like the UN do a lot of good, but there are certain basic realities they never seem to grasp. . . . Maybe the most important truth that eludes these organizations is that it's insulting when outsiders come in and tell a traumatized people what it will take for them to heal. You cannot go to another country and make a plan for it. The cultural context is so different from what you know that you will not understand much of what you see. I would never come to the US and claim to understand what's going on, even in the African American culture. People who have lived through a terrible conflict may be hungry and desperate, but they are not stupid. They often have very good ideas about how peace can evolve, and they need to be asked.
>
> That includes women. Most especially women. When it comes to preventing conflict or building peace, there's a way in which women are the experts. . . . We know our communities. We know the history. We know the people. We know how to talk to an ex-combatant and get his cooperation, because we know where he comes from. To outsiders like the UN, these soldiers were a problem to be managed. But they were our children.[46]

Gbowee and other women from WIPNET worked with UNICEF on a campaign to encourage former fighters to go back to school. The women of WIPNET continued to escort former fighters as they turned in their weapons from the war, and they even gave radio announcements explaining how the disarmament process worked. UNMIL offered to pay twenty women for their help in the process, but over fifty additional volunteers showed up to help. Each

44. Navarro, "Women of Liberia."
45. Disney and Reticker, *Pray the Devil Back to Hell.*
46. Gbowee, *Mighty Be Our Powers,* 171–72.

year, WIPNET organized a conference to bring together the most accomplished African activists to brainstorm strategies for Liberia's redevelopment.[47]

Gbowee began to travel internationally to attend peacemaking conferences and meet with diplomats from other countries. As she met with others, she realized that if she was serious about a career in peacemaking, she had to be able to speak with more knowledge. She read as many books as she could on conflict resolution, including *The Journey Toward Reconciliation* and *The Little Book of Conflict Transformation* by John Paul Lederach, and *The Peace Book* by Louise Diamond. Gbowee also spent a month in Harrisonburg, Virginia, attending a conflict resolution program at Eastern Mennonite University that she had longed to attend for years but had not been able to make time for until after the war.

While at the university, Gbowee learned the concept of restorative justice, an idea that gave her a "deep sense of recognition and relief. So my response to child soldiers . . . my desire to bring them back into the society rather than casting them out, hadn't been crazy! . . . If a community was to be made whole after war, especially civil war, perpetrators and victims had to come together."[48]

◼ A New President

For two years, women in Liberia worked to increase women's involvement in the political process and encourage them to vote so that, when the transitional government ended, women would be ready to engage. The Christian Women Peace Initiative and Liberian Muslims for Peace organized a huge voter registration campaign in the days before the registration process closed. Ten communities were targeted, and teams of twenty women traveled to each community to register voters. Another group of women, led by the minister of gender Varah Gayflor, worked to recruit women voters in rural areas. As a result of the total effort, women went from making up 15 percent of registered voters to 51 percent.[49]

On the day of the election, women monitored voting stations. Although WIPNET could not publicly take sides, its members had private conversations with voters, encouraging them to elect a candidate who would represent women's interests.

47. Ibid., 174.
48. Ibid., 179.
49. Ibid., 183.

On November 23, 2005, the people of Liberia elected Ellen Johnson Sirleaf, former chairperson of the Open Society Initiative for West Africa and the co-author of a United Nations study on women in conflict and on peacebuilding, as their first woman president. Her election returned a deep sense of pride to the women of Liberia. Sirleaf built her grassroots campaign on the promise of getting more women involved in the government and pursuing a "gender agenda." At Independence Day celebrations, President Sirleaf promised the Liberian people that she would continue to work for peace: "This democracy that we are working so hard at, we are going to keep it, we are going to make sure it stays."[50]

As President Sirleaf told one reporter, "There was a culture of impunity because of the war. There has been a complete breakdown of morality. Our approach right now is to try to empower the women to become normal again, by engaging them in productive activities, by ensuring they are part of society, by introducing education and training, to enable them to understand their potential."[51]

In the years following Sirleaf's election, she has kept her promise. She created a new Ministry of Gender and Development and the Liberian Women Media and Action Committee to work toward increasing women's access to education and policy making.[52]

Although important progress has been made in the public standing of women in the region, many challenges remain. Women are still widely treated as second-class citizens. Sexual abuse and domestic violence still frequently occur. In an article analyzing peace strategies used by West African women, Leymah Gbowee recently wrote that the goal of the women of West Africa is to continue to promote social justice and bring awareness to the barriers that continue to exclude women from major decision making.[53]

Liberian women continue to work "on the ground" in their communities. They lobby for their rights and run for election for local government. They demand a voice among the traditional village elders. And they take advantage of new property laws pioneered by the Association of Female Lawyers of

50. Etweda Cooper, interview by Amy Costello, PBS, October 18, 2011 (http://www.pbs.org /wnet/women-war-and-peace/features/what-has-ellen-johnson-sirleaf-done-for-liberian-women/).
51. Susan McKay, "Civil War's Painful Legacy for the Women of Liberia," *The Irish Times*, July 25, 2009.
52. Kwekwe, "Violence against Women," 27.
53. Leymah Gbowee, "Effecting Change through Women's Activism in Liberia," *IDS Bulletin* 40, no. 2 (2009): 50.

116

Liberia to reclaim the land that they used to farm with their husbands before the wars.[54] Women advocates and lawyers have lobbied successfully for the passage of laws such as the Rape Bill of 2006, which sets stricter conditions for what is considered rape and makes rape an unbailable offense, in an effort to work against the systemic violence against women in their society. Breaking down barriers to women's participation in the political process requires addressing both the physical violence during times of conflict and the deeper systemic lack of regard for women.

Lakshmi Puri, deputy executive director of UN Women, the United Nations Entity for Gender Equality and the Empowerment of Women, believes that women have a unique contribution to make to peacemaking: "The role, contribution and leadership of half of humanity in sustainable peace—3.5 billion women and girls—is not only a matter of numerical logic, it also has an intrinsic value. Women play an important role and have particular skills in peace-making and peace-building. These are roles and skills they have developed over many years, as mothers, wives and caretakers for family members and the community."[55]

The Future of Liberia

As the presidential election in Liberia approached in 2011, rising tensions and boycotts by opposition groups threatened chaos. Leymah Gbowee once again stepped in and met with party leaders to urge them to speak out against the violence. Party leaders later released a statement that there would be no violence on election day, and the election went on as planned. President Ellen Johnson Sirleaf was elected for a second term in November 2011 and was formally inaugurated on January 16, 2012.

At the inauguration ceremony that day, President Sirleaf modeled her second-term goal of national unity by welcoming her opponent, Winston Tubman, to sit in the front row of the celebration.[56] Since that time, Tubman has called on his party leaders to support Sirleaf's administration and

54. McKay, "Civil War's Painful Legacy."
55. UNESCO, "Culture of Peace and Non-Violence: A Vision in Action" (Paris: UNESCO, 2012), 29 (unesdoc.unesco.org/images/0021/002177/217786e.pdf).
56. "Liberian President Begins Second Term," *Voice of America*, January 16, 2012 (http://www.voanews.com/content/liberian-president-takes-oath-for-second-term-137420538/159444.html).

has spoken out in support of her efforts for greater economic justice and employment.[57]

Despite the period of unrest surrounding the election, Sirleaf's reelection was widely viewed by Liberians as a hopeful sign for their country's future. At her inauguration, Sirleaf spoke of the progress that Liberia had made in the previous four years, and she pledged to continue that work in the years ahead. "Today, we can state with conviction that our country has turned the corner," she said. "Liberia is no longer a place of conflict, war, and deprivation. We are no longer the country our citizens want to run away from, our international partners pity, and our neighbors fear. We have earned our rightful place as a beacon of democracy."[58]

More recently, Gbowee has founded the Women in Peace and Security Network, an organization that focuses on bringing West African women together to mobilize, write about, and reinvigorate women's movements. She also went on to receive a master's degree in conflict transformation from Eastern Mennonite University's Center for Justice and Peacebuilding in 2007.[59] At a women's peacebuilding conference in June 2011, Gbowee talked about the transformative nature of her continued studies in restorative justice. "Restorative justice was . . . something we could see as ours and not artificially imposed by Westerners. And we needed it, needed that return to tradition. More than we needed to punish them, we needed to undo the damage they had done."[60]

In 2008, Gbowee received the Blue Ribbon for Peace by Harvard University's Kennedy School for Government, and in 2011, she was awarded (along with Liberia's President Sirleaf) the ultimate recognition for successful peacemaking, the Nobel Peace Prize.[61]

The road ahead for women's rights in Africa will continue to pose challenges and require further support from the international community and continuing education for African women leaders. But signs of hope and progress abound. Leymah Gbowee and the women of Liberia emboldened women in Africa

57. "Liberian Opposition Leader Welcomes President's Speech," *Voice of America*, January 25, 2012 (http://www.voanews.com/content/butty-liberia-state-of-nation-opposition-tubman-25january12-138023218/159510.html).

58. *Voice of America*, "Liberian President Begins Second Term."

59. "Nobel Prize Winner Leymah Gbowee Connected to Peace-Church Tradition," *Our Weekly*, October 9, 2011 (http://ourweekly.com/news/2011/oct/09/nobel-prize-winner-leymah-gbowee-connected-to/).

60. Ibid.

61. "Leymah Gbowee," *Center for American Progress*, November 2008 (http://www.americanprogress.org/events/2008/11/inf/GboweeLeymah.html).

and from around the world to speak out for their rights and the well-being of their communities.

President Loren Swartzendruber of Eastern Mennonite University surely is right: "The impact that Leymah was able to have, first in Liberia, then in West Africa, and now all over the world, shows that another, nonviolent reality is possible."[62] Tragically, the devestation from the Ebola crisis is rapidly reversing many of the improvements made possible by the courageous nonviolent action of the women of Liberia.

62. *Our Weekly*, "Nobel Prize Winner Leymah Gbowee."

9

nonviolence in the arab spring

We are peace advocates and not advocates of violence. . . . If you see someone behaving violently, please circle around this person and take him out of the protests.

Wael Ghonim[1]

The wave of unprecedented protests that swept over the Middle East in the winter and spring of 2010–11 shocked the world.[2] Protests shook country after country ruled by authoritarian, often dictatorial leaders: Algeria, Bahrain, Egypt, Iraq, Jordan, Kuwait, Lebanon, Mauritania, Morocco, Oman, Libya, Saudi Arabia, Sudan, Syria, Tunisia, Western Sahara, and Yemen. Largely nonviolent protests successfully removed the dictators in Tunisia and Egypt.

The story is remarkably similar for both Tunisia and Egypt.[3] Both had struggling economies, high unemployment, and inflation. Both suffered under dictators who had been in power for decades. Both dictators ruled under an

---

1. Wael Ghonim, *Revolution 2.0: The Power of the People Is Greater Than the People in Power; A Memoir* (Boston: Houghton Mifflin Harcourt, 2012), 167–68.

2. I thank David Fuller for his excellent research for this chapter.

3. Ashraf Khalil, *Liberation Square: Inside the Egyptian Revolution and the Rebirth of a Nation* (New York: St. Martin's Press, 2011), 127–28; Lisa Anderson, "Demystifying the Arab Spring: Parsing the Differences between Tunisia, Egypt, and Libya," *Foreign Affairs* 90, no. 3 (2011): 2–7.

unspoken contract with the people: economic security in exchange for limited (or zero) political freedom. In both countries, the dictators failed to keep up their end of the bargain. In both countries, youth active on the Internet played a significant role. Largely unplanned nonviolent protests in both nations snowballed into widespread uprisings that eventually ousted their dictators.

Tunisia

History

To many in the West, Tunisia appeared to be the model Arab country. In fact, Tunisia "enjoyed the Arab world's best educational system, largest middle class, and strongest organized labor movement."[4] With the economy growing at 5 percent per year, the per capita GDP tripled from 1986 to 2008.[5] Education was free and compulsory to age sixteen.[6] A third of high school graduates went to college.[7] Women's rights were protected. Islamic extremism appeared to be largely eliminated.[8]

What many in the West failed to see, or simply ignored, however, was that these "benefits" came at a high cost.[9] The most humiliating cost was the rampant corruption of the ruling family. Prior to his ouster, Tunisians referred to President Ben Ali's family as "the Family" or "the Mafia." Half of Tunisia's business leaders were connected to this family through marriage.[10] The pervasive corruption that enriched them provoked a general attitude of disgust, humiliation, and, eventually, fury.[11]

Another cost was political freedom. Amnesty International reported in 2010 that the Tunisian government severely restricted freedom of expression,

4. Anderson, "Demystifying the Arab Spring."
5. John R. Bradley, *After the Arab Spring: How Islamists Hijacked the Middle East Revolts* (New York: Palgrave Macmillan, 2012), 38.
6. Anderson, "Demystifying the Arab Spring."
7. Bradley, *After the Arab Spring*, 33.
8. Vivienne Walt, "Tunisia's Nervous Neighbors Watch the Jasmine Revolution," *Time*, January 31, 2011, 24–27; see also Blake Hounshell, "Dark Crystal: Why Didn't Anyone Predict the Arab Revolutions?" *Foreign Policy* 187, July 2011 (http://www.foreignpolicy.com/articles/2011/06/20/dark_crystal).
9. Anderson, "Demystifying the Arab Spring."
10. See Scott Shane, "Cables from American Diplomats Portray U.S. Ambivalence on Tunisia," *New York Times*, January 15, 2011 (http://www.nytimes.com/2011/01/16/world/africa/16cables.html).
11. Bradley, *After the Arab Spring*, 43–48.

association, and assembly. Government critics experienced unfair trials and torture.[12]

The tradeoff of corruption and zero political freedom for economic prosperity worked as long as President Ben Ali kept economic prosperity growing. However, in the winter of 2010, Tunisia suffered from a stagnating economy, rising food prices, inflation, and a lack of jobs for educated youth. Two-thirds of the population was under thirty, and youth unemployment reached 24 percent.[13] Growing frustration over the corruption, lack of freedom, and then the economic downturn needed only a spark to ignite an explosion.[14]

A Spark That Lit the World on Fire

The last straw for one fruit vendor in the interior city of Sidi Bouzid was the public humiliation he received when a policewoman confiscated his scales, ordered him to move his cart, and, most shockingly in this patriarchal society, slapped him.[15] Mohamed Bouazizi took his humiliation to the steps of the governor's office, seeking an appointment. When his request was ignored, he threatened to set himself on fire. On December 17, 2010, Bouazizi carried out his ghastly threat, dying eighteen days later.[16]

12. Amnesty International, "Tunisia—Amnesty International Report 2010" (http://www
.amnesty.org/en/region/tunisia/report-2010).

13. John Pollock, "Streetbook: How Egyptian and Tunisian Youth Hacked the Arab Spring," *MIT Technology Review*, August 23, 2011 (http://www.technologyreview.com/featured story/425137/streetbook/). Andrew Gavin Marshall says that 53 percent (in the Middle East) are under twenty-five, and 75 percent of these youth are unemployed. See Marshall, "Are We Witnessing the Start of a Global Revolution? North Africa and the Global Political Awakening, Part 1," *Centre for Research on Globalization*, January 27, 2011 (http://www.globalresearch.ca /are-we-witnessing-the-start-of-a-global-revolution/22963); see also (cited by Marshall) Clemens Höges, Bernhard Zand, and Helene Zuber, "Tunisia's Worrying Precedent: Arab Rulers Fear Spread of Democracy Fever," *Spiegel Online International*, January 25, 2011 (http://www.spiegel .de/international/world/tunisia-s-worrying-precedent-arab-rulers-fear-spread-of-democracy -fever-a-741545.html).

14. Marshall, "Start of a Global Revolution?"; Bradley, *After the Arab Spring*, 40; Nicholas Collins, *Voices of a Revolution: Conversations with Tunisia's Youth* (Washington, DC: National Democratic Institute, 2011), 6 (pdf.usaid.gov/pdf_docs/PNADU912.pdf).

15. That she slapped him is disputed. *The Guardian* interviewed the policewoman several months after the revolution, and she claims that she never hit Bouazizi. See Elizabeth Day, "Fedia Hamdi's Slap Which Sparked a Revolution 'Didn't Happen,'" *The Guardian*, April 23, 2011 (http://www.guardian.co.uk/world/2011/apr/23/fedia-hamdi-slap-revolution-tunisia). Regardless of whether or not it actually happened, the rest of the country (and the world) thought that it did.

16. Walt, "Tunisia's Nervous Neighbors."

Tunisian rapper El Général called Bouazizi's suicide "the drop of water which made the whole cup overflow."[17] The day after his self-immolation, residents of Sidi Bouzid took to the streets in protest. The governor reacted with violence. The protestors responded with rocks and burned police vehicles. They also used their mobile phones and video cameras. Footage and pictures of the protests flooded the Internet, primarily on Facebook. Activists in Tunisia saw these images and helped to spread them further. Eventually Al Jazeera, the large Arab television network, aired footage. In a country where a third of the population has Internet access and everybody has a television tuned to Al Jazeera, it did not take long for the news of the public humiliation and self-immolation to spread.

Initially, it was widely reported that Bouazizi was a college graduate who was forced to sell fruit because he could not find any other job. Though we later learned that Bouazizi was not a college graduate, the damage had been done.[18] For Tunisians, there are few things more humiliating than for a male college graduate who is selling fruit to be slapped by a woman.[19]

The Eruption of Popular Protests

A string of further suicides and self-immolations increased the number and passion of the protestors. On December 22, Houcine Nejji[20] screamed, "No to misery, no to unemployment!" as he electrocuted himself.[21] Protests spread to other cities in the interior of Tunisia. Various organizations jumped into action to continue the protests and help them spread throughout the country. The largest trade union in Tunisia, the Tunisian General Labor Union (UGTT), along with other unions, especially teachers' and lawyers' unions, played a major role. These groups helped to politicize the demands of the protestors, who were, at first, concerned primarily with socioeconomic issues.[22]

In an attempt to quell the chaos, President Ben Ali visited Bouazizi in the hospital. But in the end, he resorted to his trump card: violent repression.

17. Ibid., 24.
18. See International Crisis Group, "Popular Protest in North Africa and the Middle East (IV): Tunisia's Way," *Middle East/North Africa Report* 106 (April 28, 2011): 2. Even as late as January 31, 2011, *Time* was still reporting that Bouazizi was a computer-science graduate. See Walt, "Tunisia's Nervous Neighbors," 24.
19. International Crisis Group, "Popular Protest," 3.
20. Some spell the last name as "Falhi."
21. Pollock, "Streetbook."
22. International Crisis Group, "Popular Protest," 4.

After Bouazizi died in the hospital on January 4, 2011, five thousand people attended his funeral. Tunisia's lawyers' and teachers' unions officially joined the protestors.[23] The most shockingly violent days were January 8–10. Police killed between twenty-one and fifty people.[24] Eyewitnesses reported that government snipers fired on the crowds. Amnesty International reported that many demonstrators died from a single bullet to the head or chest, thus obviously "fired by trained professionals with the intent to kill."[25]

In an address to the nation on January 10, 2011, President Ben Ali promised to create three hundred thousand jobs in the next two years. But he also dismissed the protestors as terrorists controlled by foreign powers.[26]

This pushed the protestors over the edge. Thousands of people took to the streets. The leaderless protests were fueled by text messages, Twitter, and Facebook updates. Mobile phones took video of police beatings and shootings, which were immediately uploaded.

Activists called for a mass protest at the Muhammad Ali Square in Tunis. The turnout was larger than anyone expected. Activists took video with their mobile phones and streamed it live on the Internet.[27] A clear message emerged from the protestors: "Down with Ben Ali!"[28] The previous weeks of protests, which began as an angry reaction to economic conditions and government indifference, had finally developed into a unified call. Ben Ali must step down.

The president deployed the army on January 12, but the army chief of staff, General Rachid Ammar, refused to fire on the protestors.[29]

On February 13, Ben Ali gave his last speech. He promised lower commodity prices, the end of censorship, unrestricted Internet access, and new elections for the legislature in six months. And he announced that he would not seek office in the 2014 election.[30] But the next day he fled to Saudi Arabia as tens of thousands of protestors filled Tunisia's capital.

23. Pollock, "Streetbook."

24. According to Mounir Saidani, twenty-one died ("Revolution and Counterrevolution in Tunisia: The Forty Days That Shook the Country," *Boundary 2* 39, no. 1 [2012]: 49).

25. As quoted in International Crisis Group, "Popular Protest," 5. There is an extremely graphic video that shows the carnage in a Kasserine hospital on one of those days (http://www.youtube.com/watch?v=Ud7aAdviWaY).

26. International Crisis Group, "Popular Protest," 5.

27. "How Facebook Changed the World: The Arab Spring [2/4]," YouTube video (http://www.youtube.com/watch?v=7WNd-Zm0K9A&feature=fvwrel).

28. Saidani, "Revolution and Counterrevolution," 50.

29. Alexis Arieff, "Political Transition in Tunisia," RS21666 (Washington, DC: Congressional Research Service, February 2, 2011) (http://fpc.state.gov/documents/organization/156511.pdf).

30. Saidani, "Revolution and Counterrevolution," 51.

■ Egypt

History

Egypt is the cultural and political center of the Arab world.[31] Egypt was also considered the United States' greatest ally in the region, receiving $1.3 billion annually in US military aid.[32] But there were deep problems festering just below the surface.

The story is very similar to Tunisia's. In Egypt, too, there was a sort of unspoken contract with the government: "The regime offered free education, employment in an expanding public sector, affordable healthcare, cheap housing and other forms of social protection, in return for obedience."[33] As in Tunisia, a long-standing dictator ruled Egypt. Hosni Mubarak had been in power for thirty years. Politically, Egyptians were powerless. Even if they bothered to go to the polls to vote, it did not matter. "Every Egyptian government in living memory cheated in elections—even when it didn't have to."[34] In 2007, 87 percent of Egyptians polled said that they were dissatisfied with their government.[35] Economic conditions were worse than in Tunisia. Unemployment among college graduates was over 25 percent.[36] More than 50 percent of Egyptians lived on less than two dollars a day.[37] And from 2006 to 2007 food prices increased 25 percent.[38]

Into this scene of economic and political despair and a sense of utter hopelessness came an unlikely martyr, Khaled Said.[39]

31. Khalil, *Liberation Square*, 145; Ashraf M. Attia et al., "Commentary: The Impact of Social Networking Tools on Political Change in Egypt's 'Revolution 2.0,'" *Electronic Commerce Research and Applications* 10 (2011): 370.

32. Adding economic aid brings the total to $2.3 billion (Alexander Kazamis, "The 'Anger Revolutions' in the Middle East," *Journal of Balkan and Near Eastern Studies* 13, no. 2 (2011): 150–51. Anour Boukhars, assistant professor of international relations at McDaniel College, says, "American interests were conceived so narrowly and rigidly that maintaining an unjust status quo was seen as preferable to chaotic dismantling of despotic controls that kept the forces of Islamist extremism and radical nationalism in check" ("The Arab Revolution for Dignity," *American Foreign Policy Interests* 33 [2011]: 61).

33. Hazem Kandil, "Interview: Revolt in Egypt," *New Left Review* 68 (March–April 2011): 17.

34. Khalil, *Liberation Square*, 90.

35. John R. Bradley, *Inside Egypt: The Road to Revolution in the Land of the Pharaohs* (New York: Palgrave Macmillan, 2012), 8.

36. Charles Kenny, "Why Recessions Are Good for Freedom," *Foreign Policy* 186 (May 2011): 31.

37. As quoted in Bradley, *Inside Egypt*, 34.

38. Ibid., 40.

39. The spelling of Khaled's last name varies: Said, Saieed, Saeed.

Unlikely Martyr

Khaled Said was a twenty-eight-year-old, shy computer nerd from Alexandria. On June 6, 2010, police dragged him into the street and savagely beat him to death. Photos of his mangled face placed next to a recent picture of him went viral.[40] "The huge thing with Khaled Said (sometimes spelled Saieed) wasn't his picture after he got killed. It was his picture before he got killed. A little innocent-looking guy who looks like your son, your cousin, your nephew. That's what galvanized people."[41]

Wael Ghonim, a thirty-year-old Egyptian Google executive living in Dubai, stumbled across Said's picture—a moment that would change his life and the history of Egypt. Moved to tears by the grotesque violence and motivated by the deep feeling of despair hovering over Egypt, Ghonim started a Facebook page called "We Are All Khaled Said." "It expressed my feelings perfectly," Ghonim later wrote. "Khaled Said was a young man just like me, and what happened to him could have happened to me. All young Egyptians had long been oppressed, enjoying no rights in our own homeland. The page name was short and catchy, and it expressed the compassion that people immediately felt when they saw Khaled Said's pictures."[42]

The government defended the police officers. At first, reports circulated that Said was a drug dealer and had simply choked to death on a baggie of hashish. The mangled face, they said, was the result of a fall down stairs as he fled from police. The Egyptian people, however, were not convinced—they were outraged. Ghonim saw the photos on June 8, two days after Khaled Said was killed, and created the Facebook page on the same day. Two minutes later, he had three hundred members. By the end of the first day, there were thirty-six thousand members and eighteen hundred comments.

Through Facebook, and in consultation with other Internet activists, Ghonim scheduled June 18 as the day of a "Silent Stand." It was a day for Egyptians to make it known that they were not going to ignore what happened

---

40. "The photo is horrific. Khaled's face is cut and mangled, several teeth seem to be missing and blood is still pooling underneath his head" (Khalil, *Liberation Square*, 76). As author Johnny West describes it, "His whole jaw has been dislocated to another part of his face. He's missing at least three teeth. Blood trickled and has dried on his mouth, his nose and a cut near his eye. His open eyes stare at the ceiling. Worst of all is the rictus, his mouth gaping. It must have been a horrific death" (*Karama! Journeys through the Arab Spring* [London: Heron Books, 2011], 148).
41. As quoted in Khalil, *Liberation Square*, 76.
42. Ghonim, *Revolution 2.0*, 60.

to Said and to express their outrage at what had been done to him. By this time, the Facebook page had one hundred thousand members. The protestors lined up along major roads in Cairo and Alexandria with their backs toward the road. All the protestors wore black and stood silently, reading the Qur'an or the Bible or meditating. Ghonim said, "We wanted to send out a clear message that although we were both sad and angry, we were nevertheless nonviolent."[43]

Ghonim had a clear strategy for his Facebook page:

> The strategy for the Facebook page ultimately was to mobilize public support for the cause. This wasn't going to be too different from using the "sales tunnel" approach that I had learned at school. The first phase was to convince people to join the page and read its posts. The second was to convince them to start interacting with the content by "liking" and "commenting" on it. The third was to get them to participate in the page's online campaigns and to contribute to its content themselves. The fourth and final phase would occur when people decided to take the activism onto the street. This was my ultimate aspiration.[44]

The Facebook page helped spark large nonviolent protests over the next several months as Ghonim and other activists worked hard to move the people of Egypt from silent submission and secret grumbling to taking a stand against the system that had deprived them of dignity.

One of the most important groups that joined the protest was the April 6 Youth Movement, which began in response to a worker strike at a textile factory in early 2008. A group of young people heard about the unsuccessful strike and, through a Facebook page, called for a general workers' strike in Egypt for April 6, 2008. Only one town took part in the strike, and the strike was violently repressed. Although the group was unsuccessful in moving people from the virtual to the real world, the group grew rapidly on Facebook, adding about three thousand followers a day. By 2010, the group had seventy thousand members. Because of the failure of the April 6 protest, the group focused on training. In April 2009, twenty-year-old Mohamed Adel went to Serbia to train with the Center for Applied Non-Violent Action and Strategies (CANVAS), founded by Ivan Marovic, a leader

43. Ibid., 70. The important role of Facebook is demonstrated in general with Ghonim's Facebook page, but it is also illustrated specifically by the fact that the idea for the stand was posted on the page on the morning of June 16 and took place in the early evening on June 18.
44. Ibid., 67.

in the peaceful Serbian revolution against Slobodan Milosěvić, in which only two people died.[45]

Helped by this training in nonviolence in Serbia, the April 6 Youth Movement began an online group, the Academy of Change, that promoted nonviolent civil disobedience. Adel continued to keep in contact with CANVAS in Serbia through email. "He conducted miniature versions of the CANVAS workshop in Egypt, stressing unity, nonviolent discipline, the importance of clear goals, and keeping members engaged."[46] April 6 Youth Movement adopted the famous clenched fist that was the logo of the Serbian opposition.

Another group that worked closely with the April 6 group was Kefaya. Kefaya (Arabic for "Enough!") began in the summer of 2004 with the primary goal of "preventing Gamal Mubarak from succeeding his father."[47] It also was a training ground for young activists who would be pivotal in the January 2011 revolution.[48]

The Youth of the Muslim Brotherhood was another major group. Only three years old when the protests began, the Youth of the Muslim Brotherhood sought to form a political party with more specific goals than the cultural movement of the Muslim Brotherhood. The Muslim Brotherhood began in 1928 as an organization committed to the idea that Islamic tenets were the solution to Egypt's problems. The group initially used violence to promote its cause but later changed tactics, professing nonviolent opposition. In 2005, the Muslim Brotherhood won 88 out of 454 seats in the parliament, but in 2010 they lost all 88—blatant proof that the elections were rigged.[49]

These three groups—April 6 Youth Movement, Kefaya, and Youth of the Muslim Brotherhood—had a more developed political agenda than the We

45. Pollock, "Streetbook"; Tina Rosenberg, "Revolution U," in *Revolution in the Arab World: Tunisia, Egypt, and the Unmaking of an Era*, ed. Marc Lynch, Susan B. Glasser, and Blake Hounsell (Washington, DC: Slate Group, 2011), 127. See p. 102 for a discussion of the successful nonviolent revolution in Serbia in 2000.

46. Rosenberg, "Revolution U," 141.

47. Khalil, *Liberation Square*, 44.

48. Ibid., 43–46.

49. Abigail Hauslohner and Andrew Lee Butters, "The Brotherhood," *Time*, February 21, 2011, 36–37. For thirty years before the Muslim Brotherhood's candidate won the presidential election in 2012, the Brotherhood embraced peaceful opposition. Since President Morisi's overthrow by the Egyptian military in 2013, they have again used violence. There is continuing disagreement about their real intentions. Famous members include notorious terrorists Ayman Al-Zawahiri, a key leader of Al-Qaeda, and Omar Abdel Rahman, the "Blind Sheik" responsible for the first bombing of the World Trade Center in New York City. For a somewhat balanced look at the Muslim Brotherhood, see James Traub, "Don't Fear the Brotherhood," *Foreign Policy*, February 10, 2011 (http://www.foreignpolicy.com/articles/2011/02/10/don_t_fear_the_brotherhood?page=full).

Are All Khaled Said group. They were better organized and were just waiting for the right opportunity to arise to mobilize support for their cause. The We Are All Khaled Said group, however, played an unprecedented and extremely important role in moving a large number of Egyptians from political apathy to political activism.[50]

Another group helped to put much of the discontent with the state of Egypt onto the national and the international stages as well as focus concrete demands for change.[51] This group was centered on Mohamed ElBaradei. ElBaradei was the former head of the International Atomic Energy Agency and shared the 2005 Nobel Peace Prize. He returned to Egypt in February 2010 and formed the National Association for Change. This group brought together an impressively wide range of people who opposed the Egyptian regime. It included former presidential candidates, leaders of the Muslim Brotherhood, Egyptian Women for Change, Revolutionary Socialists, and many others. As its name makes clear, the group was united for one cause: change. They developed a statement entitled "Together for Change." It was also known as "ElBaradei's Seven Demands for Change."[52] All these groups (and more) were at work, chipping away wherever they could find weak spots in the monolithic Mubarak regime.

On the We Are All Khaled Said group's Facebook page, Ghonim was very much aware of the role that marketing and branding played as he developed the page and garnered support. He set a standard of positivity and nonviolence. He concentrated on the abuses of the police. He thought that since the "police force was the chain that the regime tied around our [Egyptian] necks, if the police force could be neutralized, the regime would be paralyzed."[53]

Art was one of the primary mediums used to promote the change of attitude and to build the confidence that led to the mass protests. Instead of facts and figures, the use of images and song evoked an emotional response to the awful

50. Ghonim, *Revolution 2.0*, 81.
51. Ibid., 39–45.
52. Ibid., 45. The demands: (1) terminate the state of emergency; (2) grant complete supervision of elections to the judiciary; (3) grant domestic and international civil society the right to monitor the elections; (4) grant equal time in the media for all candidates running for office; (5) grant expatriate Egyptians the right and ability to vote; (6) guarantee the right to run for president without arbitrary restrictions, and set a two-term limit; (7) voting with the national identity card.
Ultimately, very little came of ElBaradei's campaign. Many Egyptians looked to him as Egypt's savior. Many thought that ElBaradei could be elected in the November 2010 elections, but he simply was not the right man for the job. However, he "deserves to be regarded and remembered for his prerevolutionary role and his willingness to publicly confront Mubarak's government" (Khalil, *Liberation Square*, 119).
53. Ghonim, *Revolution 2.0*, 123.

realities in Egypt that created solidarity among the members of the page.[54] One
of the most striking uses of image was a poster that in one column showed
all the US presidents since 1981 (Reagan, H. W. Bush, Clinton, W. Bush, and
Obama) and in the other column showed different pictures of the same man.
"Mubarak's images over thirty years showed clear change; his smile died out
and his facial features aged. It was a simple and expressive design that showed
beyond doubt that we had been ruled by a dictator for three decades."[55]

It is quite clear that the successful overthrow of the dictator in Tunisia
was crucial to what subsequently happened in Egypt. On the day (January
14, 2011) that President Ben Ali fled Tunisia, "I started to believe," Ghonim
reports, "that we could be the second Arab nation to rid itself of its dictator.
Egypt's political, economic, and social conditions were worse than Tunisia's,
and the level of anger on the street was much greater. The only thing that
separated Egyptians from a revolution was our lack of self-confidence and
our exaggerated perception of the regime's strength. Yet after what happened
in Tunisia, I thought the Egyptian masses might finally get the message and
break the psychological barrier of fear."[56]

The successful ouster of Ben Ali in Tunisia prompted Ghonim to post on
the page, "Today is the 14th . . . January 25 is Police Day and it's a national
holiday . . . If 100,000 take to the streets, no one can stop us . . . I wonder if
we can?"[57] Police Day was a national holiday commemorating the heroic resistance by the Egyptian police against the British in 1952. Ghonim wanted "to
underline the contrast between the police back then and the police now."[58] The
event was named "January 25: Revolution Against Torture, Poverty, Corruption, and Unemployment." From this point forward, events began to happen
very quickly. The Internet was a buzz of almost constant activity. Facebook and
Twitter were major platforms for discussion of where to protest and what to
demand. A major question that many had was whether or not the enthusiasm
online could be translated into real action on the street. That question was
answered on January 25.

Ghonim reiterated the peaceful nature of the protests again and again on
his Facebook page: "[It is] important for everyone who will participate on

54. Ibid., 86.
55. Ibid., 142.
56. Ibid., 133.
57. Ibid., 134 (ellipses are original).
58. Kandil, "Interview," 20.

Jan25: We are not promoting chaos or destruction or attacks on any public or private property . . . We are taking to the streets to demand our rights; we will protest, stage a sit-in, and defend ourselves only if we are attacked."[59] In another post he said, "I am taking to the street on Jan25 . . . There is no way I will react to violence with violence . . . There is no way I will strike back at anyone who strikes at me . . . But I will defend myself and protect myself . . . And I am ready to die a martyr."[60]

In the end, Facebook and Twitter were unable to fully organize the protestors, but this actually became a major strength and even tactical strategy of the protestors. Eventually, the organizers promoted the idea for January 25 that everyone was welcome to do any sort of peaceful demonstration or march anywhere they wished. This was advantageous for two reasons: (1) it allowed creativity and practicality to flow freely, thus allowing more people to join in more ways; (2) it completely confused security forces, which were unable to concentrate their resources in a single area.[61]

A week before the planned protests, Asmaa Mahfouz, a twenty-six-year-old veiled woman, posted a video in which she challenged her fellow Egyptians to quit feeling sorry for themselves and shake off their pessimistic attitudes.

> Anyone who says, "The numbers will be small and nothing will happen," I want to say that you are the traitor—just like the president, just like any corrupt official, just like the security officer who beats us. . . . Speak to your neighbors, your colleagues at work, your family and friends and encourage them to come. You don't have to come to Tahrir. Just go out in the streets anywhere and take a stand saying you are free human beings. Sitting at home following us on the news and on Facebook only leads to our humiliation. It leads to *my* humiliation.[62]

Many Egyptians credit this video as the thing that pushed them from behind their computers out into the street.

A few days before January 25, a twenty-six-page document called "Revolution 2011" circulated on the Internet. It was also printed and distributed widely. "It included detailed city maps advising protesters where to gather, tips on what to wear, recommended chants to draw out undecided citizens, and tactical advice on how to attack police lines, how to limit and treat tear-gas

---

59. Ghonim, *Revolution 2.0*, 154 (ellipses are original).
60. Ibid., 148 (ellipses are original).
61. Ibid., 158.
62. As quoted in Khalil, *Liberation Square*, 132 (ellipses and italics are original).

exposure, and how to use spray paint to obscure the windows of the Central Security vans."[63]

Two days before January 25, Wael Ghonim posted this ringing call for nonviolence on his Facebook page:

> The protests are peaceful. We are peace advocates and not advocates of violence. We are demanding our rights and must uphold the rights of others. We will not respond to any provocation from security forces and lose control. This is what they want us to do. One of the security forces' main goals is to portray the protestors as thugs who want to destroy our country. We must discipline ourselves and refrain from foolishness or any violations of the law, and we must not endanger any person's life or cause harm to any public or private property. If you see someone behaving violently, please circle around this person and take him out of the protest.[64]

The page also listed clear demands of the protestors:

> Disbanding the current Parliament and holding new and legitimate elections; instituting a two-term limit for the presidency; canceling the Emergency Laws and dismissing Interior Minister Habib al-Adly; raising the minimum wage to LE1200 [around $220] per month and establishing unemployment benefits.[65]

Liberation

On January 25, 2011, thousands of Egyptians took to the streets. Starting in various neighborhoods around Cairo,[66] protestors marched toward Tahrir (Liberation) Square. Groups converged and continued toward the square. At first, riot police tried to stop the protestors from making it to the square. An unknown number of protestors were caught and beaten viciously.

The protestors finally managed to converge on Tahrir Square. They held the square for several hours, until the police, using tear gas, rubber bullets, water canons, and batons, managed to clear the square around 1:00 a.m. on January 26.[67]

Momentarily, it appeared that Mubarak's police had quelled the revolution. But in reality they had ignited a war. The massive turnout of protestors—proof

63. Ibid., 130.
64. Ghonim, *Revolution 2.0*, 167–68.
65. As described (not quoted) in Khalil, *Liberation Square*, 136. For a fuller explanation of the demands, see Ghonim, *Revolution 2.0*, 166–67.
66. There were protests in other cities as well. The largest was in Cairo.
67. Khalil, *Liberation Square*, 186.

that the talk made in the virtual world of Facebook and Twitter had translated into revolutionary action in the real world—nullified the fact that the government shut down Facebook and Twitter on the night of January 25. That action simply sparked a new flurry of organization and mobilization that took the entire regime by surprise.

Word went out that Friday, January 28, would be a Day of Rage. The plan was for people to converge again on Tahrir Square after Friday prayers. The day before, the Muslim Brotherhood (which had not given official support for the protests up to this point) and ElBaradei and his organization, the National Association for Change, officially endorsed the protests and encouraged their members to participate.[68]

One group of activists made careful preparations to peacefully "combat" security forces. They purchased heavy gloves that would allow them to grab hot metallic tear-gas canisters and throw them away from the crowd. They also purchased shin pads, goggles, bandanas, vinegar and onions (to combat tear gas), and even industrial-strength gas masks. They set up a system of safe houses and gathering points for treating the injured and disseminating information.[69]

The government began the morning of January 28 by shutting down all cell-phone communication. But the communication blackout backfired. Organizers had already given up organizing the protests and were simply telling people, "Protest everywhere and don't stop."[70] Because no one knew what was going on, more people went to the streets to see what was going on. Because there was no way to know how other protestors were faring against the police, protestors fought desperately for themselves wherever they were.[71] As a result, participation was extremely broad. "The Egyptians who took part in January 28 came from different social classes, genders, age brackets, and educational backgrounds. Elderly men walked side-by-side with teenagers and university students as they chanted together, 'The people want to topple the regime!'"[72]

The police met them with brutal force. Despite the protestors' chants of "Peaceful, peaceful,"[73] the police used water cannons, tear gas, and rubber bullets. Dozens were killed as the police used shotguns and ran over people

68. Ghonim, *Revolution 2.0*, 211.
69. Khalil, *Liberation Square*, 157–58.
70. Ibid., 163.
71. Ibid., 162–63.
72. Ghonim, *Revolution 2.0*, 213.
73. According to Jonathan Kuttab, a Palestinian lawyer and peace activist, this phrase had not really been used before in nonviolent protests.

with their vehicles. After a while, however, many of the police stopped fighting and simply let the protestors go through. "Many of them hugged the marchers and broke into heartfelt apologies. 'Forgive us,' they pleaded, 'we had no choice, but we swear, our hearts are with you. We suffer just like you do.'"[74]

Some of the police made a final stand at the bridges that cross the Nile and connect many of the working-class neighborhoods to Tahrir Square. Some of the most astonishing images of the Egyptian revolution are seen in videos of the battle for Qasr al-Nil Bridge.[75] Marching riot police cross the bridge to meet a seemingly uncountable number of protestors. As the police fire tear gas into the crowds, the protestors scoop them up and toss them into the Nile. The police advance to the point of nearly taking the bridge, but then retreat. The protestors almost make it to the other side of the Nile, but are driven back. This back-and-forth struggle continues for a long time. At one point, protestors surround a police van, and the driver rams it in reverse and runs over several people. A man is shot in the face with a tear gas canister. The most moving scene is when the protestors line up and pray even as the police try to disperse them with a water cannon. Eventually, the persistence of the protestors overwhelms the police, and the crowds continue on their way to Tahrir Square. The several-hour-long battle is over.

The violence of the police provoked intense debate about whether to respond violently or nonviolently. "On a side street just outside of the battle zone, there was a near fistfight over just how violently to fight back. A young man in his twenties was having a meltdown and being held back by others who amazingly (a little naively, actually, given what was already happening) pleaded with him to maintain a nonviolent stance. The young man screamed back 'Peaceful? Are you serious! After this?'"[76]

It is important to acknowledge that not all the action was nonviolent. Ashraf Khalil, a long-term Egyptian-American reporter based in Cairo, puts it this way:

Much has been made of the near-obsessive dedication to nonviolence on the part of the Tahrir square protesters. For the most part, that's true. From the very start, one of the dominant chants from the protesters was *salmeya*, or peaceful.

But let's pause now to acknowledge and honor the fact that Egypt's nonviolent revolution wouldn't have happened without some people who were willing to be

74. Ghonim, *Revolution 2.0*, 213–14.
75. See, for example, "Protesting in Cairo Egypt, (full length version) Friday, Jan 28 at 3:30pm, Kasr Al Nile Bridge," YouTube video (http://www.youtube.com/watch?v=QheMJrDuTtY).
76. Khalil, *Liberation Square*, 171.

extremely violent at times. Over a four-day period, a hard-core cadre of protesters confronted and physically shattered the Egyptian police state—overwhelming the shock troops of the Interior Ministry's Central Security riot police. It was only after that vanguard had been physically destroyed and demoralized that the real revolution could begin. . . .

I witnessed scenes of incredible violence on January 28, with protesters using military-style organization and tactics to harass and pressure the police until they collapsed.[77]

Once the protestors finally managed to break through the police and cross the Nile bridges, a frenzy erupted. The NDP (National Democratic Party) head-quarters was looted and set on fire. The Egyptian Museum, which houses an enormous amount of Egypt's ancient artifacts, including King Tutankhamun's famous solid-gold mask, was also in danger of being destroyed and looted. But protestors surrounded the building, forming a human chain to protect it.[78]

Around 5:30 that afternoon (January 28, the Day of Rage), Mubarak deployed the army to enforce a curfew from 6:00 p.m. to 7:00 a.m. The curfew was ignored, but the army was not. The protestors greeted the tanks with cheers as they moved into Tahrir. Protestors climbed onto tanks for photos. The people welcomed the soldiers with flowers and hugs, chanting, "The people and the army are one hand!"[79] In a confrontation with a group of around eight hundred protestors (who wanted to invade, loot, and set on fire the Ministry of Information), a senior army officer stood before the crowd and held a debate with the protestors. "It ended with a mutual embrace between the officer and the most prominent protest leaders—an exchange that would be basically unthinkable with any senior police officer."[80]

Some protestors "openly berated and shoved soldiers—who once again showed impressive patience. The actions of a few protestors toward the soldiers were so aggressive that one could only conclude the soldiers were under direct orders not to retaliate."[81] In fact, there was much ambiguity over the army's position for the first few days. At one point, soldiers looked on while police officers used live ammunition to defend the Ministry of Interior building. On

77. Ibid., 161–62.
78. Ibid., 190–93. The situation in Alexandria was even worse. "'By four PM, you couldn't find a police officer. By six PM there was hardly a police station left standing. . . . The people were determined to destroy every police station in the city'" (as quoted in ibid., 187).
79. Ghonim, *Revolution 2.0*, 215.
80. Khalil, *Liberation Square*, 194.
81. Ibid., 195.

the last day in January, the army issued a statement that declared the demands of the people to be legitimate. The statement concluded, "Your Armed Forces have not and will not resort to the use of force against this great people."[82]

On January 25, large numbers of Egyptians had broken through the psychological barriers of fear and helplessness. On January 28, they broke "through the physical barriers of the police state."[83]

By the end of January 28, the protestors had firmly established themselves in Tahrir Square. Now they turned their attention to sustaining thousands of people for an unknown period of time. A first step was to establish checkpoints to prevent weapons or people with police IDs from entering the square. Teams of protestors set up tents, established cleanup crews and medical clinics, organized supplies of food and water, and set up bathrooms. The incredible self-organization and cooperation of the protestors inside Tahrir helped make the revolution possible. They encouraged women to participate and protected them in the square from sexual harassment (a huge problem in Egypt). Throughout the square, they set up stages that served the dual purpose of forming public opinion through speeches as well as having fun through music and comedy. "Organizers created a sense of community—of the 'new Egypt'—inside Tahrir Square."[84] The Muslim Brotherhood's well-disciplined members and organizational structure helped to sustain the revolution.[85] The most inspiring show of cooperation and national solidarity occurred between Christians and Muslims, who often have clashed in lethal violence. When security forces attacked Muslims with water cannons during prayer, Christians encircled them to protect them. An imam is reported as saying, "Look around you; do you see it is the Christians who are protecting us? Do you know why they do this? They are following the teaching of Jesus. It is because they have Jesus in their hearts."[86] Muslims also protected Christians as they celebrated Mass in the square.

On February 1, the call for a million-person march brought so many people to the square that "it was too packed to even move around comfortably."[87] The square was full of excitement and anticipation that this was indeed the end of Mubarak. But their hopes were promptly dashed when Mubarak addressed

82. As quoted in ibid., 211.
83. Ibid., 199.
84. Kathy Kamphoefner, "Best Practices in Egypt," *Sojourners* 40, no. 5 (2011): 19–20.
85. Hauslohner and Butters, "The Brotherhood," 36–37.
86. Rose Marie Berger, "Nothing Spontaneous About It," *Sojourners* 40, no. 5 (2011): 22.
87. Khalil, *Liberation Square*, 212.

the nation and promised only not to seek reelection. The people wanted him to leave immediately.

The next day, Wednesday, February 2, brought violent confrontation. The Battle of Tahrir (also known as the Camel Charge Battle) seemed to be the last-ditch effort by the regime to defeat the protestors. Pro-Mubarak protestors converged on Tahrir Square. The confrontation began with rock throwing. Then the pro-Mubarak thugs suddenly charged the square (some of them on camels, hence the name "Camel Charge") from several points. All of this caught the protestors off guard. The thugs attacked with knives, stones, glass, and Molotov cocktails. The protestors used sheet metal from a construction site to build a barrier and broke up concrete to use as ammunition. "[The pro-Mubarak protestors] would throw ten rocks, and we would throw one thousand and keep throwing. It was like carpet bombing," said one protestor.[88] Snipers began firing into Tahrir. They were stopped only after some protestors snuck up behind them and fought them hand to hand. After more than twelve hours of fighting and after at least twenty-six protestors were killed, the military (which had watched passively for hours) intervened by firing into the air, dispersing the pro-Mubarak protestors.[89]

The protesters had been tested nearly to the breaking point, but they emerged victorious. Mubarak was on his way out. Wael Ghonim, the key organizer of the powerful Facebook page, had been detained on January 27 but was released on February 7. His release added great momentum to the revolution. Ghonim gave an interview on a national television show immediately after getting out of prison and finally acknowledged publicly that he was the administrator of the We Are All Khaled Said page.[90] After his release, Ghonim and many other organizers of the protests were busy meeting ministers and having televised interviews. In all of the discussions, a single demand became nonnegotiable: Mubarak must step down. On February 11 he did.

■ The Result?

Three years and more after the dramatic, largely nonviolent revolutions in Tunisia and Egypt, the final outcome is anything but clear. In 2013, the Egyptian

88. As quoted in ibid., 229.
89. See Ghonim, *Revolution 2.0*, 233–35; Khalil, *Liberation Square*, 221–34. The question remains as to why the army waited so long to stop the fighting.
90. Ghonim, *Revolution 2.0*, 260.

army overthrew President Morsi, the first democratically elected leader of Egypt. The Muslim Brotherhood led large protests, which the army crushed brutally. A majority of Egyptians, however, seemed to accept Morsi's overthrow, fearing that Morsi had been leading the country toward becoming a rigid Islamist state. Very deep political disagreements continue to divide Egyptians. Tough economic challenges remain unsolved. Tunisia also continues to struggle as more secular and more radical Islamist factions jostle for power. The future in both countries is uncertain.

But one thing is clear. In two important Arab countries, ruled by long-standing dictators, in a part of the world where almost everyone despaired that change was possible, largely nonviolent movements succeeded. As a result, the first free elections in the history of both countries took place. In the Arab Spring of 2011, vast numbers of Arabs, not only in Egypt and Tunisia, but also in a number of other countries, discovered the power of nonviolent action. Whatever the developments in the coming years, that discovery cannot be erased from people's minds. Dictatorial rulers will inevitably feel less confident.

The Tunisian and Egyptian revolutions happened just as Erica Chenoweth and Maria Stephan were completing their groundbreaking book *Why Civil Resistance Works*, in which they study several hundred violent and nonviolent campaigns and use sophisticated statistical analysis to show that nonviolent resistance actually works better than violence. In an epilogue where they comment on the amazing results of the Arab Spring in 2011, they say, "The Egyptian uprising stands out as a particularly stunning example of why civil resistance works."[91] One can only agree.

91. *Why Civil Resistance Works: The Strategic Logic of Nonviolent Conflict* (New York: Columbia University Press, 2011), 229.

10

intervening, accompanying, and reporting

The Growth of Peacemaker Teams

Unless we are ready to die developing new nonviolent attempts to reduce conflict, we should confess that we never really meant that the cross was an alternative to the sword.

Ronald J. Sider, "Are We Willing to Die for Peace?"
Gospel Herald, December 25, 1984

In the last few decades, a number of new peacemaker teams have emerged to expand the use of nonviolent ways to reduce conflict in violent situations.[1] They intervene in situations of violent conflict, accompany people threatened with violence, and report instances of violence and oppression, always seeking to promote justice, peace, and reconciliation. In comparison to the need, their numbers remain minuscule. But the fact that these new peacemaking teams are growing both in size and number hints at the possibility of a much greater expansion

Accompaniment—almost always accompaniment of local oppressed people and human rights workers by outside, usually international, persons—is a

1. I thank my student Jake Goertz for help in researching material for this chapter.

central component of the new peacemaker teams discussed in this chapter. Increasingly careful reflection on "international accompaniment" helps us understand why it works so well.[2] At its core, international accompaniment works by deterrence: aggressors realize that the advantages resulting from attacking human rights activists are less than the disadvantages coming from bad publicity and global pressure that follow when they attack justice activists. International accompaniers make it more difficult for local oppressors to cover up their action, devalue the activists as criminals or terrorists, or frighten them into submission and silence. To be effective, international accompaniment must be able to appeal to internationally accepted norms (e.g., on human rights) and support only local activists who remain nonviolent. Also essential is the ability of international accompaniers to use global media to report local abuse and to persuade outside governments and international structures to bring international pressure to persuade local governments to end the abuse.

The modern story of peacemaker teams goes back at least to the followers of Gandhi. In 1948, pacifists worldwide had arranged a meeting with the man everyone viewed as their spiritual leader, Mahatma Gandhi. His assassination, however, forced postponement to December 1949. Out of this World Pacifist Conference came a proposal to form Satyagraha (Gandhi's word for "nonviolence") units.[3]

The proposal lay dormant until 1957, when Vinoba Bhave of India implemented one of Gandhi's dreams by creating the Shanti Sena (literally, "peace army" or "peace brigade").[4] Resolving communal conflict between Muslims and Hindus, including the quelling of raging mobs, was the special mission of this nonviolent peace brigade. When burning and killing broke out between Hindus and Muslims, the Shanti Sena marched unarmed into the middle of the mobs, protected only by their identifying sash and their record of goodwill in all communities. By 1969, there were thirteen thousand volunteers organized in local, district, state, and national levels.

2. See, for example, Brian Martin, "Making Accompaniment Effective," and Luis Enrique Eguren, "Developing Strategy for Accompaniment," in *People Power: Unarmed Resistance and Global Solidarity*, ed. Howard Clark (London: Pluto Press, 2009), 93–97, 98–107; Liam Mahony and Luis Enrique Eguren, *Unarmed Bodyguards: International Accompaniment for the Protection of Human Rights* (West Hartford, CT: Kumarian Press, 1997).

3. William Robert Miller, *Nonviolence: A Christian Interpretation* (New York: Association Press, 1964), 119–20; Charles C. Walker, *A World Peace Guard: An Unarmed Agency for Peacekeeping* (New Delhi: Academy of Gandhian Studies Hyderabad, 1981), 71–72.

4. Walker, *World Peace Guard*, 71–72.

The Shanti Sena also threw themselves into the Gramdan movement, a movement designed to create interreligious communal harmony at the village level. In some fifty thousand Gramdan villages, the Shanti Sena were responsible for guarding the village and maintaining peace.[5]

Narayan Desai, later director of the Shanti Sena, led the group during religious riots in Ahmedabad, India. In September 1969, the city erupted in Hindu-Muslim strife. Thousands died in a rampage that devastated much of the urban area. Immediately, Shanti Sena volunteers poured into Ahmedabad. They moved fearlessly throughout the city, visiting one riot-affected area after another. The Shanti Sena engaged in arbitration, cleanup, relief efforts, and education. After four months of work, the volunteers celebrated success with a procession, shouting, "We may be Hindus, we may be Muslims, but above all, we are human beings."[6]

In 1960, the Triennial Conference of War Resisters International met in India and embraced the idea of an unarmed Peace Guard serving under United Nations auspices.[7] The proposal envisioned teams of Peace Guards ready to intervene at the command of the United Nations or at the invitation of third parties in situations of violence around the world.[8] The leaders sent their proposal to Secretary General Dag Hammerskjöld at the United Nations, but they never received a response. The proposal, while bold, remained theoretical.

Small groups continued their search for concrete structures for nonviolent intervention in armed conflict in the 1960s. In 1962, the World Peace Brigade was formed. The founding statement declared its aim to "organize, train and keep available a Brigade for nonviolent action in situations of potential or actual conflict, internal and international."[9]

The fledging World Peace Brigade did assemble for action in Zambia (then Northern Rhodesia). Kenneth Kaunda, leader of the United National Independence Party, had requested that a force of primarily African marchers be

5. See Narayan Desai, "Gandhi's Peace Army: The Shanti Sena Today," *Fellowship*, November 1969, 23–25.

6. See Narayan Desai, "Intervention in Riots in India," in *Liberation without Violence: A Third-Party Approach*, ed. A. Paul Hare and Herbert H. Blumberg (Totowa, NJ: Rowman & Littlefield, 1977), 83. For the Shanti Sena, see also Thomas Weber, *Gandhi's Peace Army: The Shanti Sena and Unarmed Peacekeeping* (Syracuse, NY: Syracuse University Press, 1996).

7. Miller, *Nonviolence*, 123.

8. See Gene Keyes, "Peacekeeping by Unarmed Buffer Forces: Precedents and Proposals," *Peace & Change 5*, nos. 2–3 (1978): 8.

9. Cited in Charles C. Walker, "Nonviolence in Eastern Africa 1962–1964," in Hare and Blumberg, *Liberation*, 157.

ready to move into the country. Kaunda was concerned that white stalling of the election process might provoke a black backlash. More than five thousand unarmed persons massed on the Northern Rhodesian border in response to Kaunda's call. Though most were Africans, some had come from Europe, Asia, and the United States. In the end, the dispute was resolved peacefully and the marchers were not needed.[10]

In the 1970s, the Shanti Sena movement spread to Sri Lanka. Sarvodaya, Sri Lanka's largest people's organization, has worked for more than fifty years to promote self-reliance, community development, and intercommunal reconciliation in over fifteen thousand villages. In 1978, when communal violence threatened and often broke out across Sri Lanka, Sarvodaya's charismatic founder, Dr. A. T. Ariyaratne, issued a call for a nonviolent movement to curb the violence. The result was the emergence of a Sri Lankan Shanti Sena.

Shanti Sena units quickly organized in many places across the country, applying nonviolent methods to end the conflict. Today, Sri Lanka's Shanti Sena continues as an active youth movement. Over one hundred ten thousand youth have participated in thousands of units. The organization trains its members in nonviolent methods. Its vision is to use nonviolence to create a society of peace, justice, and cooperation in a nation where severe ethnic and religious tension has often exploded in violence.[11]

Peace Brigades International

Peace Brigades International (PBI) was born at an international consultation in Canada in September 1981. PBI is clearly based on the foundation of Gandhi, Shanti Sena, and the success of Martin Luther King Jr.'s nonviolent civil rights crusade. Its founding statement reads in part,

> We are forming an organization with the capability to mobilize and provide trained units of volunteers. These units may be assigned to areas of high tension to avert violent outbreaks. If hostile clashes occur, a brigade may establish and monitor a cease-fire, offer mediatory services, or carry on works of

10. Ibid., 160–67. For a broader discussion of nonviolence in Africa, see Charles C. Walker, "Nonviolence in Africa," in *Nonviolent Action and Social Change*, ed. Severyn T. Bruyn and Paula M. Rayman (New York: Irving, 1979), 186–212. For another attempt at nonviolent peacemaking, see A. Paul Hare, ed., *Cyprus Resettlement Project: An Instance of International Peacemaking* (Beer Sheva: Ben-Gurion University of the Negev, 1984).
11. See "About Us," Shanthi Sena, http://www.shanthisena.org/aboutus.php.

reconstruction and reconciliation. . . . We are building on a rich and extensive heritage of nonviolent action, which can no longer be ignored.[12]

PBI's first major action was its nonviolent "escort duty" for endangered mothers in Guatemala. For a time, members of PBI accompanied threatened leaders of GAM (Grupo de Apoyo Mutuo) twenty-four hours a day.

GAM was a group of parents (largely mothers) formed in June 1984 to protest the disappearance of their children.[13] In Guatemala, right-wing death squads were frequently kidnapping, torturing, and killing anyone involved in improving the lot of the poor. Very few of GAM's members had any previous political involvement. But the pain of their missing children prompted them to place newspaper advertisements, hold regular vigils, and petition the government with one simple question: "Where are our loved ones?"

For a year, GAM was tolerated. But in March 1985, General Óscar Victores, the chief of state, charged (falsely) that "forces of subversion" were manipulating GAM. A barrage of anonymous death threats followed. Within a few weeks, two key leaders of GAM had been murdered. One of these, Hector Gomez, was found with his head bashed in and his tongue cut out.

PBI offered to supply international, round-the-clock escorts to accompany the other leaders of GAM. After these international escorts from PBI arrived in May 1985, no board member of GAM was kidnapped or harmed. The task was nerve-racking. One never knew when a bullet or bomb might kill escort or friend. The work was so emotionally draining that escorts rotated out every few weeks. But it worked.[14]

PBI has expanded its activities over the last three decades. Its primary focus is on sending teams of international volunteers into violent situations to protect threatened human rights defenders by nonviolent accompaniment. When PBI's volunteers accompany endangered persons, they wear T-shirts, vests, caps, and jackets that identify them as members of PBI.[15] Volunteers make a minimum commitment of one year and receive extensive training in the philosophy and strategies of nonviolent action. Volunteers always work in

12. From a PBI brochure. See further Mahony and Eguren, *Unarmed Bodyguards*; Yeshua Moser-Puangsuwan and Thomas Weber, *Nonviolent Intervention across Borders: A Recurrent Vision* (Honolulu: Spark M. Matsunaga Institute for Peace, University of Hawaii, 2000); also the annual reviews of Peace Brigades International.

13. See Philip McManus, "Refusing to Disappear," *Fellowship*, July–August 1985, 12–14.

14. See the discussion in Martin, "Making Accompaniment Effective," 93–97.

15. Louise Winstanley, "With Peace Brigades International in Colombia," in Clark, *People Power*, 109.

a country other than their own. By providing international volunteers who both accompany endangered human rights workers and report their findings through PBI's global network, PBI provides significant safety to endangered human rights defenders. Their international volunteers send a clear message that the world is watching.

In its *Annual Review 2012*, PBI reported that three hundred volunteers risked their lives to defend others in Colombia, Guatemala, Mexico, and Nepal. In addition to providing 1,365 days of physical accompaniment for endangered human rights workers that year, PBI volunteers monitored dozens of demonstrations, hosted forty-eight workshops for human rights defenders, held over four hundred meetings with government officials, and made hundreds of phone calls to check on threatened local human rights workers. They attended over seven hundred meetings with the United Nations, diplomats, and international agencies to "raise concerns about the safety of human rights defenders." They also organized speaking tours in Europe and North America for twenty-six human rights defenders from the countries where PBI volunteers accompanied national human rights workers.

PBI has sixteen national groups in Europe, Australia, and North and South America. These support groups raise funds, help identify volunteers, and provide an international network to disseminate reports of endangered human rights defenders. They also develop relationships with government officials and other persons and agencies to urge them to use their influence to protect threatened human rights defenders. PBI's goal is "a world in which people address conflicts nonviolently, where human rights are universally upheld, and social justice and respect for other cultures have become a reality."[16]

■ Christian Peacemaker Teams

In the latter part of the twentieth century, Mennonites (also called Anabaptists) began to embrace activist nonviolent action as a proper expression of their historic opposition to war. Earlier, in the middle of the century, Mennonites typically used the term "nonresistance" to describe their understanding of Jesus's call to love one's enemies. But by the 1960s and 1970s, many younger Mennonites challenged this "passive" response to killing and injustice.

16. Peace Brigades International, *Annual Review 2012* (http://www.peacebrigades.org/file admin/user_files/international/files/annual_reviews/PBI_Annual_Review_2012_English.pdf).

In the peace lecture at the Mennonite World Conference in Strasbourg, France, in July 1984, I said,

> Over the past 450 years of martyrdom, immigration and missionary proclama-
> tion, the God of shalom has been preparing us Anabaptists for a late twentieth-
> century rendezvous with history. . . . Now is the time to risk everything for our
> belief that Jesus is the way to peace. If we still believe it, now is the time to live
> what we have spoken. . . .
>
> But . . . we must be prepared to die by the thousands. Those who believed in
> peace through the sword have not hesitated to die. Proudly, courageously, they
> gave their lives. Again and again, they sacrificed bright futures to the tragic
> illusion that one more righteous crusade would bring peace in their time, and
> they laid down their lives by the millions.
>
> Unless comfortable North American and European Mennonites and Brethren
> in Christ are prepared to risk injury and death in nonviolent opposition to the
> injustice our societies foster and assist in Central America, the Philippines, and
> South Africa, we dare never whisper another word about pacifism to our sisters
> and brothers in those desperate lands. . . . Making peace is as costly as waging
> war. Unless we are prepared to pay the cost of peacemaking we have no right to
> claim the label or preach the message. . . . Unless we are ready to die developing
> new nonviolent attempts to reduce conflict, we should confess that we never
> really meant that the cross was an alternative to the sword.[17]

In response to this speech, the Mennonite leadership in the United States and Canada engaged in two years of deliberation to decide if this activist type of nonviolent action was faithful to our Anabaptist understanding of Jesus. The decision was a clear yes. And the result was the formation of Christian Peacemaker Teams (CPT).[18]

CPT's first delegation went to Iraq in 1990.[19] Other short-term delegations and then permanent teams followed in Colombia; Iraq; the West Bank;
Mexico; the US-Mexico border; and Kenora, Canada. By 2013, CPT had thirty
full-time activists in various locations, plus over one hundred fifty trained
reservists who spend two to eight weeks a year in various locations. The two
largest Mennonite denominations in North America and the Church of the

17. Ronald J. Sider, "Are We Willing to Die for Peace?" *Gospel Herald*, December 25, 1984, 898–901.

18. See Tricia Gates Brown, *Getting in the Way: Stories from Christian Peacemaker Teams* (Scottdale, PA: Herald Press, 2005); see also the other works cited below.

19. Kathleen Kern, *In Harm's Way: A History of Christian Peacemaker Teams* (Eugene, OR: Cascade Books, 2009), 13.

Brethren were the original sponsors of CPT, but a number of Baptist, Presbyterian, and Quaker peace groups have also joined as sponsors. CPT hopes that a "larger, more ecumenical CPT will inspire Christians from all over the world . . . [and] show that the power for transforming conflicts is a miracle available to all humankind."[20]

CPT seeks to reduce violence by "getting in the way." Well-trained teams intervene in situations of conflict, accompany endangered persons, document human rights abuses, and provide information that helps supporters at home advocate with policy makers.

In 2003, the CPT team in Iraq documented numerous human rights abuses, including abuse of detainees, by US forces. But the international media largely ignored their January 2004 report. So on February 26, 2004, the team launched a public forty-day fast in downtown Baghdad to protest these abuses. When, in April, the ghastly photos of the abuse of Iraqi detainees by US soldiers at the Abu Ghraib prison captured global attention, CPT had already been reporting abuses for months.[21]

CPT received massive international publicity after four CPT volunteers were kidnapped in Iraq on November 26, 2005, while traveling to meet a group of influential Sunni Muslim religious leaders. The captors demanded the release of all Iraqi prisoners held by the United States. That, of course, did not happen, and one CPT team member was murdered. Allied Special Forces freed the other three after about four months in captivity.

The CPT team located in Colombia since 2001 has sought to protect farmers threatened by the fighting between guerrillas and "self-defense" forces. They accompany endangered people and document and report human rights abuses.[22]

CPT's work in Hebron in the West Bank provides one of the best illustrations of what the organization seeks to do. Kathleen Kern, who has written the history of CPT, says this project is a "study in 'mosts.'"[23] It has had the longest permanent team, generated the most press releases, seen more of its volunteers arrested and assaulted, and drawn the most criticism. The Hebron project has also developed strong relationships with Israeli peace and human rights organizations.

20. See "History," CPT, http://www.cpt.org/about/history.
21. Kern, *In Harm's Way*, 428–37.
22. Ibid., 361–415.
23. Ibid., 93.

Hebron—the alleged burial place of Abraham, Sarah, Rebekah, Isaac, Leah, and Jacob—is an overwhelmingly Palestinian city with a bloody history. In 1929, an Arab mob murdered about sixty-seven Jews there. After Israel took control of the West Bank in 1967, right-wing Israeli settlers forcibly established settlements in Hebron. In 1980, Palestinian militants killed six Israeli *yeshiva* students in Hebron. And in 1994, an Israeli settler shot and killed twenty-nine Palestinian Muslims worshiping in Hebron's famous Al-Ibrahimi mosque. Perhaps nowhere in the West Bank is Israeli-Palestinian tension, conflict, and hatred so persistent and violent. That was the volatile situation that four CPT volunteers faced as they established an ongoing presence in Hebron in mid-1995.

Over the next eighteen years, the permanent team and short-term volunteers have tried to prevent and document illegal seizures of Palestinian land, house demolitions, and attacks on Palestinian schoolchildren by militant Israeli settlers and soldiers. They have also protested Palestinian attacks on Israelis and worked with Israeli and other Jewish peace organizations.

In the spring of 1997, Prime Minister Netanyahu's government began a new effort to demolish Palestinian houses. The legal reason given was that they had been built without permits, which the Israeli authorities regularly made very hard for Palestinians to obtain. The actual reason was that they were on land close to Israeli settlements in the West Bank that wanted more Palestinian land for expansion.

In the fall of 1997, CPT began the Campaign for Secure Dwellings, and the Israeli Committee Against House Demolitions joined CPT in the campaign. (An Israeli activist later said that CPT had provided the inspiration for the founding of this Israeli committee.) In a number of cases, CPT had a team member stay with Palestinian families threatened with house demolition. CPT and other cooperating organizations orchestrated an international letter-writing and fax campaign. One report indicated that the US State Department received more letters on the Israeli house demolitions than on any other issue in the Middle East. US Secretary of State Madeleine Albright started to quietly pressure the Israeli government to end the house demolitions.[24]

On February 25, 1996, the Palestinian militant organization Hamas bombed an Israeli bus (No. 18) in Jerusalem. The next Sunday, Hamas again bombed bus No. 18. In response, CPT members sent press releases to Israeli and Arab

24. Ibid., 122–36.

newspapers announcing that CPT members would ride bus No. 18 the next Sunday. They explained that they were opposed to all violence, both Palestinian attacks on Israelis and Israeli injustice and violence against Palestinians.[25]

Accompaniment of Palestinian schoolchildren became an important CPT activity in 2000–2003. Substantial sections of Hebron were under curfew, and the Israeli military frequently prevented Palestinian children from going to school. CPT knew, and the Israeli military acknowledged, that international law demanded that children be allowed to go to school, even during a curfew. But the local Israeli soldiers often stopped children on the way to school or entered classrooms and forced the students to leave. CPT volunteers regularly accompanied the Palestinian schoolchildren, trying to persuade the soldiers to let them pass the checkpoints on the way to school. On some occasions, CPT volunteers witnessed Israeli soldiers using tear gas and percussion grenades on students returning from school. Some soldiers drove their jeeps at children. In one famous incident, CPT volunteer Art Gish stood between Israeli soldiers and Palestinian schoolgirls as the soldiers pointed their guns at the girls. Art said, "Aren't you ashamed of threatening little girls? Just let the girls go to school."[26]

In the summer of 2001, a number of international groups—Jewish, Christian, and secular—came to visit and learn from CPT's work in Hebron. The World Council of Churches visited CPT in Hebron and then announced their decision to "develop an accompaniment program that would include ecumenical presence similar to Christian Peacemaker Teams in Hebron."[27]

CPT in Hebron has been criticized for being partisan and pro-Palestinian. In fact, they sometimes tried to befriend Israeli settlers.[28] They also condemned Palestinian attacks on Israelis. But not even the most ardent CPT members would claim that they always got the balance right.

Nor did they end the violence. Prominent Palestinian lawyer Jonathan Kuttab, an evangelical Christian and peace activist, actually called for the placement of a thousand CPT teams spread throughout the West Bank. Perhaps, if that had happened, things might have improved greatly. But CPT did offer a courageous attempt to deter violence, correct injustice, and promote peace in one of the most intractable situations in the world today.

25. Ibid., 118–21.
26. Ibid., 189.
27. Quoted in ibid., 177.
28. See Arthur G. Gish, *Hebron Journal: Stories of Nonviolent Peacemaking* (Scottdale, PA: Herald Press, 2001).

150

◼ Muslim Peacemaker Teams

Muslim Peacemaker Teams (MPT) was inspired by Christian Peacemaker Teams. Sami Rasouli, the founder and director of MPT, was impressed when he met CPT team members in Iraq. CPT agreed to his request to train Muslims in the principles of nonviolence, and MPT was born.[29] MPT's website says that "the mission of the Muslim Peacemaker Teams (MPT) is to bring all Iraqi groups together in peace to work for the good of the country by getting in the way of violence."

MPT provides training to help people understand the roots of nonviolence in Islamic thought and sponsors art exhibits promoting nonviolence.[30] MPT also sponsors the Water for Peace program, helping schools and hospitals in southern Iraq acquire life-saving water filters.

MPT is a young, tiny organization. But its very existence illustrates the spread of the idea of nonviolent peacemaking in diverse countries and cultures.

◼ Ecumenical Accompaniment Programme in Palestine and Israel (EAPPI)

In 2002, the World Council of Churches (WCC) responded to a call from Jerusalem churches requesting international organizations to send people to the Palestinian West Bank, occupied by Israel. After the outbreak of the second intifada, the United Nations Security Council tried to pass several resolutions sending peacekeepers to protect civilians in the West Bank, but the United States vetoed these resolutions. So the Jerusalem churches requested the help of nongovernmental organizations. The WCC's response has been to send about a hundred Ecumenical Accompaniers (EAs) to the West Bank each year.

Mostly from Europe and North America, EAs receive several weeks of training in the history of the Israeli-Palestinian conflict and the techniques of nonviolent action. Then they move in teams of three or four into different locations in the West Bank. EAs do a number of things: provide protection by presence (e.g., by accompanying young children to school when settlers harass them); monitor checkpoints and gates in the wall, helping Palestinians deal with the numerous obstacles; partner with and accompany Israeli peace

29. See reconciliationproject.org/2012/history.
30. See http://www.reconciliationproject.org/2012/muslim-peacemaker-teams.

movement organizations, which often are strongly disliked by other Israelis. And when they return home, EAs give speeches, write articles, and speak to government officials.[31]

One EA, Ann Wright, tells about her experience with EAPPI in Tulkarem. Tulkarem is only fifty miles from Jerusalem, but the Israelis have placed six hundred physical obstacles to movement in the West Bank, and so traveling the fifty miles regularly took about seven hours. Even when Palestinians managed to get exit permits to pass through the wall, soldiers often made passage through the checkpoints humiliating and uncertain. So Ann and her team often accompanied Palestinians and checked with commanders to make sure soldiers were following the rules.

Local Palestinian farmers also needed support. They often could not get permits to farm their land. The farmers also had to pass through checkpoints to work on their land. Under the catchall of "security," the Israelis frequently refused passage and sometimes impounded tractors. The presence of Ann's team helped the farmers get through the checkpoints. "People in Tulkarem told us that checkpoint abuse decreased when we were there monitoring."[32]

■ Nonviolent Peaceforce

Nonviolent Peaceforce (NP) is one of the newest and also one of the largest organizations using nonviolent action to prevent violence. NP defines its mission as implementing "unarmed civilian peacekeeping as a tool for reducing violence and protecting civilians in situations of violent conflict."[33] NP was conceived when two men from the United States, David Ray Hartsough (a Quaker) and Mel Duncan (an activist formerly engaged in opposing the Contras in Nicaragua in the 1980s), met at a peace conference in the Netherlands in 1999. Three years later, in 2002, a founding conference in India launched NP. By 2012, NP had about two hundred field staffers working in the Philippines, South Sudan, and South Caucasus and a budget of almost $7 million.

NP's central concept is "unarmed civilian peacekeeping" (UCP). Key components of their strategy include physical presence in conflict zones, protective

31. See http://www.oikoumene.org/en/what-we-do/eappi.

32. Ann Wright, "The Work of the Ecumenical Accompaniment Programme in Palestine and Israel (EAPPI)," in Clark, *People Power*, 137.

33. Nonviolent Peaceforce, *2012 Annual Report*, 2 (http://www.nonviolentpeaceforce.org /sites/nonviolentpeaceforce.org/files/attachments/NP%202012%20AR_FINAL.pdf).

accompaniment of threatened persons and groups, relationship building with all parties in a conflict, rumor control to prevent the outbreak of violence, interpositioning between conflicting groups, monitoring compliance with agreements, and capacity building for local groups.[34]

NP differs from most of the other groups discussed in this chapter in several ways. NP pays its workers, who thus are called "staff," not "volunteers." Partly because NP pays its staff, large numbers of its team are able to come from places other than Europe and North America. In addition, a large portion of NP's income comes from national governments and large governmental bodies, such as the European Union and the United Nations.

NP has a large program in South Sudan. By 2012, there were almost one hundred staffers in nine teams in six states in the new country of South Sudan. The following story illustrates how NP works. When NP staff learned that youth in two clans had started fighting over cattle, an NP leader, Asha Asokan, a petite woman from India, set to work shuttling back and forth between the clans. Eventually, the youth agreed to let clan chiefs mediate a deal, which the NP team then monitored at the chiefs' request.[35]

NP also has major teams in the Philippines and the South Caucasus. NP has worked since 2007 on the Philippine island of Mindanao to protect civilians and support the peace process. At a United Nations briefing in Geneva in 2012, the Philippine ambassador had high words of praise for NP: "Civilian, neutral, impartial, and cost-effective. We are grateful for the contributions of Nonviolent Peaceforce as practitioners of unarmed civilian peacekeeping. The concept has been tested in our country—and it works."[36] In the South Caucasus, NP teams have helped develop and train local unarmed civilian peacekeeper teams. They have also taken representatives from several countries in the region to visit NP's successful program in the Philippines.

In 2012, for the first time, a national government invited NP to come to the country. The government of Myanmar asked NP to come and use its successful experience in South Sudan and the Philippines to help the country strengthen its ambitious peace process. NP will run a training program that will include members of the parliament, members of opposition groups, and representatives from local civil society.[37]

34. Ibid.
35. Ibid., 6–7.
36. Ibid., 12.
37. Ibid., 10.

The year 2012 was a breakthrough year for NP. Fifty-eight countries sent representatives to a briefing at the United Nations on unarmed civilian peace-keeping. Ambassadors and United Nations officials had high praise for NP's work. Excellent media coverage of the event led to a long-awaited public relations breakthrough, including a national television special on Christmas Day. NP now has staff in New York, meets frequently with ambassadors on the United Nations Security Council, and makes high-level presentations at the United Nations. Also in 2012, NP received its largest grant ever: €2.4 million from the European Union. That grant demonstrated, NP's executive director noted, "that unarmed civilian peacekeeping is gaining mainstream support and is here to stay."[38]

The evidence in this chapter supports that claim. But that is not to assert that nonviolent peacemaking organizations such as Nonviolent Peaceforce, Peace Brigades International, and Christian Peacemaker Teams are anywhere close to realizing the vision of tens of thousands of trained nonviolent peace-makers ready to move into violent situations to deter injustice and violence. The total numbers are still tiny, indeed minuscule in comparison to the need. But the stories in this chapter demonstrate that the vision is expanding rapidly. The number and size of organizations using nonviolent action are growing significantly. The idea, as well as awareness of concrete success, has gone mainstream. One can hope that in the next decade the number of trained practitioners of unarmed civilian peacemaking will jump from the hundreds to the thousands, even tens of thousands.

38. Ibid., 1.

the time to act

If what exists is possible, then a vast expansion of nonviolent action is possible today. In fact, it has already happened. Successful nonviolent campaigns against injustice and oppression have become much more frequent in the last one hundred years, especially the last fifty. We now know that often, even in extremely difficult circumstances, nonviolent action succeeds. Now is the time to invest vast new resources to see how much more can be done nonviolently.

truly testing the possibilities of nonviolent action—for the first time in christian history

Most movements of social change have only begun to experiment with the real power and flexibility of nonviolence. . . . One of the greatest discoveries of [the twentieth] century is in the real power of mass nonviolent movements.

Richard B. Deats[1]

Now is the time to test the full range of possibilities of nonviolent resistance to injustice and oppression. Never in our history has the Christian community done that in a sustained, carefully organized, and solidly financed way. Nor has any other community. In the early twenty-first century, however, there are compelling reasons for experimenting with nonviolence on a scale never before attempted in human history.

■ Why We Must Seriously Explore Nonviolent Alternatives

The first and most important reason to explore nonviolent action is that unless we do so, all Christians—both just-war Christians and pacifists—blatantly

1. Richard B. Deats, "The Way of Nonviolence," in *Essays on Nonviolence*, ed. Thérèse de Coninck (Nyack, NY: Fellowship of Reconciliation, n.d.), 18.

defy their own explicit teaching. Just-war Christians (the majority of all Christians since the fourth century) have always claimed that war must be a last resort. Before Christians dare go to war, they must have tried all reasonable nonviolent alternatives. But contemporary just-war Christians who would claim that all reasonable nonviolent alternatives have been tried must face two hard facts: (1) even without much preparation, nonviolent approaches have worked again and again in the last one hundred years; (2) we have never systematically trained thousands of our people to explore the full possibilities of nonviolence in a serious, sustained way. In order to engage in a large-scale test of nonviolence, just-war Christians do not have to believe that nonviolence will always prevent war; all they must do is implement their own rule that war must be a last resort.

Pacifists have long claimed that they have an alternative to war. But that claim remains empty unless they are willing to risk death, as soldiers do, to stop injustice and bring peace.

The theological/ethical commitments of both just-war and pacifist Christians demand that they invest serious time and resources in sustained nonviolent peacemaking. Unless they do, they should admit to the world that they never meant what they said.

A second reason for an unprecedented exploration of nonviolent action is the sheer success of increasingly numerous nonviolent campaigns. That alone warrants increased exploration and implementation. The previous chapters have chronicled story after story where even spontaneous, ill-prepared nonviolent resistance succeeded beyond anyone's wildest dreams. In more recent decades, more careful study of the techniques of nonviolent action has increased the success of this approach.

Furthermore, nonviolent campaigns have again and again proved more effective than lethal violence. That is true in at least three ways: (1) nonviolent campaigns have often accomplished their goals with far less loss of life than their violent alternatives; (2) nonviolent campaigns accomplish their goals more often than do violent methods; and (3) nonviolent campaigns are more likely to lead to democratic societies.

Again and again, fewer people get killed in nonviolent campaigns. When one compares the numbers of people who died in the campaigns for independence in India and Algeria, the figures are astonishing. India's nonviolent struggle for independence from the British took longer than Algeria's violent victory over French colonialism (twenty-eight years, 1919–46, compared to seven years,

1955–61). But only eight thousand Indians died, whereas a million Algerian lives were lost. Even more staggering is the comparison of the numbers of dead with total population figures. Of India's three hundred million, only one in four hundred thousand died. Of Algeria's ten million, one in ten was sacrificed.[2]

The revolutions of Solidarity in Poland, Castro in Cuba, and the Sandinistas in Nicaragua point in the same direction. Only three hundred Poles died, whereas in the Cuban revolution twenty thousand died. There were at least that many deaths (and probably more) in the Nicaraguan revolution against Somoza.[3]

Second, nonviolent campaigns are more likely to succeed. A recent extensive scholarly study and comparison of all the known cases (323) of major armed and unarmed insurrections from 1900 to 2006 dramatically confirms the claim that nonviolent strategies are more effective. In *Why Civil Resistance Works*, Erica Chenoweth and Maria J. Stephan report that "nonviolent resistance campaigns were nearly twice as likely to achieve full or partial success as their violent counterparts."[4]

Third, nonviolent campaigns are more effective in that they are more likely to lead to a democratic society. A nonviolent struggle involves large numbers rather than a handful of highly trained and well-equipped armed elites, who possess enormous power after their violent revolution has succeeded. Gandhi pointed out that "in nonviolence the masses have a weapon which enables a child, a woman, or even a decrepit old man to resist the mightiest government successfully."[5] Nobel Peace Prize winner Adolfo Pérez Esquivel has underlined this strength of nonviolence with his humorous discussion of the "battle of the elephant and the ants." "True the elephant is stronger. But the ants . . . well, there are more of us."[6] Hence comes the repeated success of nonviolent masses, even when pitted against powerful and ruthless military machines.

But the virtue of nonviolence lies not only in the fact that it enables unarmed masses to conquer armed opponents; there also is a better chance of democratic results after the revolution, precisely because the process itself is

2. Figures from Walter Wink, *Violence and Nonviolence in South Africa: Jesus' Third Way* (Philadelphia: New Society, 1987), 41–42.

3. Ibid., 42.

4. Erica Chenoweth and Maria J. Stephan, *Why Civil Resistance Works: The Strategic Logic of Nonviolent Conflict* (New York: Columbia University Press, 2011), 7 (for a discussion of the reasons for this greater success, see 58ff.).

5. Quoted in de Coninck, *Essays on Nonviolence*, 2.

6. Adolfo Pérez Esquivel, *Christ in a Poncho: Testimonials of the Nonviolent Struggles of Latin America*, ed. Charles Antoine, trans. Robert R. Barr (Maryknoll, NY: Orbis Books, 1983), 32.

more democratic. Chenoweth and Stephan have discovered from their extensive comparative studies that nonviolent campaigns are far more likely to lead to democratic results and avoid future societal conflict than violent campaigns. "The probability that a country will be a democracy five years after a campaign ends is 57 percent among successful nonviolent campaigns but less than 6 percent for successful violent campaigns."[7]

A major study by Freedom House discovered the same results: nonviolent campaigns are three times more likely to lead to free democratic societies than are violent struggles.[8]

When a small group of armed elites has seized power, even in the name of "justice for the people," the result has very often been further repression. One need only think of Stalin in Russia, Mao in China, Ben Bella in Algeria, Castro in Cuba, or Pinochet in Chile. Once chosen, violence is not easily abandoned. Violent revolution by an armed elite is one of the least effective training grounds for democratic cooperation. "Those who win by the gun tend to rule by the gun."[9]

Advocates of nonviolence have sometimes been accused of naiveté about human nature and the pervasive power of evil. David Hoekema turns this argument on its head, precisely at the point of the abuse of lethal weapons intended only to restrain evil. "The reality of human sinfulness means that the instruments we intend to use for good are certain to be turned to evil purposes as well. There is therefore a strong presumption for using those means of justice that are least likely to be abused and least likely to cause irrevocable harm when they are abused."[10]

It is easy to see why a nonviolent revolution increases the prospects of a democratic future. Its very nature prevents the emergence of small, armed elites who consequently possess enormous power that is regularly abused. At the same time, nonviolence schools large numbers of people in the tough skills of political struggle and respect for the humanity even of opponents.[11] The tragedy of Karl Marx is not that he saw the reality of class conflict, but

7. Chenoweth and Stephan, *Why Civil Resistance Works*, 213–14.

8. Adrian Karatnycky and Peter Ackerman, "How Freedom Is Won: From Civic Resistance to Durable Democracy," *International Journal of Not-for-Profit Law* 7, no. 3 (2005): 50; David Cortright, *Gandhi and Beyond: Nonviolence for a New Political Age*, 2nd ed. (Boulder, CO: Paradigm, 2010), 229–30.

9. Cortright, *Gandhi and Beyond*, 230.

10. David A. Hoekema, "A Practical Christian Pacifism," *Christian Century*, October 22, 1986, 918.

11. I owe this point to Wink, *Violence and Nonviolence in South Africa*, 56–57.

rather that his way of solving the problem elevated violent conflict to a necessary law of history.[12] Rather than exacerbating conflict between groups in a society, on the contrary, nonviolence reduces the hostility. That in turn makes more possible a future democratic society where all can coexist in relative harmony, freedom, and justice.

The past century of carnage and the future prospects of much worse to come also compel us to search for nonviolent alternatives. The twentieth century was the bloodiest in human history. A nuclear holocaust would make all past bloodshed seem like child's play. The ever-upward spiral of violence and counterviolence seems not only unending but also ever more colossal in its destructive dimensions. Surely at a time such as this, an exploration of nonviolent alternatives must be high on everyone's agenda.

In May 1983, I was one of the speakers at a large conference in California on "The Church and Peacemaking in the Nuclear Age." In my speech, I urged the kind of nonviolent peace team on the Honduras-Nicaragua border that took shape later that year with Witness for Peace.[13] What surprised me was the positive response of another speaker, General Robert Mathis, who had recently retired as vice-chief of staff of the US Air Force. Subsequent conversation helped me understand why General Mathis liked my proposal. General Mathis was so terrified by what he knew about the deadly dangers posed by nuclear weapons that he was eager to explore any realistic approach that offers nonviolent alternatives for resolving international conflict. That is not to claim that large numbers of top military leaders will quickly join a coalition to implement nonviolence. Such a claim would be naive. But the episode does indicate that the desire for nonviolent alternatives has become more widespread and urgent in our time.

A fourth reason for a vast expansion of nonviolent action is that, contrary to widespread belief, it works even against vicious dictators and ruthless regimes. The prominent scholar Michael Walzer reflects a common view when he asserts that nonviolence simply does not work with brutal rulers prepared to torture and kill opponents.[14] A bishop in the Philippines reflected this view

12. Bernard Häring, *The Healing Power of Peace and Nonviolence* (New York: Paulist Press, 1986), 83–84.

13. I later served on Witness for Peace's advisory board, but I do not mean to suggest that my speech prompted the emergence of Witness for Peace later that year.

14. Michael Walzer, *Just and Unjust Wars: A Moral Argument with Historical Illustrations*, 2nd ed. (New York: Basic Books, 1977), 331–33. See further Cortright's reply in *Gandhi and Beyond*, 231–32.

when he told Richard Deats, who was training Filipinos in nonviolence, that it would not work against President Marcos, who was the "Hitler of Asia."[15] But just a few months later, People Power defeated Marcos.

In fact, nonviolent action has worked in the case of many brutal dictators. In Poland, East Germany, and Russia, nonviolent movements defied and overcame one of the most ruthless dictatorships of modern history. Nonviolent action did not defeat Hitler, but it did save the lives of tens of thousands of Jews.

Near the end of their analysis and comparison of nonviolent and violent campaigns, Chenoweth and Stephan insist that their data contradicts the widespread view that nonviolent action works only with "more humane" adversaries:

> The argument that using violent resistance is the only effective way to win concessions from a repressive adversary simply does not stand up to the evidence. Nonviolent resistance has the strategic edge. The evidence presented also rejects the claim that there are some types of states against which only violence will work. We were able to discern no such states in this study.[16]

Again and again, nonviolent resistance has worked against even the most ruthless rulers.

In the light of these compelling reasons for a new, sustained exploration of the possibilities of nonviolent action, it is not surprising that more and more official church documents have issued the call. Indeed, the number, diversity, and increasing frequency are impressive.

■ Church Leaders' Calls for Nonviolent Options

The Latin American Catholic bishops appealed for nonviolence in their official statements at Puebla in 1979: "Our responsibility as Christians is to use all possible means to promote the implementation of nonviolent tactics in the effort to re-establish justice in economic and political relations."[17] One commentator concluded that at Puebla conservative, moderate, and progressive thinkers agreed that "the future struggle in Latin America will depend on . . . the techniques used by Martin Luther King and Mahatma Gandhi."[18]

15. Stephen Zunes, Lester R. Kurtz, and Sarah Beth Asher, eds., *Nonviolent Social Movements: A Geographical Perspective* (Oxford: Blackwell, 1999), 309.
16. Chenoweth and Stephan, *Why Civil Resistance Works*, 226.
17. No. 533 of their declaration, quoted in Esquivel, *Christ in a Poncho*, 52.
18. Penny Lernoux, *Cry of the People: The Struggle for Human Rights in Latin America—The Catholic Church in Conflict with U.S. Policy* (New York: Penguin Books, 1982), 447.

In 1983, Belgian and Dutch Catholic bishops affirmed the importance of nonviolence. In July, the Belgian bishops said, "Maybe the Church of earlier times and of today should have given more emphasis to the witness of nonviolence."[19] In May, the Dutch bishops had been more emphatic: "The development of methods which enable people to resist injustice and to defend themselves without using violence is in keeping with the spirit of the Gospel and may not be labeled as utopian and unrealistic."[20]

In their widely acclaimed peace pastoral of the same year, the US Catholic bishops spoke even more vigorously. Noting that Vatican II had praised those who renounce the use of violence in favor of other methods of defense, they insisted, "Nonviolent means of resistance to evil deserve much more study and consideration than they have thus far received."[21] At the conclusion of this lengthy appeal for developing nonviolent means of conflict resolution, the bishops declared, "No greater challenge or higher priority can be imagined than the development and perfection of a theology of peace suited to a civilization poised on the brink of self-destruction."[22]

Ten years later, in 1993, in a reflection on the earlier peace pastoral, the US Catholic bishops noted "the success of nonviolent methods in recent history." They specifically referred to the "lessons of the nonviolent revolutionaries in Eastern Europe in 1989 and the former Soviet Union in 1991."[23] They quoted John Paul II's 1989 encyclical, in which the Polish pope shared his amazement at the success of nonviolent action against Communist dictators: "It seemed that the European order resulting from the Second World War . . . could only be overturned by another war. Instead, it has been overcome by the nonviolent commitment of people."[24]

The US Catholic bishops argued that "these nonviolent revolutions challenge us to take into full account the power of organized, active nonviolence." "What is the real potential power of serious nonviolent strategies and tactics and their limits?" they asked. National leaders, they insisted, have "a moral

19. Quoted in Häring, *Healing Power*, 34.
20. Quoted in ibid.
21. National Conference of Catholic Bishops, *The Challenge of Peace: God's Promise and Our Response; Pastoral Statement of the National Conference of Catholic Bishops* (Boston: St. Paul Editions, 1983), no. 222, 58.
22. Ibid., no. 230, 60–61.
23. National Conference of Catholic Bishops, *The Harvest of Justice Is Sown in Peace: A Reflection of the National Conference of Catholic Bishops on the Tenth Anniversary of "The Challenge of Peace"* (Washington, DC: United States Catholic Conference, 1993), 9.
24. John Paul II, *Centesimus Annus*, paragraph 23, quoted in *The Harvest of Justice*, 8.

obligation" to seriously consider nonviolent alternatives. And they urged the nation to "promote research, education and training in nonviolent means of resisting evil." "Nonviolent strategies," they concluded, "need greater attention in international affairs. . . . In some future conflicts, strikes and people power could be more effective than guns and bullets."[25]

In 2004, the National Association of Evangelicals, the largest evangelical group in the United States, unanimously adopted a new public policy platform called "For the Health of the Nation." The vast majority of the member denominations of this association stand in the Just War tradition, and the document reflects that fact. But in the section on peacemaking, this official document says, "We urge governments to pursue thoroughly nonviolent paths to peace before resorting to military force." The section ends with a call to Christians: "As followers of Jesus, we should, in our civic capacity, work to reduce conflict by promoting international understanding and engaging in nonviolent conflict resolution."[26]

In 2007, the Vatican's Pontifical Council for Promoting Christian Unity and the Mennonite World Conference issued a joint statement on peace. Together, they affirmed "Jesus' teaching and example on nonviolence as normative for Christians"[27] and declared that "Christian peacemaking embraces active nonviolence."[28] They noted that "Catholics have increasingly emphasized nonviolence as central to the Gospel," and Mennonites had recently embraced "the exercise of active nonviolence."[29] Together, they sought to promote "nonviolence in the resolution of domestic and international disputes."[30] They also insisted that "the education, training and deployment of Christians in the practice of active nonviolence is an essential contribution of the church and church-sponsored organizations in our time."[31]

"An Ecumenical Call to Just Peace" was a key document at the International Ecumenical Peace Convocation in Kingston, Jamaica, in 2010. The Central

25. Ibid.
26. Ronald J. Sider and Diane Knippers, eds., *Toward an Evangelical Public Policy* (Grand Rapids: Baker Books, 2005), 374.
27. Pontifical Council for Promoting Christian Unity and Mennonite World Conference, "A Mennonite and Catholic Contribution to the World Council of Churches' *Decade to Overcome Violence*," 8 (http://www.overcomingviolence.org/fileadmin/dov/files/iepc/Mennonite_and_Cath olic_contribution_to_DOV.pdf).
28. Ibid., 4.
29. Ibid., 5–6.
30. Ibid., 4.
31. Ibid., 7.

Committee of the World Council of Churches received this call and recommended it for study. The call declared, "Nonviolent resistance is central to the Way of Just Peace," and noted, "Well-organized and peaceful resistance is active, tenacious and effective." It also observed that "peace education promotes active nonviolence as an unequalled power for change."[32]

The General Assembly of the Presbyterian Church (USA) adopted a document in 2010 that mandated a four-year study on nonviolence and peacemaking. It had two basic goals: "1. Seek clarity as to God's call to the church to embrace nonviolence as its fundamental response to the challenges of violence, terror, and war; 2. Identify, explore, and nurture new approaches to active peacemaking and nonviolence." The study group was directed to "explore new thinking on nonviolence" and "explore new models," including "nonviolent direct action."[33]

Perhaps the boldest and most explicit call for nonviolent action came in a study document for the 2010 General Assembly of the National Council of Churches. After noting some of the many instances of successful nonviolent action (including Mahatma Gandhi, Martin Luther King Jr., Solidarity in Poland, and People Power in the Philippines), this document notes that "the possibilities of Jesus' nonviolent way of righting wrong are being explored, practiced and promoted in unprecedented fashion."[34] The document celebrates the fact that "inspired by the development of the numerous large-scale, effective nonviolent social change movements of the last decades, many churches or church-related groups have initiated training programs in active nonviolence."[35] As a result, several different organizations are training and placing dozens of peacemakers in areas of conflict.

But the document is blunt about how meager such efforts still are:

> Compared to the numbers of Christians who are each year extensively trained in war and killing through the military, these efforts can only be described as puny. Compared to the financial contributions American Christians make to war efforts each year through our tax payments, the resources devoted by churches to peacemaking efforts are likewise minuscule.[36]

32. World Council of Churches, "An Ecumenical Call to Just Peace," 4, 10 (http://www .overcomingviolence.org/fileadmin/dov/files/iepc/resources/ECJustPeace_English.pdf).

33. Presbyterian Peace Fellowship, "Nonviolence Discernment Overture—Final Version" (http://www.presbypeacefellowship.org/node/398).

34. General Assembly of the National Council of Churches in the USA and Church World Service, "Studies 2010: Christian Understanding of War in an Age of Terror(ism)," 6 (http:// www.ncccusa.org/witnesses2010/christian-understanding-of-war.pdf).

35. Ibid., 12.

36. Ibid.

It calls for a vast increase in the use of nonviolent action:

> The moment has come for Christians to dramatically increase their commitment to active peacemaking, particularly to further developing the movement of unarmed Christian soldiers for peace, trained and disciplined to work creatively, sacrificially and courageously in high conflict situations. Can our churches imagine working together to field an army of one thousand international, trained, disciplined Christian peacemakers who would be engaged in one or more situations of significant, long-term conflict? This would require the commitment of the most gifted and experienced peacemakers and trainers among us, the readiness of many ordinary Christians to take courageous risks, serious financial and spiritual support of the churches, the prayers of the faithful, and a powerful movement of God's own Holy Spirit.[37]

The document ends this bold call by noting that both just-war and pacifist Christians are compelled by their own principles to rise to this challenge:

> Christians in the Just War tradition who have always taught that war must be a last resort will be challenged to engage in serious large-scale testing of nonviolent peacemaking. Pacifist Christians who reject violence and claim there are alternatives to war will be challenged to be prepared to make similar sacrifices as soldiers as they engage in active and risky peacemaking.[38]

■ Common Ground for Pacifists and Nonpacifists

Nonviolent action against injustice and oppression is clearly on the Christian church's agenda in a dramatic new way. Not only historic Anabaptist pacifists but also Catholics and Protestants in the Just War tradition are calling for a new, vigorous exploration. As the US Catholic bishops have pointed out, nonviolent resistance offers "a common ground of agreement" between Christians who stand in the Just War tradition and those who stand in the pacifist tradition.[39]

In fact, as I have argued, one must put it much more strongly. To have any integrity, both the pacifist and Just War traditions demand a massive commitment to nonviolent action.

According to the Just War tradition, as we have seen, lethal violence must always be a last resort. How, then, can Christians in the Just War tradition

37. Ibid.
38. Ibid.
39. National Conference of Catholic Bishops, *Challenge of Peace*, no. 224, 58.

166

claim that they are justified in resorting to war until they have devoted vast amounts of time and money to explore the possibilities of nonviolent action? At a time when Martin Luther King Jr. and Mahatma Gandhi are two of the most revered international religious leaders; after a century where success after success has been registered in nonviolent campaigns against oppression, injustice, and dictatorship; at such a time, no one can honestly deny that nonviolent action is often a realistic alternative to war or violent revolution. The only way that the just-war criterion "last resort" can have any integrity at all in our time is if Christians in that tradition commit themselves to a sophisticated and sustained testing of the possibilities of nonviolent alternatives.[40]

Pacifist premises demand a similar commitment. Pacifists hotly reject the charge that their refusal to bear arms is a callous or cowardly disregard of their obligation to defend the weak and defenseless against bullies and tyrants. If pacifists think that they have an alternative to war, then they must have the guts and integrity to prove it in the brutal world in which dictators such as Hitler, Somoza, Stalin, and Marcos kill and destroy. If pacifists are not ready to run the same risk as soldiers in nonviolent struggle against evil, then they have no moral right to pretend they know a better way. Only pacifists ready to risk death by the thousands will have credibility after a century that has witnessed the greatest bloodshed in human history. Costly pacifist involvement in successful nonviolent campaigns is perhaps the most effective way to convince doubting contemporaries that there is an alternative to war. Pacifist premises and goals demand a much more vigorous commitment to nonviolent defense of freedom, justice, and peace.

A new nonviolent movement in the Christian church possesses a twofold virtue: (1) it offers the promise of greater integrity to the stated positions of both pacifist and just-war Christians; (2) it offers a channel, not for ending the ongoing debate, but for emphasizing mutual cooperation in nonviolent resistance as both groups focus on what the US Catholic bishops have rightly called the "common ground of agreement."[41]

■ A Call for a Vast Exploration of Nonviolent Alternatives

Now is the time to move from frequently spontaneous, ill-prepared nonviolent skirmishes to a serious and sustained global exploration of the full power of

40. See further John Howard Yoder, *When War Is Unjust: Being Honest in Just-War Thinking* (Minneapolis: Augsburg, 1984), 76–78.
41. National Conference of Catholic Bishops, *Challenge of Peace*, no. 224, 59.

nonviolent alternatives. Gene Sharp, probably the most important contemporary analyst of nonviolent action, has underlined the difference:

> Nonviolent action has almost always been improvised without significant awareness of the past history of this type of struggle. It has usually been waged without qualified leadership, or without . . . wide popular understanding of the technique, without thorough comprehension of its requirements for effectiveness, without preparations and training, without analyses of past conflicts, without studies of strategy and tactics, without a consciousness among the actionists that they were waging a special type of struggle. In short, the most unfavorable circumstances possible have accompanied the use of this technique. It is amazing that the significant number of victories for nonviolent struggle exists at all, for these conditions of the lack of knowledge, skill and preparations have been to the highest degree unfavorable.
>
> In contrast, for many centuries military struggle has benefited from conscious efforts to improve its effectiveness in all the ways in which nonviolent action has lacked.[42]

Sharp wrote that more than thirty years ago, and it is still substantially true, even though scholarly analyses and study programs have increased significantly in recent years. However, a study of nonviolent social movements published almost two decades after Sharp's comments still lamented that "nonviolent strategies have not been developed or analyzed with the same energy and resources as military and other violent means" and regretted that "we have no large nonviolent academies that parallel our military academies or widespread units of peace brigades stationed to intervene nonviolently in crisis situations."[43] The study concludes that "we have scarcely begun to explore the implications of nonviolent direct action."[44] We spend hundreds and hundreds of billions of dollars every year on military research, academies, sophisticated weapons, and military bases, all preparing for violent conflict. Almost nothing is spent preparing for nonviolent action.

It is true that there are now many, indeed hundreds of, "peace studies" programs of various sorts at both Christian and secular universities.[45] But

42. Gene Sharp, "The Significance of Domestic Nonviolent Action as a Substitute for International War," in *Nonviolent Action and Social Change*, ed. Severyn T. Bruyn and Paula M. Rayman (New York: Irving, 1981), 245.

43. Zunes, Kurtz, and Asher, *Nonviolent Social Movements*, 1. Note also Walter Wink's comment that "'people power' is still in its infancy" (quoted in Cortright, *Gandhi and Beyond*, 121).

44. Zunes, Kurtz, and Asher, *Nonviolent Social Movements*, 303.

45. For example, the Joan B. Kroc Institute for International Peace Studies at the University of Notre Dame and the peace studies majors at Eastern Mennonite University. The website of

none of these programs even begins to match the size and sophistication of the military academies around the world.

It is also true, as we have seen, that several organizations, such as Peace Brigades International and Christian Peacemaker Teams, train and deploy small numbers of nonviolent peacemakers in conflict situations. But they number in the hundreds, not tens of thousands.

Many today honestly believe that we must maintain massive nuclear and nonnuclear weaponry. Others disagree. Without settling that disagreement, however, both can unite in a new exploration of the possibilities and limits of nonviolent action. Could we not all agree that it would be worthwhile to see what would happen if for two decades we spent at least one-tenth as much on nonviolent methods as we do on preparation for lethal violence? Concretely, that would mean massive new activity in at least three areas: (1) more, better-funded study centers to analyze the history of previous nonviolent successes and failures; (2) training centers to prepare large numbers of people in the strategy and tactics of actual nonviolent campaigns; (3) the launching of new or greatly expanded nonviolent organizations. In different ways, study centers, training centers, and active organizations all would serve to popularize the possibilities of nonviolent action.

Study centers. If the Christian church is serious about exploring nonviolence, then we must develop financial resources and the scholars needed to make possible large numbers of new and expanded study centers on nonviolence around the world. Individuals, foundations, denominations, and governments can provide the money. Colleges and universities can develop the centers to produce both scholarly studies and popular materials.

We need large study centers that can analyze all the past and present instances of nonviolent action to discover with much more precision what works best and why. We can only guess what we would learn if for several decades there existed large study centers on nonviolence that paralleled in sophistication and funding the many superb military academies around the world that have for decades engaged in rigorous analysis of what does and does not work in war.

Training centers. We also need new training centers—parallels to the military academies and military training programs that annually train hundreds of thousands of soldiers for battle. We saw in chapter 5 how important were the short-term training seminars conducted for key Philippine leadership by the

---

the Kroc Institute says that about four hundred colleges and universities around the world offer a variety of peace studies programs.

Goss-Mayrs. Witness for Peace did short training sessions for its volunteers in Nicaragua. Organizations such as Christian Peacemaker Teams do the same. In the last few decades, a significant number of training centers and training manuals have emerged.[46] But much more is required. We need hundreds of action-oriented training centers to produce thousands of trained nonviolent activists who are familiar with the tactics of Gandhi, King, and the many other nonviolent campaigns described in this book, and who are ready to lead nonviolent campaigns.

Some training centers could concentrate on producing generalists—trainers of trainers. Others could prepare people for specific campaigns. In both cases, key components would include spiritual formation and the techniques of nonviolent direct action. For Christians, the development of a biblical spirituality of prayer, Bible study, and worship focused on the heavy emotional demands of costly nonviolent intervention would be essential. Each volunteer should be supported by a "hometown" support group and prayer chain committed to regular prayer plus all-night intercession during emergencies. All the concrete strategies, techniques, and tactics learned in the many successful nonviolent campaigns need to be studied carefully.[47] Role-playing scenarios of intervention, ambush, crowd control, and injury would be important.

Organizations for nonviolent peacekeeping. Small organizations such as Christian Peacemaker Teams (CPT), Peace Brigades International (PBI), and the World Council of Churches' Ecumenical Accompaniment Programme in Palestine and Israel (EAPPI) field a few small teams in various conflict zones. But their numbers are minuscule compared to the need. Groups such as CPT need thousands of people, not dozens. If the Christian church wants to seriously test what could be done to replace violence with nonviolent action, then we need a vast expansion of present organizations and the emergence of new organizations. If we are serious—if we want to meet the moral obligation that pacifist and just-war Christians have to genuinely test the possibilities of nonviolent action for the first time in our history—then we must train and deploy tens of thousands of CPT-like peace activists in the next two decades.

What might happen if the top leaders of the "Historic Peace Churches" (i.e., denominations that have a long history as pacifist bodies) that founded

46. See "Annotated Bibliography of Nonviolent Action Training" at www.nonviolencein ternational.net/biblio.htm.

47. We need much more of what Gene Sharp has done so well in *The Politics of Nonviolent Action*, 3 vols. (Boston: Porter Sargent, 1973), 2:117–435.

Christian Peacemaker Teams would take the initiative (perhaps in conjunction with the World Council of Churches' EAPPI) to invite key leaders from all the Christian communities (Catholic, Orthodox, Protestant) to a global conference? The agenda: to take seriously the stated ethical commitments of just-war and pacifist Christians and therefore commit themselves to explore seriously for the first time in Christian history what could be done to vastly expand nonviolent peacemaking. The goal would be to fund, train, and deploy at least ten thousand peacemakers using the techniques of CPT, PBI, and EAPPI, as well as other techniques and strategies developed by the new study centers on nonviolent action.

It is important to understand that the peacemaking techniques of CPT, PBI, and EAPPI are not by any means the only effective ways to work nonviolently for peace and justice. The book *Just Peacemaking: Ten Practices for Abolishing War* discusses nine other very important peacemaking activities in addition to a massive expansion of the techniques of King, Gandhi, and CPT.[48] There are many urgent, significant ways to work for peace with justice. But the numerous successful nonviolent campaigns of the last hundred years and the achievements of even a handful of CPT-type volunteers indicate that one urgent task for the global Christian community is to train and deploy thousands of peacemaker teams in conflict situations around the world.

Any serious program of this sort would, of course, reach out to people of other faiths. We would invite them to form similar teams and join us in joint peacemaking ventures. One wonders what would have happened in the mid-1980s when apartheid was the law of the land in South Africa if Billy Graham, Pope John Paul II, and Archbishop Robert Runcie had led a few thousand praying Christian peacemakers into South Africa's governmental buildings and vowed to stay there until the government abandoned apartheid. One wonders what would have happened if top Catholic, Orthodox, and Muslim leaders had led a couple thousand praying peacemakers into Bosnia before ethnic hatred exploded in lethal violence.

What would happen today if top Christian and Muslim leaders led a few thousand praying Christians and Muslims into Syria to stand between warring

---

48. Glen Stassen, ed., *Just Peacemaking: Ten Practices for Abolishing War*, 2nd ed. (Cleveland: Pilgrim, 2004). For a book that illustrates the way Anabaptist Christians have engaged in a wide range of peacemaking activities, see Cynthia Sampson and John Paul Lederach, eds., *From the Ground Up: Mennonite Contributions to International Peacebuilding* (New York: Oxford University Press, 2000). See also John Paul Lederach, *Building Peace: Sustainable Reconciliation in Divided Societies* (Washington, DC: United States Institute of Peace Press, 1997).

factions in Aleppo and Damascus and demand an end to the bloodshed? What would happen if Jewish, Christian, and Muslim leaders led a few thousand praying followers into Israel and Palestine and vowed to stay there until the Israelis and Palestinians negotiated a just-peace agreement?

▓ The Power of Nonviolent Action

Too often, power is understood only in terms of lethal coercion. Mao Zedong said that power is what comes from the barrel of a gun. Certainly power includes the ability to control people's actions by the threat or use of lethal violence; however, the people also possess nonviolent collective power because they can choose to withdraw their support from rulers. Political scientist Karl Deutsch has pointed out that "the voluntary or habitual compliance of the mass of the population is the invisible but very real basis of the power of every government."[49] The potential choice by large numbers to withdraw that compliance represents enormous collective power. Consequently, without any arms at all, the people can exercise nonviolent power either by doing what they are not expected to do or by not doing what they are required to do.[50] Large numbers of people using nonviolent techniques possess enormous nonviolent collective power.

But nonviolent action does not require large numbers to have power. Witness for Peace and Peace Brigades International have demonstrated that even small groups can exercise substantial power.

Nonviolent activists possess strong moral power. Praying, reconciling teams of Christian peacemakers risking their lives for others would share something of the moral power that Jesus exercised in the temple. He was able single-handedly to drive the crowds of angry, oppressive moneychangers out of the temple, not because he was stronger or his disciples were more numerous. It was because deep in their hearts they knew that he was right.

International public opinion would also be influential. The daring of the teams of Christian peacemakers would sometimes make headline news around the world. Any group or nation that battered or killed prominent, internationally famous Christian leaders or even ordinary peacemakers would suffer substantial international disapproval.

49. Karl W. Deutsch, *The Analysis of International Relations* (Englewood Cliffs, NJ: Prentice Hall, 1978). See the discussion in the excellent book by Duane K. Friesen, *Christian Peacemaking and International Conflict: A Realist Pacifist Perspective* (Scottdale, PA: Herald Press, 1986), 147–49.
50. Friesen, *Christian Peacemaking*, 148, summarizing Gene Sharp.

A mandate also provides authority and therefore power. A mandate to intervene internationally, if issued by an organization such as the Organization of African States or the United Nations, could legitimize nonviolent teams of peacemakers. So too—at least to a certain, if lesser, degree—would an invitation by prominent Christian leaders and established churches, as well as recognized leaders of other religious groups.

Self-sacrificial love has innate power. It often weakens even vicious opponents—though not always, of course. People ready to suffer for others sometimes get crucified. But often, too, they evoke a more human, loving response, even from brutal foes.

The discipline, training, and coordination of an organized body with visible symbols of identity and cohesion are also powerful. Part of the power of a large group of police or soldiers lies in their uniforms, careful coordination, and ability to act quickly, decisively, and collectively. Highly trained and disciplined peacemaker teams would possess some of this same power.

Finally, there is the divine power of the Lord of history. What the Almighty will do if thousands of praying, loving Christians nonviolently face death in the search for peace and justice will remain shrouded in mystery—at least until we have the courage to try it. But what believer will doubt that there may be surprises ahead?

We do have to be honest and realistic. We never dare pretend that no one will get hurt. Tyrants and bullies callously torture and murder. Opponents will sometimes intimidate, threaten, wound, torture, and massacre even praying peacemakers. But we have always assumed that death by the thousands, indeed even millions, is necessary in war. Would it not be right for nonviolent teams of Christian peacemakers to be ready to risk death in the same way soldiers do? Certainly we must not seek death. Martyr complexes are wrong. But a readiness to lay down one's life for others lies at the heart of the gospel.

Death will be tragically intertwined with any serious test of the effectiveness of nonviolent action. But that will not prove that the effort has failed; it will only underline the depth of human sin, and also the fact that Christians are willing to imitate the One they worship. Nor is that all. The death of courageous nonviolent activists will also lead to the birth of a more powerful belief in and practice of successful nonviolent movements for peace and justice.

12

---

the moral equivalent of war

The War against war is going to be no holiday excursion or camping party.

William James[1]

In a now famous essay, "The Moral Equivalent of War," William James argued that the struggle for nonviolent alternatives would be a long and costly battle. Why? Because "history is a bath of blood."[2] War has been central to human history because violent instincts are deeply embedded in the human heart.

■ The Costly Demands of Nonviolent Action

Anyone seeking to reduce war, James argued, must realize that in important respects war represents human nature at its best. Not only does war smash the dull boredom of ordinary life; it also evokes high virtues, such as courage, self-sacrifice, intense discipline, and total dedication. War disciplines the slack,

1. William James, "The Moral Equivalent of War," in William James, *The Moral Equivalent of War, and Other Essays*, ed. John K. Roth (New York: Harper & Row, 1971), 3. The essay originally appeared in 1910.
2. Ibid., 4.

rewards the daring, elicits one's last ounce of energy, and breeds loyalty to the larger community. How, James concluded, can any peace movement succeed unless it offers meaningful substitutes for the glamour and appeal of war?

If James's essay poses a valid question, then vigorous nonviolent action offers the answer. Nonviolent resistance to tyrants, oppressors, and brutal invaders is not for fools or cowards. It demands courage and daring of the highest order. It requires discipline, training, and willingness to face death. It produces collective pride in the group or society, as in the Philippines and other places we have examined, that successfully stands together and overcomes a brutal foe.

Are there tough, brave volunteers for that kind of costly, demanding battle? Would the people be there if the Christian church, as well as other faith communities, called for a vast multiplication of our efforts in nonviolent alternatives to violence? Would the scholars and trainees emerge if we doubled and then quadrupled our study and training centers on nonviolent action? Would the nonviolent troops be available to be trained by the thousands and then tens of thousands to form a disciplined team of Christian peacemakers ready to walk into the face of danger and death in loving confrontation of injustice and oppression? We will not know until courageous Christian leaders, organizations, and denominations issue the call and spend the money.

The time has never been more right. At no time in history, perhaps, has the concrete evidence of the tangible success of nonviolent action been clearer. At no time has the need to break the escalating cycle of violence and counterviolence been greater. As we glance back in anguish at history's most violent century and peer ahead fearfully to far worse potential catastrophes, a new, sustained exploration of the possibilities of nonviolent action seems to be a prerequisite of sanity.

■ The Ultimate Risk

The battle will be long and costly. To argue that nonviolent action is less costly in human lives than is violence is not to pretend that no one will be wounded or killed. Some will die. Everyone must be ready to face death.

Are there enough people for such a struggle? The history of warfare proves that danger does not deter volunteers. Throughout history, millions of bold souls have gladly risked death for a noble cause and a grand vision. Walter

Wink is surely right that "there is a whole host of people simply waiting for the Christian message to challenge them for once to a heroism worthy of their lives."[3]

Death, of course, is not the goal. To seek martyrdom would be naive and immoral. The way of Christ is the way of life, not death. But the Christian martyrs of all ages provide testimony that the way to abundant life sometimes passes through the dark valley where the cross stands stark and rugged. Those who dare in loving obedience to shoulder that old rugged cross will exchange it some day for a crown of *shalom* in the peaceful kingdom of the reconciling Lamb.

3. Walter Wink, *Violence and Nonviolence in South Africa: Jesus' Third Way* (Philadelphia: New Society, 1987), 34.

bibliography

Ackerman, Peter, and Jack DuVall. *A Force More Powerful: A Century of Nonviolent Conflict*. New York: Palgrave, 2000.

Adams, John P. *At the Heart of the Whirlwind*. New York: Harper & Row, 1976.

Americas Watch. *Human Rights in Nicaragua: 1985–1986*. New York: Americas Watch Committee, 1986.

Amnesty International. *Nicaragua: The Human Rights Record*. London: Amnesty International, 1986.

Anderson, Lisa. "Demystifying the Arab Spring: Parsing the Differences between Tunisia, Egypt, and Libya." *Foreign Affairs* 90, no. 3 (2011): 2–7.

Arieff, Alexis. "Political Transition in Tunisia." RS21666. Washington, DC: Congressional Research Service. February 2, 2011.

Ash, Timothy Garton. *The Polish Revolution: Solidarity*. New Haven: Yale University Press, 2002.

———. *We the People: The Revolution of '89 Witnessed in Warsaw, Budapest, Berlin and Prague*. Cambridge: Granta Books, 1990.

Belli, Humberto. *Breaking Faith: The Sandinista Revolution and Its Impact on Freedom and Christian Faith in Nicaragua*. Westchester, IL: Crossway Books, 1985.

Bondurant, Joan V. *Conquest of Violence: The Gandhian Philosophy of Conflict*. Princeton, NJ: Princeton University Press, 1988.

Boserup, Anders, and Andrew Mack. *War without Weapons: Non-Violence in National Defence*. New York: Schocken Books, 1975.

Boukhars, Anouar. "The Arab Revolution for Dignity." *American Foreign Policy Interests* 33 (2011): 61–68.

Bradley, John R. *After the Arab Spring: How Islamists Hijacked the Middle East Revolts.* New York: Palgrave Macmillan, 2012.

————. *Inside Egypt: The Road to Revolution in the Land of the Pharaohs.* New York: Palgrave Macmillan, 2012.

Branch, Taylor. *Parting the Waters: America in the King Years 1954–63.* New York: Simon & Schuster, 1988.

Brody, Reed. *Contra Terror in Nicaragua: Report of a Fact-Finding Mission: September 1984–January 1985.* Cambridge, MA: South End Press, 1985.

Brooks, Thomas R. *Walls Come Tumbling Down: A History of the Civil Rights Movement, 1940–1970.* Englewood Cliffs, NJ: Prentice Hall, 1974.

Brown, Archie. *The Rise and Fall of Communism.* New York: HarperCollins, 2009.

Brown, Tricia Gates. *Getting in the Way: Stories from Christian Peacemaker Teams.* Scottdale, PA: Herald Press, 2005.

Bruyn, Severyn T., and Paula M. Rayman, eds. *Nonviolent Action and Social Change.* New York: Irving, 1979.

Bultman, Bud. *Revolution by Candlelight: The Real Story behind the Changes in Eastern Europe.* Portland, OR: Multnomah, 1991.

Campuzano, Elizabeth, et al. *Resistance in Latin America: The Pentagon, The Oligarchy and Nonviolent Action.* Philadelphia: American Friends Service Committee, 1970.

Charry, Frederick B. *The Bulgarian Jews and the Final Solution, 1940–1944.* Pittsburgh: University of Pittsburgh Press, 1972.

Chenoweth, Erica, and Maria J. Stephan. *Why Civil Resistance Works: The Strategic Logic of Nonviolent Conflict.* New York: Columbia University Press, 2011.

Clark, Howard, ed. *People Power: Unarmed Resistance and Global Solidarity.* London: Pluto Press, 2009.

Conser, Walter H., Ronald M. McCarthy, David J. Toscano, and Gene Sharp, eds. *Resistance, Politics, and the American Struggle for Independence, 1765–1775.* Boulder, CO: Lynne Rienner, 1986.

Cortright, David. *Gandhi and Beyond: Nonviolence for a New Political Age.* 2nd ed. Boulder, CO: Paradigm, 2010.

Dalton, Dennis. *Mahatma Gandhi: Nonviolent Power in Action.* New York: Columbia University Press, 2000.

de Coninck, Thérèse, ed. *Essays on Nonviolence.* Nyack, NY: Fellowship of Reconciliation, n.d.

DeFronzo, James. *Revolutions and Revolutionary Movements.* Boulder, CO: Westview Press, 1991.

del Vasto, Lanza. *Warriors of Peace: Writings on the Technique of Nonviolence*. Edited by Michel Random. Translated by Jean Sidgwick. New York: Knopf, 1974.

Deutsch, Karl W. *The Analysis of International Relations*. Englewood Cliffs, NJ: Prentice Hall, 1978.

Disney, Abigail, producer, and Gini Reticker, director. *Pray the Devil Back to Hell*. Fork Films, DVD. 2008.

Dobbs, Michael, Dessa Trevisan, and K. S. Karol. *Poland, Solidarity, Walesa*. New York: McGraw-Hill, 1981.

Dziwisz, Stanislaw. *A Life with Karol: My Forty-Year Friendship with the Man Who Became Pope*. Translated by Adrian J. Walker. New York: Doubleday, 2008.

Elwood, Douglas J. *Philippine Revolution, 1986: Model of Nonviolent Change*. Quezon City: New Day, 1986.

―――, ed. *Toward a Theology of People Power: Reflection on the Philippine February Phenomenon*. Quezon City: New Day, 1988.

Esquivel, Adolfo Pérez. *Christ in a Poncho: Testimonials of the Nonviolent Struggles in Latin America*. Edited by Charles Antoine. Translated by Robert R. Barr. Maryknoll, NY: Orbis Books, 1983.

Estey, George F., and Doris A. Hunter. *Nonviolence: A Reader in the Ethics of Action*. Waltham, MA: Xerox College Publishing, 1971.

Frank, Jerome D. *Sanity and Survival: Psychological Aspects of War and Peace*. New York: Vintage Books, 1968.

Franklin, John Hope. *From Slavery to Freedom: A History of Negro Americans*. 3rd ed. New York: Random House, 1969.

Friesen, Duane K. *Christian Peacemaking and International Conflict: A Realist Pacifist Perspective*. Scottdale, PA: Herald Press, 1986.

Gandhi, Mohandas K. *All Men Are Brothers: Life and Thoughts of Mahatma Gandhi as Told in His Own Words*. Edited by Krishna Kripalani. Ahmedabad: Navajivan Publishing House, 1960.

―――. *Gandhi's Autobiography: The Story of My Experiments with Truth by M. K. Gandhi*. Translated by Mahadev Desai. Washington, DC: Public Affairs Press, 1948.

Gbowee, Leymah. *Mighty Be Our Powers: How Sisterhood, Prayer, and Sex Changed a Nation at War*. New York: Beast Books, 2011.

Ghonim, Wael. *Revolution 2.0: The Power of the People Is Greater Than the People in Power; A Memoir*. Boston: Houghton Mifflin Harcourt, 2012.

Gish, Arthur G. *Hebron Journal: Stories of Nonviolent Peacemaking*. Scottdale, PA: Herald Press, 2001.

Glover, Jonathan. *Humanity: A Moral History of the Twentieth Century*. New Haven: Yale University Press, 2000.

Griffin-Nolan, Edward. *Witness for Peace: A Story of Resistance*. Louisville: Westminster John Knox, 1991.

Hare, A. Paul, ed. *Cyprus Resettlement Project: An Instance of International Peacemaking*. Beer Sheva: Ben-Gurion University of the Negev, 1984.

Hare, A. Paul, and Herbert H. Blumberg, eds. *Liberation without Violence: A Third-Party Approach*. Totowa, NJ: Rowman & Littlefield, 1977.

Häring, Bernard. *The Healing Power of Peace and Nonviolence*. New York: Paulist Press, 1986.

Hunter, Allan A. *Courage in Both Hands*. New York: Ballantine Books, 1962.

James, William. *The Moral Equivalent of War, and Other Essays*. Edited by John K. Roth. New York: Harper & Row, 1971.

Juhnke, James C., and Carol M. Hunter. *The Missing Peace: The Search for Nonviolent Alternatives in United States History*. Kitchener, ON: Pandora Press, 2001.

Kandil, Hazem. "Interview: Revolt in Egypt." *New Left Review* 68 (March–April 2011): 17–55.

Karnow, Stanley. *In Our Image: America's Empire in the Philippines*. New York: Ballantine Books, 1989.

Kennedy, Michael D. *Professionals, Power, and Solidarity in Poland: A Critical Sociology of Soviet-Type Society*. Cambridge: Cambridge University Press, 1991.

Kern, Kathleen. *In Harm's Way: A History of Christian Peacemaker Teams*. Eugene, OR: Cascade Books, 2009.

Khalil, Ashraf. *Liberation Square: Inside the Egyptian Revolution and the Rebirth of a Nation*. New York: St. Martin's Press, 2011.

Kwitny, Jonathan. *Man of the Century: The Life and Times of Pope John Paul II*. New York: Henry Holt, 1997.

Laba, Roman. *The Roots of Solidarity: A Political Sociology of Poland's Working-Class Democratization*. Princeton, NJ: Princeton University Press, 1991.

LaFeber, Walter. *Inevitable Revolutions: The United States in Central America*. 2nd ed. New York: W. W. Norton, 1993.

Lederach, John Paul. *Building Peace: Sustainable Reconciliation in Divided Societies*. Washington, DC: United States Institute of Peace Press, 1997.

Lernoux, Penny. *Cry of the People: The Struggle for Human Rights in Latin America—The Catholic Church in Conflict with U.S. Policy*. New York: Penguin Books, 1982.

Lim, David S. "Consolidating Democracy: Filipino Evangelicals between People Power Events, 1986–2001." In *Evangelical Christianity and Democracy in Asia*, edited by David H. Lumsdaine, 235–84. Oxford: Oxford University Press, 2009.

Maggay, Melba. "People Power Revisited." In *Following Jesus: Journeys in Radical Discipleship; Essays in Honor of Ronald J. Sider*, edited by Paul Alexander and Al Tizon, 124–32. Oxford: Regnum Books International, 2013.

Mahony, Liam, and Luis Enrique Eguren. *Unarmed Bodyguards: International Accompaniment for the Protection of Human Rights*. West Hartford, CT: Kumarian Press, 1997.

Mallick, Krishna, and Doris Hunter. *An Anthology of Nonviolence: Historical and Contemporary Voices*. Westport, CT: Greenwood Press, 2002.

McGinnis, James B. *Solidarity with the People of Nicaragua*. Maryknoll, NY: Orbis Books, 1985.

Mercado, Monina Allarey, ed. *People Power: The Philippine Revolution of 1986: An Eyewitness History*. Manila: James B. Reuter, S.J., Foundation, 1986.

Meyer, Michael. *The Year That Changed the World: The Untold Story Behind the Fall of the Berlin Wall*. New York: Scribner, 2009.

Miller, Webb. *I Found No Peace: The Journal of a Foreign Correspondent*. New York: Simon & Schuster, 1936.

Miller, William Robert. *Nonviolence: A Christian Interpretation*. New York: Association Press, 1964.

Monshipouri, Mahmood, and John W. Arnold. "The Christians in Socialism—and After: The Church in East Germany." *Journal of Church and State* 38 (1996): 751–73.

Morley, Morris H. *Washington, Somoza, and the Sandinistas: State and Regime in U.S. Policy toward Nicaragua, 1969–1981*. New York: Cambridge University Press, 1994.

Moser-Puangsuwan, Yeshua, and Thomas Weber. *Nonviolent Intervention across Borders: A Recurrent Vision*. Honolulu: Spark M. Matsunaga Institute for Peace, University of Hawaii, 2000.

Parkman, Patricia. "Insurrection without Arms: The General Strike in El Salvador, 1944." PhD diss., Temple University, 1980.

Rummel, R. J. *Statistics of Democide: Genocide and Mass Murder Since 1900*. Piscataway, NJ: Transaction Publishers, 1997.

Sampson, Cynthia, and John Paul Lederach, eds. *From the Ground Up: Mennonite Contributions to International Peacebuilding*. New York: Oxford University Press, 2000.

Schock, Kurt. *Unarmed Insurrections: People Power Movements in Nondemocracies*. Minneapolis: University of Minnesota Press, 2005.

Schwenk, Richard L. *Onward, Christians! Protestants in the Philippine Revolution*. Quezon City: New Day, 1986.

Sharp, Gene. *The Politics of Nonviolent Action*. 3 vols. Boston: Porter Sargent, 1973.

————. *Waging Nonviolent Struggle: 20th Century Practice and 21st Century Potential*. Boston: Porter Sargent, 2005.

Sider, Ronald J. *Christ and Violence*. Scottdale, PA: Herald Press, 1979.

Sider, Ronald J., and Diane Knippers, eds. *Toward an Evangelical Public Policy: Political Strategies for the Health of the Nation*. Grand Rapids: Baker Books, 2005.

Sider, Ronald J., and Richard K. Taylor. *Nuclear Holocaust and Christian Hope: A Book for Christian Peacemakers*. Downers Grove, IL: InterVarsity; New York: Paulist Press, 1982.

Smith, Christian. *Resisting Reagan: The U.S. Central American Peace Movement*. Chicago: University of Chicago Press, 1996.

Solaún, Mauricio. *U.S. Intervention and Regime Change in Nicaragua*. Lincoln: University of Nebraska Press, 2005.

Stassen, Glen. *Just Peacemaking: Ten Practices for Abolishing War*. 2nd edition. Cleveland: Pilgrim, 2004.

Stokes, Gale. *The Walls Came Tumbling Down: The Collapse of Communism in Eastern Europe*. New York: Oxford University Press, 1993.

Stürchler, Nikolas. *The Threat of Force in International Law*. Cambridge: Cambridge University Press, 2007.

Swoboda, Jörg. *The Revolution of the Candles: Christians in the Revolution of the German Democratic Republic*. Edited by Richard V. Pierard. Translated by Edwin P. Arnold. Macon, GA: Mercer University Press, 1996.

Taylor, Richard K. *Blockade: A Guide to Non-Violent Intervention*. Maryknoll, NY: Orbis Books, 1977.

————. *Nonviolent Direct Action as a Spiritual Path*. Pendle Hill Pamphlets 424. Wallingford, PA: Pendle Hill Publications, 2013.

Thompson, Mark. *Democratic Revolutions: Asia and Eastern Europe*. New York: Routledge, 2004.

Touraine, Alain, et al. *Solidarity: The Analysis of a Social Movement; Poland 1980–1981*. Translated by David Denby. Cambridge: Cambridge University Press, 1983.

Tyndale, Wendy R. *Protestants in Communist East Germany: In the Storm of the World*. Burlington, VT: Ashgate, 2010.

Von der Heydt, Barbara. *Candles Behind the Wall: Heroes of the Peaceful Revolution That Shattered Communism*. Grand Rapids: Eerdmans, 1993.

Walesa, Lech. *A Way of Hope*. New York: Henry Holt, 1987.

Walker, Charles C. *A World Peace Guard: An Unarmed Agency for Peacekeeping*. New Delhi: Academy of Gandhian Studies Hyderabad, 1981.

Wallis, Jim, ed. *The Rise of Christian Conscience: The Emergence of a Dramatic Renewal Movement in the Church Today*. New York: Harper & Row, 1987.

Walzer, Michael. *Just and Unjust Wars: A Moral Argument with Historical Illustrations*. 2nd ed. New York: Basic Books, 1977.

Washington, James Melvin, ed. *A Testament of Hope: The Essential Writings of Martin Luther King, Jr.* New York: HarperOne, 1991.

Weber, Clare. *Visions of Solidarity: U.S. Peace Activists in Nicaragua from War to Women's Activism and Globalization*. Lanham, MD: Lexington Books, 2006.

Weber, Thomas. *Gandhi's Peace Army: The Shanti Sena and Unarmed Peacekeeping*. Syracuse, NY: Syracuse University Press, 1996.

Wehr, Paul. *Conflict Regulation*. Boulder, CO: Westview Press, 1979.

———. "Nonviolent Resistance to Nazism: Norway, 1940–45." *Peace & Change* 10, nos. 3–4 (1984): 77–95.

Weigel, George. *The Final Revolution: The Resistance Church and the Collapse of Communism*. New York: Oxford University Press, 1992.

———. *Witness to Hope: The Biography of Pope John Paul II*. New York: Harper Perennial, 2005.

Weinberg, Arthur, ed. *Instead of Violence: Writings by the Great Advocates of Peace and Nonviolence throughout History*. New York: Beacon, 1963.

West, Johnny. *Karama! Journeys through the Arab Spring*. London: Heron Books, 2011.

Williams, Juan. *Eyes on the Prize: America's Civil Rights Years, 1954–1965*. 15th anniversary ed. New York: Penguin Books, 2002.

Wink, Walter. *Violence and Nonviolence in South Africa: Jesus' Third Way*. Philadelphia: New Society, 1987.

Witness for Peace Documentation Project. *Kidnapped by the Contras: The Peace Flotilla on the Rio San Juan, Nicaragua, August 1985*. Santa Cruz, CA: Witness for Peace Documentation Project, 1985.

Wolpert, Stanley. *Gandhi's Passion: The Life and Legacy of Mahatma Gandhi*. New York: Oxford University Press, 2001.

Yoder, John Howard. *When War Is Unjust: Being Honest in Just-War Thinking*. Minneapolis: Augsburg, 1984.

Zunes, Stephen, Lester R. Kurtz, and Sarah Beth Asher, eds. *Nonviolent Social Movements: A Geographical Perspective*. Oxford: Blackwell, 1999.

Index